Crime, Truth and Justice

Crime, Truth and Justice

Official inquiry, discourse, knowledge

Edited by George Gilligan and John Pratt

Routledge
Taylor & Francis Group

LONDON AND NEW YORK

First published by Willan Publishing 2004

This edition published by Routledge 2013
2 Park Square, Milton Park, Abingdon, Oxfordshire OX14 4RN
711 Third Avenue, New York, NY 10017

First issued in paperback 2014

Routledge is an imprint of the Taylor & Francis Group, an informa business

ISBN 13: 978-1-84392-027-4 (hbk)
ISBN 13: 978-1-138-00193-0 (pbk)

British Library Cataloguing-in-Publication Data

A catalogue record for this book is available from the British Library.

Project management by Deer Park Productions, Tavistock, Devon
Typeset by PDQ Typesetting, Newcastle-under-Lyme, Staffordshire

Contents

Notes on contributors

David Brown is a Professor at the University of New South Wales, Sydney, Australia teaching criminal law and criminal justice. He has been active in criminal justice movements, issues and debates for three decades and is a regular media commentator and has published widely in the field. He has co-authored or co-edited *The Prison Struggle* (1982), *The Judgments of Lionel Murphy* (1986), *Death in the Hands of the State* (1988), *Criminal Laws* in three editions (1990; 1996; 2001), *Rethinking Law and Order* (1998) and *Prisoners as Citizens* (2002).

Pat Carlen is Honorary Professor of Criminology at Keele University, Staffordshire, and Visiting Professor of Criminology at Westminster University, London. She has published 15 books and many articles on the relationships between criminal and social justice, the latest being *Women and Punishment: The Struggle for Justice* (Willan 2002). Presently engaged in an EC-funded six-nation project on social exclusion and women prisoners, she is also an editor of the *British Journal of Criminology* and book review editor of *Punishment and Society*. In 1997 she was awarded the Sellin-Glueck Prize by the American Society of Criminology for outstanding international contributions to criminology.

Nils Christie is Professor of Criminology, Faculty of Law, University of Oslo. He is the author of numerous scientific articles and many books, some of them published in a great number of languages. Among them are *Limits to Pain* (Oslo University Press 1981) and *Crime Control as Industry. Towards Gulags, Western Style?* (Routledge, revised and enlarged edition 2000). Most of his writing has been in the field of crime and crime control, but he has also published books on education, on drugs and drug control (*Suitable Enemies* [with Kettil Bruun])) and on alternative communities (*Beyond Loneliness and Institutions*, on villages for extra-ordinary people, by many called mentally retarded). He has worked as a visiting professor in Berkeley, Jerusalem and Oxford, and also given lectures in a great number of other universities in Latin America and in Eastern Europe. His particular interest during the last few years has been an analysis of the development in prison figures in industrialised countries. Another major interest has been analysis of mediation as an alternative to punishment. A new book soon to be published is *A Suitable Amount of Crime* (Routledge, London, Winter 2003).

David Dixon is Professor and Associate Dean (Research) in the Faculty of Law, University of New South Wales, Sydney, Australia. He has researched and published widely on policing and crime control in Britain, Australia and the USA. His publications include *From Prohibition to Regulation: Bookmaking, Anti-Gambling and the Law* (Oxford University Press), *Law in Policing: Legal Regulation and Police Practices* (Oxford University Press) and *A Culture of Corruption: Changing an Australian Police Service* (Hawkins Press). His current research includes: 'Q&A: Police Interviewing of Suspects', a study of videorecorded police interrogations, and 'Policing, Law and Order', a comparative study of developing crime control strategies.

George Gilligan is Logan Senior Research Fellow at Monash University in Melbourne. He is a criminologist who has taught at the universities of Cambridge, Exeter, La Trobe, Melbourne, Middlesex and Monash. His research interests centre on the regulation of financial markets, white-collar crime and organised crime, and he has published extensively in these areas.

Nigel Hancock is a senior manager in HM Prison Service, England and Wales and currently leads the Safer Custody Group, which focuses on work to reduce suicide and self-harm. During a long Home Office career he has also worked in such areas as police efficiency and civil defence. He has degrees from Lancaster, Essex and Cambridge universities, the latter following completion of a research thesis on independence in investigations, and also works for the *Prison Service Journal*.

Carol LaPrairie obtained her Ph.D. in sociology at the University of British Columbia and is currently Principal Researcher in the British Columbia Regional Office of Justice Canada. For many years she has been undertaking research on justice and policing issues in Aboriginal communities across Canada, and on Aboriginal offenders in correctional institutions. She has also been involved in evaluation research on sentencing reforms, crime prevention programmes, an experimental drug treatment court and therapeutic programmes for correctional inmates. In 1994 she published *Seen but Not Heard: Native People in the Inner City* (Ottawa: Department of Justice), an in-depth study of the experiences of Native people in Canada's inner city areas.

John Lea is Professor of Criminology at Middlesex University, London. He is the author with Jock Young of *What Is to Be Done About Law And Order?* (1993) and has published on issues concerning crime in postmodern society and racism in criminal justice agencies. His most recent book is *Crime and Modernity* (London: Sage Publications, 2002).

Stéphane Leman-Langlois wrote his PhD thesis on post-conflict justice in the South African Truth and Reconciliation Commission at the University of Toronto's Center of Criminology. He is now studying terrorism and international law as a post-doctoral fellow at the University of Montreal's International Center for Comparative Criminology.

Alison Liebling is a Lecturer and Director of the Prisons Research Centre at Cambridge University's Institute of Criminology. She is also a Fellow of Trinity Hall. Since 1992 she has conducted a wide range of empirical research into prisons, prisoners and young offenders, and published and contributed to numerous books and journals, including several edited books on deaths in custody and two empirical studies of suicides in prison. She has just completed a book called *Prisons and Their Moral Performance* (Oxford: Clarendon Press).

Ronnie Lippens is a Senior Lecturer in Criminology at Keele University in the UK. His research interests currently include images and imagery of law, peace and justice. He has published extensively on this topic in numerous scholarly books and journals.

John Pratt is Professor of Criminology at Victoria University, Wellington, New Zealand. He has published extensively on the sociology and history of punishment, including *Punishment in a Perfect Society* (1992), *Governing the Dangerous* (1997) and *Punishment and Civilization* (2002). He has also edited (with Mark Brown) *Dangerous Offenders: Punishment and Social Order* (2000). Since 1997 he has been editor of the *Australian and New Zealand Journal of Criminology*.

Phil Scraton is Professor of Criminology in the Institute of Criminology and Criminal Justice at Queen's University, Belfast. Until recently he was Professor and Director of the Centre for Studies in Crime and Social Justice at Edge Hill University College. His primary research interests include: the regulation and criminalisation of children and young people; controversial deaths and the state; the rights of the bereaved and survivors in the aftermath of disasters; the politics of truth and official inquiry; critical analysis and its application. He is the author of numerous books such as *The State of the Police* (Pluto, 1985) and *Hillsborough: The Truth* (Mainstream, 2000), co-author of *In the Arms of the Law* (Pluto, 1987), *Prisons Under Protest* (Open University Press, 1991) and *No Last Rights* (LCC/Alden Press, 1995) and editor of *Causes for Concern* (Penguin, 1984), *Law, Order and the Authoritarian State* (Open University Press, 1987), *'Childhood' in 'Crisis'?* (UCL Press, 1997) and *Beyond September 11* (Pluto, 2002). He has also written extensively on a range of human rights and social justice issues.

Clifford D. Shearing is a Professor in the Law Program, Research School of Social Science, Australian National University. He directs projects on developments in governance in Australia, Argentina, Northern Ireland and South Africa. His most recent book, *Governing Security: Explorations in Policing and Justice* (written with Les Johnston), was published by Routledge in 2003.

Philip Stenning obtained his S.J.D. (doctorate in law) at the University of Toronto and in 2003 accepted the position of Professor of Criminology at Victoria University of Wellington, New Zealand. Prior to that he was at the Center of Criminology, at the University of Toronto, for over thirty years. In addition to research on Aboriginal policing and justice issues, he has recently written on Canadian policy and law with respect to the sentencing of Aboriginal offenders. His principal research interests over the last thirty years have been in the areas of public and private policing, the prosecution process, accountability in criminal justice, firearms abuse and gun control laws, and occupational victimisation of police officers and taxi drivers.

Loïc Wacquant is Professor of Sociology at the University of California-Berkeley and Researcher at the Centre de sociologie européenne du Collège de France. A MacArthur Prize Fellow, his interests include comparative urban inequality and marginality, ethnoracial domination, penal institutions as instruments for the management of dispossessed and dishonoured groups, the body and violence, and social theory. His recent books include *Body and Soul: Ethnographic Notebooks of an Apprentice Boxer*, *Punir les pauvres* and *Deadly Symbiosis: Race and the Rise of Neoliberal Penality* (forthcoming with Polity Press). He is co-founder and editor of the interdisciplinary journal *Ethnography* and a regular contributor to *Le Monde diplomatique*.

Introduction: crime, truth and justice – offical inquiry and the production of knowledge

John Pratt and George Gilligan

'That's the trouble with judicial inquiries. They may be set up to shed light on one thing, but you never know what else will be illuminated' (*The Economist*, 23 August 2003, p. 46).

As we write these lines people have recently been queuing all night in London to attend the judicial inquiry, chaired by Lord Hutton, into the death of United Nations weapons expert Dr David Kelly. Not only are journalists, senior civil servants and security officials required to give evidence, but so too are a cabinet minister and even Prime Minister Tony Blair. While few such inquiries have ever generated this much interest before, Hutton highlights the key strategic role that public inquiries can play in the production of knowledge and understanding in relation to issues of crime, truth and justice. Of course, many people have strong opinions on matters of crime, criminal justice and punishment. They are regular themes of everyday discourse, letters to the editor columns of the press, calls to talkback radio and so on. What is it, though, that their knowledge of these matters is based on? How do they know what is happening in these worlds, other than becoming a criminal, or a victim, or having some involvement in the administration of criminal justice or punishment? One of the most obvious sources of this knowledge beyond everyday experience is the mass media, of course – as much criminological research in the last two decades or so has confirmed. But it is not the only source. A much less recognised one (but which actually provides a very healthy diet for the mass media which then relays it to us) is 'official discourse'. This ranges from the formal, extraordinary inquiry or commission convened to review, comment and advise on a particular crisis or scandal to the more mundane information usually released in annual reports, statistics and so on by government organisations.

Official discourse is thus very wide ranging in its scope: it can be designed to bring closure to controversial incidents or signal a break from the past, and it can seem little more than simple documentation of the work, expenditure and functions of a particular criminal justice bureaucracy written by its chief executive. What such discourse does, however, is to provide an official, objective truth about crime, criminal justice and punishment which puts a particular stamp on the available beliefs that individuals and social groups have of such matters – official discourse becomes the formal way of giving definition to the issue in hand. Thus the *official* crime statistics are exactly this and consequently set the terms of debate about the level of crime. Most importantly, for many, official discourse provides an objective truth – *the truth* – on the matters they are reflecting or adjudicating on. Commissions and inquiries, precisely because their constituency of senior civil servants and other authoritative figures makes them appear as 'impartial, expert and representative' (Cartwright 1975), must surely be telling the truth and constituting *the truth*. How could they not be doing so?

We know, however, as Burton and Carlen (1979) brought to our attention, that notwithstanding the claims to objectivity and the pursuit of impartial, rational analysis these formal bodies are unlikely to arrive at some irrefutable version of the truth, whatever the claims they may make for themselves in this regard. Instead, it becomes possible to see such inquiries as a way of repairing 'crises of legitimacy' (*ibid.* 13; see also Scraton this volume). Official discourse can thus lead to 'the systematization of modes of argument that proclaim the state's legal and administrative rationality. The discourse is a necessary requirement of political and ideological hegemony' (Burton and Carlen 1979: 48). One reading of the Hutton inquiry is that it was instigated as a way of stabilising the crisis of the Blair government brought on by Kelly's death amidst growing concerns about Britain's role in the war on Iraq.

As the opening chapter by Gilligan emphasises, such inquiries thus become crucial forms of governance in modern democratic societies, even if the mechanisms that produce them may vary according to different jurisdictions, cultures and legal traditions. He examines Royal Commissions of Inquiry as a lens with which to consider how official inquiry may perform a variety of roles for the state in contributing to official discourse, and in particular the capacities held by various forms of official inquiry for legitimation and representations of *truth*. He stresses not only that truth may often be a contestable space and so these capacities of official inquiry are especially influential in the criminal justice context, but also that the strategic importance of specific forms of official discourse can change and differ sharply across different eras. Dixon also shows in his chapter on police governance how certain types of inquiry are suited to particular state forms and the way in which they can assist in the establishment of governance. As central government in the United Kingdom has become more authoritative and directive in relation to its public services at least, the recourse to some varieties of inquiry, such as royal commissions, for reassurance or legitimacy, may become redundant. As part of the new meritocracy and efficient bureaucracy being constructed, new sources of official discourse – consultants' reports, for example – could be purchased; meanwhile the annual police reports have undergone a process of reconstruction, now providing generous documentation as to how their organisation conformed to the imperatives of efficiency and effectiveness.

Nonetheless, the legitimation theme and the assumed closure of debate that this brings with it is pursued in the chapter by Pratt who argues that one of the ways in which prisons became acceptable in Britain in the late nineteenth century, after considerable debate and conflict about prison policy direction, was because of successive Royal Commissions so regularly adjudicating in favour of the prison authorities on contentious issues, to the point where it came to be understood that they were always telling the truth, and their opposition – prisoners and their supporters – were by definition untruthful and unbelievable. Even in post-1980s Britain, where neo-liberal orthodoxy has become hostile to establishment pillars of support, Scraton shows that official discourse can still play such a role. In his chapter he looks in depth at inquiries into policing, school shootings, crowd control and civil and military intervention in Northern Ireland: when establishment forces coalesce around the establishment of 'truth', familiar issues such as lack of transparency, their very constitution, limited public involvement and so on simply fit the authorities' preconceived ideas of what really happened.

Equally, it has to be recognised that even in this new era when establishment institutions may be suspect because they put impediments in the way of government, governments may in some circumstances still prefer to institute formal commissions rather than draw on some of the competing sources of knowledge that would otherwise be available to them. This is because, as Stenning and LaPrairie show in their chapter on inquiries into Aboriginal justice and criminality in Canada, they are able as a result of the selection process to fly in the face of more neutral,

3

objective, scientific knowledge – the claims that once were associated with them. In this particular example, political correctness seemed to have much higher priority. They thus show how three such commissions between 1991 and 1996 formulated a public understanding of these matters and shaped policy so that it fitted the objectives of government: the devolution of the administration of justice onto Aboriginal communities themselves. To ensure that this would be perceived and understood as justifiable, the commissions became the way to assess the validity of such proposals – replacing standard social science research as the leading investigative methodology into such matters and their implications. The subsequent inquiry processes simply ignored a large body of such research which argued that Aboriginal over-representation in the justice system did not solely revolve around culture conflict and racial discrimination but was tied into a more complex web of demography, education, employment, migratory patterns and so on which also had to be addressed. And which, after the findings of the commissions, were not.

It would seem then that this rationality/hegemony linkage may still be important to the legitimacy of the late modern state and its institutions. Indeed, as the impacts of globalisation gather pace, the importance of this linkage assumes supra-national and international dimensions in the management of global markets and contemporary conflicts such as the war on terrorism, the management of social disorder and the conduct of war crimes tribunals. Loïc Wacquant discusses how a 'new penal common sense' is in the process of being diffused around the globe by complex networks of interests associated with official discourse within, and across, different jurisdictions. These new 'doxa' on security have been incubated by certain US think tanks and their supporters in the fields of government, academe and the media, and are being exported around the world, where they have been adapted to suit better the state traditions and cultural idioms of the different jurisdictions importing their ideology and methods. From a different perspective, Nils Christie shows how the Nuremberg trials, post-Second World War, set the agenda for subsequent inquiries in this mode (these preliminary thoughts of Christie are set out in more detail in his forthcoming book *A Suitable Amount of Crime* (Routledge, 2003)). They focused on the personal guilt of some of the Nazi high command – and so did not address questionable Allied activities: the bombing of Dresden, Hiroshima and Nagasaki and the formation of Russian gulags. Today, the International Crime Tribunal in The Hague perpetuates the principle that war winners should be the prosecutors and losers the defendants. He then goes on to discuss the potential of the proposals for the International Penal Court to break out of this framework.

Legitimation, then, is one role that official discourse can play – but it seems to us that it can also play a number of others. Far from simply supporting the status quo, acting as a deflector of public criticism or presenting a preferred government viewpoint, it may actually embarrass the government's own bureaucratic organisations. Thus, here, Hancock and Liebling demonstrate how the British Prison Inspectorate, established in 1981 as part of the Thatcherite drive towards 'open government' amid a general climate of distrust of many institutions and organisations of government, has frequently castigated the government's own prisons. As such, official discourse has a different role to play in the new model of the British state that superseded the postwar consensual welfare state. In this new state form, official discourse no longer simply tries to bring 'closure' or pretends that 'all is for the best in the best of all possible worlds'. Instead, it may become an aide-de-camp to government in exposing further layers of bureaucratic incompetence and inefficiency (providing ideological support for strategies such as privatisation and the emasculation of public sector unions). In these respects, the Woolf Report into British prisons in 1991 serves as an outstanding example of how such inquiries can indeed open up to public scrutiny previously closed off regions of public affairs; conducted in a liberal, open manner, it revealed successive layers of incompetence, inefficiency and corruption, peeling back from the actions of individuals and going all the way down to the very structure of the institution itself.

What happens next, though, with such inquiries that perhaps surpass all expectations in what they uncover and which, in terms of truth telling, are actually too successful? They not only embarrass bureaucracies but governments as well for having presided over such shortcomings. While no doubt a successful inquiry in terms of getting towards the truth they were seeking out, if they do not fit easily within the prevailing political ethos they may only have short-term 'scandal' impact rather than facilitating longer term-change. Here, Woolf was succeeded by two much narrower, restrictive inquiries, but more in keeping with climatic change, and the recommendations of which were more readily activated. What this points to is the need to take into account factors extraneous to the commissions and inquiries themselves, as David Brown illustrates in his contribution. That is to say, we have to take into account not simply the selection process to decide who will sit on the inquiry body and the terms that are set down for them; in addition we have to note what is not spoken or addressed – what effectively disappears. Thus if police corruption was so endemic in New South Wales as the Wood Commission in the mid-1990s indicated, how did this escape the notice of judges, prosecutors and all the other 'players' in the criminal justice system of that state for so long? Equally, commissions do not suddenly form themselves out of thin air – we have to note the important advance work that might take such forms as priming the media, briefings and leaks that help to secure the ground and terms on which the commission is to be set down.

It does seem the case, though, that our understanding of official discourse should be one that is less formulaic and more fragmented than that provided in Burton and Carlen (1979). It would seem clear that it can, *in addition to* the legitimation role prescribed for it, function as a form of social repair, a kind of healing process, as Leman-Langlois and Shearing demonstrate in their chapter. Their analysis emphasises the socially constituted nature of truth seeking within the context of Truth Commissions, and in particular how the South African Truth Commission promoted normative agendas that were oriented towards reconciliation in the post-apartheid South Africa.

There may be occasions when governments will resort to official inquiries as a reaction, a kind of panic rather than closure, to events well beyond the 'normal' parameters of their knowledge and experience. Although governments have retracted their role and responsibilities in the era of the neo-liberal state, paradoxically this may now open up new kinds of social problems that are 'beyond them' and they have to fall back on the old remedy of a formal inquiry. Lea demonstrates these processes at work in his chapter that discusses official inquiries into race riots in England. He shows how during the relatively short period of twenty years (1981–2001), a series of official inquiries changed dramatically in their approach to issues of race and urban violence in response to changing broader structural pressures such as globalisation, different state priorities regarding citizenship and a shrinking welfare state. By adopting such a perspective, Lea shows how official inquiries can be seen as 'museums of official discourse'.

Again, Lippens shows in his analysis of the Belgian child abduction, abuse and murder cases of 1996 how formal inquiries can, as it were, act as a kind of bridge between an outdated set of social arrangements and understandings and their replacements. In this case, the inquiries were extremely critical of the way the Belgian police and judiciary, and by extension the government, seemed only able to respond to these horrors that had been uncovered in a language that was cold and impartial, seemingly uncaring, making only superficial gestures towards redress, leading to suspicions of high level cover-ups and complicity. During the era of welfare-state bureaucratic governance, these gestures may have been enough towards establishing the truth about what had happened.

But in 1996 this was no longer the case. The social forces necessary to shut down debate and leave these matters in the hands of trusted authorities were themselves crumbling away before the marketisation of Belgian society, causing a collapse of confidence in formerly trusted points of reference. The subsequent inquiries allowed the possibilities of a new criminal justice framework to be glimpsed as much more victim oriented: a realignment that was much more in keeping with the more general shift away from the welfare-bureaucratic model of the Belgian state towards the consumerist democracy it was then turning into.

Finally, Carlen provides reflection and reconsideration of her work with Burton in the 1970s on official discourse. Clearly, the production of 'truth' in official discourse was something that had come to be largely taken for granted. Their work demonstrated how it had been able to deny or nullify alternative truth accounts. This is one effect, but not the only one, however; nor should the power of official discourse lead to an abandonment of belief in both truth and justice as fundamentally desirable attributes worth striving for. She goes on to illustrate, by reference to her work with prison reform groups, how various contestable spaces are likely to open up in the opposition between official discourse and its Others, allowing for some reshaping and realignment, but with uncertain, unrecognised and unknown consequences. Official discourse, as in her example, may actually incorporate elements to which it is opposed, transforming itself, but with entirely different effects from those intended from the source of the previously oppositional voice. Rather than closure of the issue though, this was only the end of one act in a timeless play, with no known finish to it, as the next episode in the interplay of discourse unfolds.

References

Burton, F. and Carlen, P., (1979) *Official Discourse: On Discourse Analysis, Government Publications, Ideology and the State*. London: Routledge, Kegan & Paul.

Cartwright, T.J., (1975) *Royal Commissions and Departmental Committees in Britain – A Case Study in Institutional Adaptiveness and Public Participation in Government*. London: Hodder & Stoughton.

Part I
Official discourse and modern societies

Chapter 1

Official inquiry, truth and criminal justice

George Gilligan

Introduction

The initial impetus for this collected volume of papers came upon my completing research upon the historical conditions surrounding the evolution of Royal Commissions of Inquiry (RCIs), and the political and ideological functions that such inquiries may serve (Gilligan, 2002). When writing that analysis I found that most of the academic texts that examined RCIs as a category of inquiry either discussed: (1) the legal and procedural aspects of RCIs, for example: Borchhardt (1978, 1991), Cartwright (1967, 1975), Clokie and Robinson (1937), Donaghue (2001), Gosnell (1934), Hallett (1982) and Hanser (1965); or (2) the subject of judges serving as royal commissioners, for example: Holmes (1955), McInerny (1978) and McInerny, Moloney and McGregor (1985). These issues are of course significant to an extent, but what most interested me regarding RCIs was the role that they might play in the nexus between official modes of inquiry and prevailing knowledge/power contexts. The most informative critique that I could find in this area was the work of Frank Burton and Pat Carlen on official discourse (Burton and Carlen, 1979). Given the critical importance of the linkages between official inquiry, representations of truth and governance to societal structures in so many countries around the world, I found it disappointing that my various web-based literature searches produced only a relatively small number of focused critical analyses of these linkages (as they applied to RCIs at least) in the intervening period of almost twenty-five years since Burton and Carlen's appraisal of official discourse. Some of the most relevant studies are those of McEachern (1987), Prasser (1982, 1985), Sheriff (1983), Woodward (1984), and collections of papers edited by Smith and Weller (1978) and Weller (1994). So, it was with these issues in mind that I approached my co-editor John Pratt to help gather together a group of scholars from around the world to analyse the linkages between official inquiry, truth and criminal justice as they impact in a range of contexts, including among others, policing and prisons. This book is the product of that collaboration.

For me, the most important question about the interactions between official inquiry, truth and criminal justice is, if I might paraphrase from Pat Carlen's chapter in this volume, *why bother*? Pat poses the question in the context of explaining the unease back in the early 1970s that she and Frank Burton felt about the nihilistic capacity of relentless analytic deconstruction to cloud the moral and political capacity of knowledge and law. I pose the *why bother* question in a different way. If one believes (and I certainly do) that linkages between official inquiry, representations of truth and governance to societal structures are critical to how societies function, and subsequently can have substantive effects on the lives of millions of people, then how can social scientists and others who are committed to notions of social justice justify *not bothering*? The need for critical analysis of these linkages is even greater in a criminal justice context, given the capacity of official inquiry and official representations of the *truth* to help shape the structure and operation of criminal justice systems, and the capacity of these systems to deprive people of their livelihood, possessions, reputation, liberty and, in the case of far too many jurisdictions around the world, their lives.[1] In recognition of this, many of the chapters in this volume focus on specific aspects of the criminal justice system in different jurisdictions. However, all academic outputs have pragmatic limitations of time, space and other resources. A consequence of this practical reality is that the contents of this book focus largely on the effects of official inquiry in certain developed western capitalist societies that are committed to principles of democracy and secular freedom. Nevertheless, some of the themes that recur throughout the book have universal application, for example notions of legitimation, the effects of prevailing sets of power relations, the classification of crime or deviance and the representation of truth.

Official discourse may be defined as: '... the systemisation of modes of argument that proclaim the state's legal and administrative rationality' (Burton and Carlen, 1979: 48). It is important to remember that the field of official discourse is characterised by its heterogeneity. At one level this is of course an unsurprising and indeed almost blindingly obvious statement to make, as one would expect the mechanisms that produce official discourse and specific modes of official inquiry to reflect the societal structures and cultural history of different societies. For example, RCIs are a category of official discourse production peculiar to British

Commonwealth jurisdictions. Nevertheless, some mechanisms that produce official discourse are common to most countries, such as inquiries conducted by government ministries or departments. It is necessary to restate these truisms, because what is both important and interesting is to consider the discursive frameworks and other social and political structures and processes that dictate first how modes of official inquiry develop, and then how they are utilised in different ways in some jurisdictions in comparison to others, and indeed how over time they are used in different ways in the same jurisdiction. For example, in this volume Lippens notes that in Belgium between 1830 and 1980 there were only nine parliamentary inquiries, but between 1980 and 2000 there were 16. Lippens discusses some of the broader structural socio-political changes in Belgium in the last twenty years that have contributed to this relative surge of parliamentary inquiry activity. The brief analysis below of RCIs acts as a window on the broader debate about the purposes and utility, social, political or otherwise, of official inquiry in general. Many jurisdictions around the world do not have RCIs, but instead utilise comparable mechanisms of official inquiry such as judicial inquiries, Senate Committees or other forms of parliamentary inquiry.

The contributions to this book seek to draw out the interactive linkages between official discourse, modes of official inquiry and notions of truth as they impact in the context of criminal justice. Consequently, core themes for this book are why are public inquiries deemed to be such a necessary component of official discourse in so many countries around the world, and how should such official inquiries be evaluated? If answers to these core questions can be found that can be generalised across countries and cultures (and this is a big if), there are likely to be multiple perspectives and explanations. A discussion of RCIs can start to highlight some of the key issues.

Royal Commissions of Inquiry – a window on official inquiry as a discourse mechanism of the state

As an example of the fluctuating popularity of different types of official inquiry let us consider for a moment Royal Commissions of Inquiry (RCIs). Within Britain and in some of its former colonies such as Australia and Canada, RCIs are an ad hoc, flexible, adaptive and adaptable mode of inquiry available to centralised authority, but their frequency can vary sharply between jurisdictions. For example, in the period 1970 to 2002 there have been 74 RCIs in Australia, 89 RCIs in Canada and by comparison only 11 RCIs in Britain (Gilligan, 2002: 290). Contrast this latter total of 11 with the fact that in Britain in their heyday of the mid-Victorian era there were 75 RCIs established between 1850 and 1859 (Clokie and Robertson 1937: 26).

The state apparatuses of mid-Victorian Britain were obviously less developed than those that exist today. In contemporary Britain individual government ministries have much greater managerial and technocratic capacity than their Victorian counterparts, a capacity that often includes units dedicated to research and policy development. Such units are arguably a much more efficient and less expensive tool for inquiry by the state than the cumbersome machinery that may be an RCI or other form of public inquiry. However, Australia and Canada also have developed similar fact-finding and policy development resources within their governmental infrastructures, so why do RCIs remain such a regular feature of the political landscape in Australia and Canada but have almost faded from view in Britain? It is not simply that the British have tired of RCIs, but rather a mix of constitutional, historical and political factors. Of these, one of the most significant is the constitutional reality that both Australia and Canada have a federal system of government and RCIs remain a functional mechanism for mediating some of the jurisdictional limitations of co-operative inquiries between individual states/provinces and between states/provinces and the federal government. This is especially important concerning crime-related issues that have a national context, such as the growth in recent years in the extent and impact of organised crime, because the bulk of criminal justice administration occurs at a state/provincial level. So, the intrinsic flexibility that RCIs offer, allied to the fact that their findings and/or recommendations are not binding, seem likely to ensure their continuing popularity in somewhere like Australia or Canada, where co-operation and flexibility may be required across constitutional paradigms in a variety of investigative contexts.

However, how effective as a mode of official inquiry are RCIs? Alan Herbert saw RCIs as a prima facie case of a failure to govern and believed that they are: '...generally appointed not so much for digging up the truth, as digging it in' (Herbert 1960: 17). Herbert mercilessly lampooned RCIs: 'The Royal Commission is not a new joke...It is the Ascot of the sport of inquiry' (*ibid*. 23). As George Bernard Shaw is reputed to have said: 'When a thing is funny, search it carefully for a hidden truth.' There is more than a smidgen of truth in Herbert's insults, but is he too harsh in his criticism of RCIs? Herbert is correct that RCIs are definitely not new. The first RCI in England is better known as the Domesday Book, ordered by the Norman Conqueror William I and compiled between 1080 and 1086. Essentially it was a taxation-oriented exercise in ascertaining land ownership (Clokie and Robinson 1939: 28). However, are RCIs as Herbert and other critics have suggested merely an expedient instrument of political management by governments in response to some public controversy, or do they present meaningful opportunities for the broader community to impact upon government policy and practice? My own research on RCIs (Gilligan 2002) found them (like I would suggest many other forms of official inquiry around the world) to be deeply ambiguous, both in their process and in their effects. RCIs like many other mechanisms of official inquiry perform two broad functions for the state:

- a pragmatic and/or legal function to investigate an issue for a government, collect information, submit a report and make recommendations; and

- a broader political or ideological function as a technique of governance, in particular a capability for crisis management of an issue or of a range of issues.

Most RCIs usually fall into the category of either being an information gatherer or a mechanism that provides *breathing space* for governments. The capacity of RCIs and other public inquiries as an information gatherer should not be underestimated, nor should their ability to provide a public forum for a wide array of interest groups to express their views. For example, Stenning and LaPrairie in this volume, while they are critical of various aspects of the Marshall Inquiry established by the Nova Scotia government in 1986, note that it did provide an opportunity for a '... wide variety of interested parties ...' to make submissions and became a '... broad-ranging inquiry into the entire administration of criminal justice in the province'. Also in this volume, Pratt, in his analysis of various English nineteenth-century RCIs and other official inquiries into prisons, discusses how they provided a high-visibility platform, not only for the promotion of those perspectives favoured by the state, but also for critics of the official regime (including prisoners) to voice their criticisms.

So given that official inquiries such as RCIs may offer a platform to attack *official versions of the truth* regarding issues or structures, why do governments take the risk with such inquiries? Prasser (1994: 6–8) offers ten possible explanations: to provide a perceived independent response to a crisis situation; to investigate allegations of impropriety; to obtain information; to define policy problems; to provide government with policy options; to review policies, programmes or organisations; to resolve public controversy; to help governments manage policy agendas; to justify government decisions; and to help governments determine what to do about previous promises. Some of these motivations may be true for some RCIs but not for others, and in terms of how they conduct themselves RCIs can be investigatory, inquisitorial or a combination of both. Their capacity for coercive powers of investigation varies between jurisdictions but in Australia for example, not only do they include both the ability to compel the attendance of witnesses and/or the production of documents, but also to examine witnesses under oath or affirmation (Moore 1913: 508). Such inquisitorial powers make RCIs an extremely powerful mode of inquiry with considerable political attractiveness. This is because a minister or a government not only has influence over the selection of commissioners and their terms of reference, but also in many contexts can distance themselves (if they so desire) from the operation and/or effects of the RCI. Often governments and state bureaucracies seek to reduce any political risk associated with official inquiries such as RCIs by defining the terms of an inquiry, appointing an *appropriate* head for the inquiry and selecting those involved in the administration of the inquiry (Moffitt 1985: 185).

Generally civil servants advise government ministers and draft the actual terms of reference for official inquiries such as RCIs, a process that might be described as an art form or a murky process depending on one's point of view. The civil service usually provides the secretary and draws up a short list of appropriate potential commissioners or inquiry heads from a pool of available notables often referred to in bureaucratic circles as 'The Book of the Great and the Good' (Hennessy 1986). The majority of those chosen to act as royal commissioners have been judges and lawyers (Holmes 1955: 266). This tendency can be explained in part by the acknowledged ability of experienced legal practitioners 'to get up the brief' and also a widespread assumption that they bring impartiality and independence to an inquiry (Wheare 1955: 85). This assumption is challenged by Scraton in this volume who argues that those who head public inquiries are likely to be: 'plumbed into the ideological "ways of seeing" and political "ways of doing" that constitute the routine expressions of civil service practice'. There are other types of pressure that the state can exert on official inquiries, such as financial restrictions and other budgetary pressures (Hallett 1982: 80–5). Also, RCIs may be terminated at the discretion of a government. So, given this range of pragmatic constraints and the almost impossible attempt to measure impacts of interest groups on any, or perhaps in the case of some RCIs and official inquiries, all of these constraints, it is probably fair to say that RCIs are not truly independent mechanisms of inquiry.

These various procedures that may lead to definitional and operational closure can contribute to what Burton and Carlen refer to as techniques of discursive affirmation, which seek to ensure that explanations acceptable to official discourse are always likely to be predominant (Burton and Carlen 1979: 51). Nevertheless, despite all the constraints listed above, it should be noted that the extensive and flexible powers that some official inquiries such as RCIs may possess empower them with the potential to resist being channelled into some sort of programme of discursive affirmation. Also RCIs, like many other forms of public inquiry, tend not to be subject to performance indicators, day-to-day executive oversight or other very specific forms of accountability. In turn, these characteristics may increase their capability (if they so choose) perhaps to be more entrepreneurial in their relations with the mass media and/or adopt positions that may run counter to the preferred positions of the apparatuses of the state that have appointed them.[2]

Nevertheless, it is reasonable to assert that an RCI or any mechanism of official inquiry that is subversive is a relatively *rare bird*, and it far more common for official inquiries to perform an issue management and/or legitimation role for governments and/or state agencies. This more common practice of official inquiries such as RCIs helped to inform Burton and Carlen's (1979: 48) view, that the purpose of such inquiries is 'to represent failure as temporary, or no failure at all, and to re-establish the image of administrative and legal coherence and rationality'. Inherent in this interpretation is the capacity that official discourse possesses for legitimation, a legitimating capacity to enhance the rationality of the state's view of specific events or issues in particular, and the state's view of the world in general, and then subsequently to persuade the state's citizens and those abroad of the truth and/or appropriateness of these state perspectives. This somewhat *darker* capacity of official discourse is discussed in the contributions of Lea, Scraton and Wacquant in this volume. Wacquant is critical of how networks of certain powerful official discourse interests in the US and Europe, especially certain influential US think tanks, are exporting around the globe specific ideologies of penal reasoning that in Wacquant's view are harmful to the interests of many sectors of the community in Europe and elsewhere. Both Lea and Scraton are critical of the activities of a number of official inquiries in Britain in recent years. Lea, writing in the context of race and urban violence in the United Kingdom, stresses that official inquiries can, over time, serve as 'museums of official discourse through which the practical working out, and metamorphosis, of dominant political ideologies about the relationship between ethnicity and social stability are revealed.'

However, there are inquiries, or series of inquiries, that seem to defy specific classification as a tool of vested interests of the state, for example the Stevens Inquiry/Inquiries into collusion between security forces and loyalist paramilitaries in Northern Ireland.[3] The third Stevens Inquiry produced damning indictments of some of the activities of security forces in Northern Ireland including 'collusion, the wilful failure to keep records, the absence of accountability, the withholding of intelligence and evidence, and the extreme of agents being involved in murder' (Stevens 2003: 3). Stevens also reported that all three of his inquiries endured widespread obstruction from the British Army and the Royal Ulster Constabulary (RUC) (*ibid*. 13). Together the three inquiries gathered 9,526 statements, seized 16,194 exhibits and recorded 10,391 documents totalling more than 1 million pages and as such comprise the largest investigation ever undertaken in Britain (*ibid*. 15). The Stevens Inquiry revelations are deeply prejudicial to the reputations of the British Army and the RUC, but how damaging are they to the current British government and why were the Stevens Inquiries allowed to become such an expensive juggernaut? This is probably an impossible question to answer but a complex cocktail of factors contributes. They include political influences such as the election of a Labour government in that country in 1997 replacing a Conservative government which had only a small majority of seats and was dependent on the support of the Ulster Unionists, and also the developing momentum of the Good Friday Peace Process as the British and Irish governments tried to broker a permanent and meaningful peace in Northern Ireland. There are broader cultural influences, such as the sheer community horror of the way in which Mr Finucane was murdered in front of his family, and the fact that both Mr Finucane and Mr Lambert were not members of terrorist or criminal groups. Also, sometimes the quest or desire for truth can develop an irresistible momentum for an inquiry that hurdles barriers political, financial, sectarian or otherwise. The effects of the Stevens Inquiries are ongoing and are likely to be a force for positive reforms concerning some of the activities of security forces, but not many official inquiries provide such impact. More common is the capacity that official inquiries possess to act as a convenient mechanism of legitimation for the state. It is one of their most important and contentious characteristics, and merits intense scrutiny of both their form and function.

The capacity of official inquiry for legitimation and representations of truth

When the reputation of a particular structure or process is threatened, state agents may activate any of a range of responses intended to engender a sense of reassurance and the promotion of social harmony.

The most symbolically valuable (and therefore among the most attractive) responses for the state are those that are popularly perceived to be objective, politically independent and of high status, such as official inquiries. These characteristics combine to provide official inquiries with an aura of authority in the public consciousness regarding their interpretation of facts and issues. This aura, whether it has a regal ring as is the case with RCIs, or not, can at certain times be extremely seductive *to* the state, and at times can be used seductively *by* the state. Some official inquiries may be seen more clearly to act as a legitimation device for the state than others; see for example in this volume Scraton's criticism of the inquiry by the then Lord Chief Justice, Lord Widgery, into the fatal shootings of 13 civilians by British soldiers in Derry, Ireland in 1972. That inquiry, like many other official inquiries, acted as a conduit to help bridge a current, often problematic situation to whatever might be the desirable context or development for the interests of government and/or state bureaucracies. The Widgery Inquiry was quite proactive in its efforts to legitimate the activities of the state agents that were under investigation. However, the legitimation processes undertaken by official inquiry can also be quite passive as is demonstrated by David Brown's analysis in this volume of a number of official inquiries in New South Wales. The inquiry into the wrongful conviction of Ziggy Pohl simply maintained a discursive strategy of silence on the glaring failures of the system that produced such a blatant miscarriage of justice. The Wood Royal Commission was silent about the failures of the judiciary, Director of Public Prosecutions and the legal profession to utilise the prosecutorial and judicial processes to help combat the corrosive effects of process corruption among the police force of New South Wales. Brown is critical of both these inquiries and also of the New South Wales Police Integrity Commission for their inability to be reflexively critical of the 'routines, structures, practices and assumptions of the criminal justice system'.

When official inquiries neglect to be reflexive regarding structural and/ or habitual weaknesses of state agencies then they are failing in what one might reasonably assume should be a core public interest duty for such inquiries – a commitment to the improvement of public services. But, viewed from another perspective, turning a Nelsonian eye to problematic situations or being overly gentle in lines of inquiry may sometimes not only be politically helpful, but also provide a boost in legitimacy to state actors under pressure. However, it is very difficult to assert the extent to which official inquiries as a generic grouping perform a legitimation function for the state, because historical experience demonstrates that such inquiries are capable of manufacturing their own forms of legitimacy or belief that may be contrary to the position that the state would prefer them to adopt (Gilligan 2002: 301). It is this intrinsic capacity for variety and political risk that make official inquiries '...challenging to theoretical generalization' (Althaus 1994: 197). However, as stated earlier, despite this capacity for variety the reality is that a subversive official inquiry is much more rare than a legitimating one.

At the heart of debates about official inquiry and a key question that all the contributions in this volume seek to investigate in their different ways is how is truth discovered, socially constructed and disseminated within the context of official discourse. These processes are not a given. Indeed they are worked upon by various interested parties, as well as affected, whether knowingly or unknowingly, by broader structural pressures such as the effects of everyday routinisation or protocols such as legal or constitutional conventions. In this volume Scraton reiterates Foucault's observation that representations of truth are inextricably intertwined with prevailing sets of power relations, and as such power continually interrogates, inquires, registers, institutionalises and professionalises regimes of truth (Foucault 1980: 93). It is these regimes of truth that constitute much of official discourse. RCIs and other official inquiries are specific forms of truth regimes but there are many more types. They include what to many may seem the mundane, such as the annual reports on a myriad of agencies, in the criminal justice infrastructure and elsewhere, each signed off as a true record of that agency's performance by its chief executive or by its relevant inspectorate. These annual reports, whether in the fields of policing, prisons, social services or transport, may be voluminous records of resources, expenditure, activities and achievements, and some may appear impenetrable, intimidating or hopelessly distant and/or boring to many in the community. However, it is important to remember that in some instances these official reports may be the only significant data available. So, almost by default, they provide the empirical *truth* on which to evaluate the effectiveness or otherwise of that agency. It is almost inevitable in these circumstances that the assertions of some of these reports are not challenged by many, as most people seek to simply get on with all the daily challenges that they face in their own social and working lives. This is not to say this is always so or that such reports will automatically offer glowing reports of agency performance. In an era of new managerialism in the public sector, with a growing emphasis on smaller government, or at least a diminishing of the role of the welfare state, or a 'depillarisation', to employ the term used by Lippens in this volume, there seems to be a growing willingness to demand more accountability and cost efficiency for the resources expended in the provision of public services. This is a new variable in the seemingly never-ending creation and interpretation of truth in official discourse.

Thus there can be many competing, complementary or contradictory truths about the same sets of social facts as various actors evaluate these facts from perspectives that are premised on their own inherent assumptions or presumptions. The chapter by Pratt in this volume highlights the power, both explanatory and political, that assumed truth can come to wield as he analyses how 'the contestable prison for much of the nineteenth century became the acceptable prison for much of the twentieth.' In deconstructing the 'garrulous discourse' that constituted penal reform politics from 1850 to 1895, Pratt demonstrates that how prisons should be organised was in fact a fiercely contested discourse site in that period. Of crucial importance were a succession of formal inquiries into prisons, culminating in the Report of the Gladstone Committee (1895) that won 'the battle for truth', in the sense that they helped establish the central bureaucratic control of the state over prisons that in turn ensured that official prison discourse would for a very long period from then on be the only voice with sufficient power to present a view of the truth about prisons that was widely accepted as legitimate. Hancock and Liebling examine similar issues one hundred years later as they consider the interaction between reliability and effectiveness in truth seeking and in reform in the context of inquiries into prisons. Their focus is on the relative power and legitimacy of official inquiries into contemporary English prisons and how these newer, and in some cases more critical, forms of inquiries into prisons sought to establish 'both the *reality of what happened* in a given set of circumstances and *knowledge-as-understanding about the organisation concerned* more generally'. In these contexts, evaluations regarding the legitimacy of the processes of official inquiry themselves were seen as being heavily dependent on meaningful levels of fairness and impartiality – in short the *truthfulness* of the various accounts, including official discourse perspectives, that were on offer.

This reflexive interaction between truthfulness and official inquiry is discussed in interesting ways by Lippens in this volume as he analyses the Belgian Parliamentary Inquiry into the Dutroux and Consorts Case. He draws on the work of Marcel Mauss (1980) to show how the Dutroux Inquiry might be viewed as a 'gift' to representations of truth. By implication, almost any official inquiry or other form of official discourse might carry a similar potential as a gift to the truth. However, as Lippens cautions, from a Maussian perspective a gift 'is essentially, ontologically, a multiplicity, and is therefore able to hold and generate a multitude of discourses about it.' Lippens argues that the Dutroux Inquiry was both a 'gift as a consumer item' intended for passive consumption and a 'gift as a piece of technology' intended for active consumption, as well as a form of management practice, i.e. as a practice of managing the enormous outburst of emotion at the time of the Dutroux affair. One might extrapolate this analogy to certain other official inquiries and other forms of official discourse as they are offered by the state to its citizens as gifts and/or managerial strategy as part of the everyday business of governing. For example, Leman-Langlois and Shearing in their chapter on the South African Truth Commission examine what the function of truth is in the context of a specific type of official inquiry – truth commissions. They found that the truth-seeking mechanism was utilised in the South African context for the purposes of national reconciliation, restorative justice, community education and victim rehabilitation.

It should be becoming clear to the reader that truth in official discourse can be an atomistic concept, or indeed mechanism, subject to fluctuating pressures and interpretations. Thus if truth can be a technology, then like any technology or commodity it can be worked on and in some instances owned, whether by official discourse or by other interests.

Conclusion

So, what are we to make of official discourse in general and official inquiry in particular, especially as they affect criminal justice issues and structures? First, the importance of national and cultural differences regarding prevailing forms of official inquiry should be acknowledged, for example the effects on official inquiry of different constitutional structures. Second, as Stone emphasises, official inquiries should be seen as a normal and continuing feature of parliamentary democracies, and a reflection of the dispersion of expertise and authority in society that helps to reflect the meaning of the state in society (Stone 1994: 248–58). However, this expertise component of inquiries should not be conflated with effectiveness. For example, RCIs in Australia can be over-reliant on costly and inefficient methodologies based on cross-examination and inquisitorial praxis – see Leader Elliott (1982, 1983) and Egger (1985). The relatively poor performance of RCIs in Australia in utilising social sciences research methodologies contrasts with a country like Sweden '... where commissions of inquiry are integrated into the policy process' (Prasser 1994: 2). Also, the ad hoc nature of RCIs in Australia in particular means that they 'may run out of control, undermine a reputation on hearsay, drone expensively and ineffectively on and on, expand their powers' (Weller 1994: 266).

Many Australian RCIs, indeed many inquiries in many countries, are totally ignored or quickly forgotten. However, some have more influence than others and as Dixon notes in this volume an individual inquiry 'may achieve totemic status, so that its influence goes beyond its specific recommendations.' The latter type of official inquiry may become a force for the public good but as Scraton cautions, if considering official inquiries as an overall category, '... their representation and justification as independent, impartial and value-free, as apolitical antidotes to the partisanship of politics and the polarisation of the law, cannot be accepted uncritically.' This legitimation capacity of official discourse in general and official inquiry in particular should not be underestimated. It is undeniable that some inquiries are utilised as symbolic instruments of agenda manipulation or management by state agencies, but as noted earlier there are examples of other inquiries that can play a subversive role to the vested interests of state agencies. Nevertheless, official inquiry as a policy mechanism may not necessarily be against the public interest and indeed can help to produce a range of practical benefits to the general community. In addition, official inquiry can play a social repair or healing role, as seen in the case of the South African Truth Commission discussed in this volume by Shearing and Leman-Langlois.

So, in closing, might I once again paraphrase from Pat Carlen in this volume when she is describing her preferred form of poststructuralism, and offer this thought to the reader as a conceptual lens to carry through the remainder of this book and beyond. The challenge regarding official inquiry, truth and criminal justice is to construct analytic models that simultaneously both recognise and deny the power of official discourse without eulogising it as truth.

Notes

1. For example, in its *Annual Report 2002*, Amnesty International (AI) reports that during 2002 at least 1,526 people were executed in 31 countries and that at least 3,248 people were sentenced to death in 67 countries. These figures include only those cases that were known to AI and it is almost certain that the true totals in reality were higher. It should be noted that the vast majority of executions worldwide are carried out in a tiny handful of countries, for, as AI comments, in 2002, 81% of all known executions took place in China, Iran and the USA. See: http://web.amnesty.org/library/Index/ENGACT500072003.
2. For extended discussion of this almost subversive potential held by certain forms of official inquiry such as RCIs see Gilligan (2002).
3. In fact the saga that is the Stevens Inquiry is really three separate inquiries. John Stevens was first appointed to head an inquiry into collaboration between

security forces and loyalist paramilitaries in September 1989 when he was Deputy Chief Constable in the Cambridgeshire Constabulary. In January 1990, the allegedly secure headquarters of that inquiry suffered a fire in suspicious circumstances hours before the inquiry team was to launch a series of arrests, but the inquiry's efforts still led to 43 subsequent convictions. In April 1993, following sustained criticism from nationalist politicians, the media and other interest groups, Stevens (by then Chief Constable of Northumbria Police) was appointed to begin a second inquiry into security forces in Northern Ireland. In April 1999, Stevens (now Sir John and Commissioner of the Metropolitan Police Service) began a third inquiry specifically into the circumstances surrounding the murder of Catholic solicitor Patrick Finucane and Protestant student Brian Lambert. On 12 February 1989, in front of his wife and three children in their family home in Belfast, Mr Finucane was shot 14 times by two masked gunmen and on 13 February 1989 the Ulster Freedom Fighters claimed responsibility for his murder. Mr Lambert was shot at a building site in Belfast on 9 November 1987.

References

Althaus, C. (1994) Legitimation and agenda-setting: development and the environment in Australia and Canada's North. In P. Weller (ed.) *Royal Commissions and the Making of Public Policy*. Melbourne: Macmillan, pp. 186–97.

Borchhardt, D.H. (1978) *Checklist of Royal Commissions, Select Committees of Parliament and Boards of Inquiry, Part V, Queensland, 1859–1960*. Sydney: Wentworth Books.

Borchhardt, D.H. (1991) *Commissions of Inquiry in Australia*. Sydney: La Trobe University Press.

Burton, F. and Carlen, P. (1979) *Official Discourse: On Discourse Analysis, Government Publications, Ideology and the State*. London: Routledge & Kegan Paul.

Cartwright, T.J. (1967) Review of Guide to Decision: the Royal Commission. *Canadian Journal of Economics and Political Science*, 33: 482–4.

Cartwright, T.J. (1975) *Royal Commissions and Departmental Committees in Britain – A Case Study in Institutional Adaptiveness and Public Participation in Government*. London: Hodder & Stoughton.

Clokie, H.M. and Robinson, J.W. (1937) *Royal Commissions of Inquiry, The Significance of Investigations in British Politics*. Stanford, CA: Stanford University Press.

Donaghue, S. (2001) *Royal Commissions and Permanent Commissions of Inquiry*. Sydney: Butterworths.

Egger, S. (1985) Drugs: high on commission. *Australian Society*, April: 6–8.

Foucault, M. (1980) *Power/Knowledge: Selected Interviews and Other Writings 1972–1977*, ed. C. Gordon. Brighton: Harvester Wheatsheaf.

Gosnell, H.F. (1934) British royal commissions of inquiry. *Political Science Quarterly*, 49: 84–118.

Gilligan, G.P. (2002) Royal commissions of inquiry. *Australian and New Zealand Journal of Criminology*, 35(3): 289–307.

Hallett, L.A. (1982) *Royal Commissions and Boards of Inquiry, Some Legal and Procedural Aspects*. Sydney: Law Book Company.

Hanser, C.J. (1965) *Guide to Decision: The Royal Commission*. Totowa, NJ: Bedminster Press.

Hennessy, P. (1986) *The Great and the Good: An Inquiry into the British Establishment*. London: Policy Studies Institute.

Herbert, A.P. (1960) *Anything but Action? A Study of the Uses and Abuses of Committees of Inquiry*, Hobart Paper No. 5. London: Barrie & Rockliff.

Holmes, J.D. (1955) Royal Commissions. *Australian Law Journal*, 29: 253–72.

Leader Elliot, I. (1982) Heroin: mythologies for law enforcers. *Criminal Law Journal*, 6: 6.

Leader Elliot, I. (1983) Heroin myths revisited: the Stewart Report. *Criminal Law Journal*, 7: 333.

McEachern, W.A. (1987) Federal advisory commissions in an economic model of representative democracy. *Public Choice*, 54: 41–62.

McInerny, M. (1978) The appointment of judges to commissions of inquiry and other extra-judicial activities. *Australian Law Journal*, 52: 540–53.

McInerny M., Moloney, G.J. and McGregor, D.G. (1985) *Judges as Royal Commissioners and Chairmen of Non-Judicial Tribunals*. Adelaide: Australian Institute of Judicial Administration Incorporated.

Mauss, M. (1980) *The Gift*. London: Routledge & Kegan Paul.

Moffitt, A. (1985) *A Quarter to Midnight, The Australian Crisis: Organised Crime and the Decline of the Institutions of the State*. North Ryde, NSW: Angus & Robertson.

Moore, W. Harrison (1913) Executive commissions of inquiry. *Columbia Law Review*, 13: 500–23.

Prasser, S. (1982) Public inquiries: their use and abuse. *Current Affairs Bulletin*, 68(9): 4–12.

Prasser, S. (1985) Public inquiries in Australia: an overview. *Australian Journal of Public Administration*, 44: 1–15.

Prasser, S. (1994) Royal commissions and public inquiries: scopes and uses. In P. Weller (ed.) *Royal Commissions and the Making of Public Policy*. Melbourne: Macmillan, pp. 1–21.

Report of the Gladstone Committee (1895) London: PP LVII.

Sheriff, P. (1983) State theory, social sciences and governmental commissions. *American Behavioral Scientist*, 26(5): 669–80.

Smith, R.F.I. and Weller, P. (eds) (1978) *Public Service Inquiries in Australia*. St Lucia: University of Queensland Press.

Stevens, J. (2003) *Stevens Inquiry 3, Overview and Recommendations*, http://www.met.-police.uk/commissioner/MP-Stevens-Enquiry-3.pdf.

Stone, B. (1994) Success in public inquiries: an analysis and a case study. In P. Weller (ed.) *Royal Commissions and the Making of Public Policy*. Melbourne: Macmillan, pp. 244–58.

Weller, P. (1994) Royal commissions and the governmental system in Australia. In P. Weller (ed.) *Royal Commissions and the Making of Public Policy*. Melbourne: Macmillan, pp. 259–66.

Weller, P. (ed.) (1994) *Royal Commissions and the Making of Public Policy*. Melbourne: Macmillan.

Wheare, K.C. (1955) *Government by Committee: An Essay on the British Constitution*. Oxford: Clarendon Press.

Woodward, E. (1984) An insight into royal commissions. *Law Institute Journal*, Vol 58, pp. 1459–61.

Chapter 2

Royal commissions and criminal justice: behind the ideal

David Brown

Introduction

A re-reading of Burton and Carlen's *Official Discourse* (1979) more than two decades after its publication is instructive in various ways. Like all research, *Official Discourse* is a product of its conjuncture, specified as a meeting of 'the discourses of linguistics, psychoanalysis and Marxism' (1979: 20). It evoked for this re-reader a sense of how much the conjuncture has changed, along with a sneaking nostalgia for the theoretical rigour and political militancy of the times which it reflects. Volosinov, Lacan and Althusser meet at the textual crossroads of *Official Discourse*, while Hindess and Hirst (1978) point a path out of epistemology and Hall *et al.* (1978) signpost shifts in the balance of hegemony in a period of constant 'legitimacy crises'. The result is an ambitious, challenging and theoretically dense text, open, with the benefit of hindsight, to charges of functionalism.

Five specific inquiries – James on the Challenor case (1965); Devlin on identification evidence after specific miscarriages (1976); Scarman on Grunwick (1977); Scarman on violence and civil disturbances in Northern Ireland in 1969 (1972) and Diplock on legal procedures to deal with terrorist activities in Northern Ireland (1972) – are deconstructed within a theorised 'general textual function' (1979: 8) of 'intellectual collusion' and 'the constant renewal of hegemonic domination ... in the process of reproducing specific ideological social relations, a strategy of discursive incorporation through which legitimacy crises are repaired ...' (1979: 7–8). The 'Official Discourse' of royal commissions is the work of 'professional functionaries' ('the state's men') who further the 'overall hegemonic and legitimating strategies of the state' through 'discursive incorporation', legitimacy repair, celebration and reaffirmation (1979: 51–2).

But if this seems to rather decisively and reductively foreclose the why questions, the how questions are specifically left open as a 'product of the subject, objects, themes and theories created within the discursive regularities of the work' necessitating a 'consideration of the conditions of existence of official discourse and a discursive deconstruction of selected texts' (1979: 8). The 'main problem' for 'Official Discourse' is seen to be 'that all problems have to be discussed in terms of an ideal of distributive justice which cannot admit to the material conditions which render that ideal impossible' (1979: 95). In order to overcome this problem 'the alternative, unofficial version the Other of the discourse' has to be confronted, incorporated and suppressed (1979: 70). Here the identification of particular paradigms and syntax through which this attempt to effect a 'discursive closure' is conducted is instructive, as is the recognition that such attempts are always partially unsuccessful as 'the Other constantly obtrudes, demanding a recognition at the limits of discourse' (1979: 138). So that, despite its overarching functionalism, *Official Discourse* makes a substantial contribution to the study of the 'paradigmatic' and 'syntagmatic' techniques of selected official discourse.

This chapter will attempt in a much less theorised, more mundane and pragmatic way, to add a few observations to the politico-legal discussion of the strategies, techniques and outcomes of certain criminal justice oriented royal commissions in the Australian, indeed New South Wales (NSW), context. It will not be suggested that these commissions can be accounted for in terms of some legitimation-repair function carried out on behalf of the state. The analysis will be conducted at a more conjunctural level, stressing specificity and local context. Royal commissions will be given a broad interpretation to include not only the traditional judicial royal commissions but also the new hybrids in the form of crime and corruption commissions, task forces, standing committees and special judicial inquiries into specific miscarriage cases.

The various inquiries will be approached not as always and already exercises in legitimation and closure but as sites of political, legal, moral and discursive struggle, sites heavily traversed by power relations but open nevertheless to the voices and influence of 'alternative, unofficial' pressure groups, social movements and individuals. As Gilligan points out against Burton and Carlen, royal commissions are not all responses to crisis situations; they can be effective information gatherers; they can generate accountability; some can escape their origins and have profoundly 'destabilising' effects on governments (Gilligan 2002: 294).

27

The conditions of existence, conduct and outcomes of specific inquiries are diverse and contingent on a whole host of factors such as the political imperatives behind their establishment, the broader conjuncture, the type of commission agency involved, the particular appointments of commissioner and of key staff, the level of resources supplied by government, the terms of reference, decisions as to rights of standing and legal representation, the level of media interest and coverage and its terms and themes, the timetable involved, types of evidence produced and chance events, to mention just a few of the more obvious.

The main aim of the chapter will be to explore aspects of the hegemony of legal methodology and discourse apparent in the conduct of particular inquiries. Central to this hegemony is the institutionalised climate of adversarialism centred on the practice of cross examination and, as Burton and Carlen point out, the (always partly unattainable) discursive attempt to celebrate an 'idealised conception of justice' (1979: 138). This aim will be approached by examining in greater detail three inquiries. The first is a single-case miscarriage inquiry into the conviction of Ziggy Pohl, the second the wide ranging Wood Royal Commission into the NSW Police Service (1997) and the third a spin-off inquiry by the NSW Police Integrity Commission (PIC), a creature of the Wood Royal Commission, into certain matters surrounding the Leigh Leigh rape/murder case.

The Ziggy Pohl inquiry will show the difficulty apparently experienced by the inquiring judge in explaining how it is that the normal, and in his view quite unexceptional and proper operation of the criminal justice system could produce a shocking miscarriage of justice. The discussion of the Wood Royal Commission will show how the 'judicial stare ... the ideological site where common law, common-sense and epistemology are conflated' (Burton and Carlen 1979: 69) can sometimes be revelatory of the activities and practices of police, while simultaneously blinkered in relation to the practices of other criminal justice agencies such as prosecutors, the legal profession and the judiciary. The third inquiry will show how commissions, in this case the NSW PIC, can seek to discipline and exclude bearers of non-legal methodologies and discourses such as feminist criminologists in the process of conducting what is increasingly a hybrid endeavour of investigation, public hearings and media management, geared at least in part to shoring up their own practices and legitimacy, rather than those of 'the state', 'the criminal justice system' or 'justice'.

Ziggy Pohl: a miscarriage of justice, but nothing went wrong

In March 1971 a Queanbeyan carpenter came home from work around midday to find his wife, Joyce, dead in the bedroom of their flat. He had called home from work around 9.30 am and she was still alive. Medical evidence put the time of death as between 8.45 am and 9.45 am. Pohl's sister in law had visited the flat around 11.30 am but had not gone into the bedroom and so had not seen the body. Pohl said that the gas was turned on when he came home at 12 noon and there was a small hole in the door but his sister in law did not notice these things. He said a watch and some money had been taken from the flat. He was arrested one month later and charged with his wife's murder. In November 1973 a jury convicted him of murder after a trial lasting five days. He was sentenced to life imprisonment. He appealed against the conviction to the NSW Court of Criminal Appeal but his appeal was dismissed. Pohl sought legal advice on a leave to appeal application to the High Court but was advised not to appeal. He served ten years' imprisonment before being release on licence and his licence was discharged five years later in 1988.

In September 1990 a man called Roger Bawden walked into Queanbeyan police station and confessed to the murder of Joyce Pohl some 19 years previously. To the embarrassment of police, his detailed confession closely fitted the facts of the crime. He drew an accurate map of the interior of the flat and said he had taken a watch and some money, later pawning the watch. A Commission of Inquiry by a Supreme Court judge was established into Pohl's conviction and it reported in May 1992 (McInerney 1992). The report concluded that there were substantial doubts about Pohl's guilt and recommended that he be pardoned. Bawden was later charged with the murder of Joyce Pohl and pleaded guilty. The inquiry acknowledged that 'had it not been for the confession of Bawden no doubt would have arisen as to Pohl's guilt' (1992: 76). The inquiry notes that 'his continuous protestations of innocence were regarded initially by probation and parole officers as a factor inhibiting his rehabilitation' and one report noted that 'he seemed to have little faith in the justice system' (1992: 43), which is perhaps hardly surprising.

Amazingly, it seemed no one was at fault; a tragic miscarriage of justice had occurred but nothing went wrong in the criminal justice process. According to the inquiry no fault lay with the investigating detectives who had 'carried out a careful and thorough investigation' (1992: 18) even though it came up with the wrong man. More generally the Commissioner was:

Satisfied that the Crown case was presented fairly to the jury. There was no suggestion of any impropriety by any of the police officers in their investigation or in the evidence that they gave, nor is there any suggestion that the lay witnesses gave their evidence other than to the best of their recollection. Looking at the whole of the circumstances as they appeared at the trial, no criticism can be levelled at the trial process, the decision of the jury, nor the decision of the Court of Criminal Appeal. (1992: 20–1)

This conclusion echoed the certainty of the NSW Court of Criminal Appeal some 15 years earlier when McClemens CJ and Lee J concluded, despite the trial judge having expressed surprise at the jury verdict:

Once it is seen that the death took place at a time when the appellant, on his own admission, could have been at the house, then the convincing evidence that someone altered the condition of the house after Mrs Pohl visited it later in the morning, leads inevitably to the conclusion that the possibility of a casual intruder being the killer is rationally not open. (1992: 20)

'Inevitability' and 'rationality' are, it seems, not all they are cracked up to be. As Hogg notes:

Ziggy Pohl made the transition from grieving husband to convicted murderer with remarkable ease. But if this is scary, what is truly remarkable is that this apparently happened without anybody being at fault. At least this was the conclusion of the inquiry. If this can be the outcome in a case of murder (where we might reasonably expect adherence to the highest investigative and forensic standards), what can be expected in case of a more typical, less serious nature? (2001: 312)

Here then in the Pohl case, confronted with a spectacular miscarriage of justice, a point at the limits of justice where Burton and Carlen's 'Other' has rather obviously raised its head in the form of the confession of Roger Bawden, the real killer, no explanation of how that point was reached is offered by the inquiring judge. Faced with a justice that is patently less than ideal, yet where no evidence of obvious malpractice is evident, the discursive strategy simply becomes one of silence, of offering no explanation at all. However obviously unsatisfactory, such a strategy and 'lack of unease' (Hogg 2001: 341) is apparently preferable to addressing the way in which the routine and apparently unproblematic practices of the criminal process can result in shocking miscarriages of justice, even in cases supposedly invoking the 'highest investigative and forensic standards'. As Hogg notes: 'It is the very ordinariness of the circumstances that led to Ziggy Pohl's conviction that make it such a singular tragedy' (2001: 343).

Issues which might have been addressed by a commission prepared to face up to the fallibility of the criminal justice system include: what the presumption of innocence and proof beyond a reasonable doubt actually mean in practice; the fact that standards of sufficiency of evidence are subordinated to the pragmatics of an adversarial contest; the imbalance in access to investigative resources between prosecution and accused; the lack of a right to competent legal counsel; the dubious precision accorded to medical evidence of the time of death; the lack of supervision over police investigation and the ease with which investigation blurs into accusation and evidence assembly becomes a partisan and highly selective process which seeks to confirm the original 'case theory' (for example because the police discounted the intruder theory, no check was made of local pawnbrokers for a watch); and the inadequacy and irrelevancy of avenues of appeal. 'The judge evinces no conception of what a careful and competent investigation might have looked like independently of the investigations the police actually undertook. There is not even any notion that this might be an issue' (Hogg 2001: 342). An attempt at 'closure' hardly seems the word to describe the discursive strategy in operation here, unless it is closure of the 'leave the door open and hope no one will notice and wander in' sort.

Process corruption and the lack of judicial reflexivity in the Wood Royal Commission Report

Introduction

The Wood Commission into NSW Police was established in 1994 when the then opposition Australian Labor Party (ALP) backed a motion by long-time anti-corruption independent MP, John Hatton. The inquiry was bitterly opposed by the governing Liberal Party/National Party Coalition government and the then Police Commissioner. Within a relatively short period of time, certainly by the release of its Interim Report (1996) the Commission had been remarkably successful in revealing extensive entrenched corruption in a wide range of areas. These included: process corruption; gratuities and improper associations; substance abuse; fraudulent practices; assaults and abuse of police powers; compromise or favourable treatment in prosecutions; theft and extortion; protection of the drug trade; protection of club and vice operators; protection of gaming and betting interests; drug trafficking; interference with internal investigations and the code of silence; and other circumstances suggestive of corruption (*Final Report*, 1997: Vol. 1, 83–4).

The success in revealing extensive 'entrenched' and 'systemic' corruption was brought about in part by the 'power and resources' accorded the Commission (1997: Vol. 1, 144), by some innovative investigative techniques, particularly the production of video evidence, and the 'roll-over' of some key police witnesses such as Trevor Haken relatively early in the process. Selective examples of the video surveillance, in particular the 'crotch-cam' shots of 'Chook Fowler' trousering wads of cash and uttering endless permutations on the 'f' word, achieved international media cult status. Such readily understandable and widely conveyed images grabbed public attention, helped build up a strong momentum for further revelation, swept aside the remnants of the 'rotten apple' thesis and created a strong public and political demand for reform. While not making specific published findings against individuals the inquiry resulted in a significant number of police being dismissed or resigning ('separations' as the Commission puts it), and cleared the ground for later dismissal, and possible prosecutions or internal disciplinary actions (see generally Dixon 1999; Dixon this volume).

Process corruption

Direct evidence of police 'on the take' or dealing in drugs tends to fall within most definitions of corruption. The Commission was suitably alert to concentrating only on the easy cases and broad in its definition of corruption which importantly included process corruption, which it listed as comprising variously: perjury; planting of evidence; verbals in the form of unsigned records of interview and note book confessions; denial of basic rights in respect of matters such as the use of a caution or detention for the purpose of interview; assaults and pressure to induce confessions; gilding the evidence to present a better case; posing as a solicitor to advise suspects to co-operate with police; tampering with the product of electronic interception to remove any matter that might prove embarrassing; unofficial and unauthorised practices such as putting suspected street drug dealers onto a train and 'banning' them from an area; and 'taxing' criminals who are seen as beyond the law (1997: Vol. 1, 84).

As the Commission notes, process corruption 'is often directed at those members of the community who are least likely or least able to complain, and it is justified by police on the basis of procuring the conviction of persons suspected of criminal activity or anti-social conduct, or in order to exercise control over sections of the community' (Vol. 1, 26). The reports give numerous examples of the various process corruption practices and some useful case studies across a range of different police sections. Many of the forms of process corruption were common across these quite different sectors, indicating its entrenched (police witnesses used the word 'routine' (1996: Interim Report, 46)) nature. Among the consequences of corruption the Commission includes the observation that 'the innocent may be convicted of crimes they did not commit, and the guilty may escape justice' (1997: Vol. 1, 46). It pointed out that process corruption 'commonly becomes linked with extortion, theft and other forms of corruption', going on usefully to 'expose the hypocrisy of the tag of "noble cause corruption" sometimes given to this activity' (1997: Vol. 1, 85). The Commission stated in its Interim Report that process corruption

> strikes at the very heart of the administration of the criminal justice system, bringing it into disrepute. Moreover, once learned and practised, it can become an effective method of extortion in the hands of an officer lacking in integrity. If it is not checked, it will eventually destroy or so destabilise the Police Service and other institutions of criminal justice, such as the Courts, to the point where all confidence in and respect for them is lost. (1996: Vol. 1, 46)

Notice that at this point, process corruption is seen as having a significant effect on the conduct of the criminal process and the operation of the courts.

However, in the subsequent analysis of the Commission there is a systematic failure to squarely confront three key institutional components of the criminal justice system central to any analysis of the reasons for both the emergence of entrenched corruption and the failure to pick it up in the prosecutorial and judicial process. The judiciary, the DPP and the legal profession are to a significant extent missing players in the Reports of the Commission, indicating an inability to be reflexive about institutional conditions conducive to corruption. An earlier review (Brown 1998; and see Brown 1997) scours the published reports of the Wood Commission and demonstrates how at key points the judiciary, the DPP and to a lesser extent the legal profession emerge as potential ethical agencies of responsibility and regulation in relation to police misconduct and corruption, only to disappear again very quickly. The following treatment will give selective examples only.

Appearance and disappearance 1

In Chapter 1 of the Interim Report under the heading 'The Disciplinary Structure' a list of eight organisations follows: 'Commissioner of Police; Police Tribunal; Police Board; Government and Related Employees Appeal Tribunal; Minister of Police; Governor; **Director of Public Prosecutions; and courts**' (1996: 19, emphasis added). Yet the discussion which follows concentrates almost entirely on all the other agencies. It seems not to be envisaged at this stage that the DPP and the courts have any responsibility or role to play in bringing police misconduct and corruption to light. This omission is repeated in the 'Complaints and Discipline' chapter in Vol. 2 of the Report (1997: 327–72), only here the DPP and courts have disappeared altogether.

Appearance and disappearance 2

The courts next pop up in Chapter 2 of the Interim Report assessing 'The Inquiry So Far' (1996: 1). There we find some acknowledgment of the inadequacies of the court hearing as a forum for ventilating complaints about police fabrication of evidence. But such an acknowledgment is not followed up in any way; the court process is characterised as having little or no role to play in bringing process corruption to light.

> Complaints made by accused persons of fabricated evidence being provided against them are rarely, if at all, investigated beyond the limitations of the trial process. It must be recognised that the trial process is an inappropriate forum for such complaints to be determined. Often this is because it is perceived that it may not be in the best interests of an accused to complain, either formally, or during the course of the trial process. To do so may only paint that person in a worse light in the eyes of the tribunal of fact. Alternatively, if such an allegation is maintained, it is commonly discounted as the standard response of a guilty accused. The confidence so derived largely permitted the 'police verbal' and 'loading' of accused to become an art form within certain sections of the NSW Police Service. (1996: 40)

Fleeting appearance 3 (but kept entirely in the dark)

Later in Chapter 2 of the Interim Report in the discussion of 'Process Corruption' the prosecution and judiciary do make a fleeting appearance, but only to be absolved – they have alas, been completely hoodwinked. In a discussion of 'misplaced loyalty which is at the core of organised corruption in the Police Service' it is noted that:

Police spoke of its existence as routine, and as something they believe was expected of them. Intelligence received and evidence yet to be called suggests that it was not confined to these areas. On the contrary, the suggestion is that it has been widespread, and has **escaped the attention of the Judiciary, and of those involved in the prosecution process, from whom the truth has been concealed**. (1996: 46, emphasis added)

The missing judges: non-appearance 4

A few pages later in the Interim Report in Chapter 3, 'The Inquiry So Far (II)', under 'Problems Arising in Dealing with Police Misconduct and Corruption' it is noted that 'investigation of police is potentially the most difficult area of criminal investigation, for many reasons, including': "they are not easily fazed by interview, they are experienced in giving evidence, and they are capable of lying; their credibility and character are readily assumed by jurors and tribunals"' (1996: 49). Interestingly this absolution approach is followed a few pages later by a discussion of the 'stumbling block' which 'police culture' presents to the internal investigation process of police. 'In very many cases' we are informed, 'investigations have ground to a halt in the face of police turning a blind eye to obvious misconduct or corruption ...' (1996: 50). At the end of this chapter it is noted that 'the role of the other external bodies', which seem to include the Police Board, the Auditor-General, the Inspector-General and the State Coroner, but not the DPP or judiciary) 'is not such that they have played any real part in discouraging or investigating serious misconduct or corruption' (1996: 69).

Disappearance 5

In Chapter 5 of the Interim Report, 'A New System', under the heading 'The Complaints and Corruption Investigation System' three possible sources of complaints are listed as 'members of the public, police, and other government agencies, including courts' (1996: 100). And yet there is no further discussion of any role the courts might play in dealing with these complaints. Again, courts as an institutional site and judges as agents with some responsibility for presiding over the criminal justice system within which police misconduct and corruption might come to light, seem to have disappeared.

Final Report: when cultures collide

The relationship between police culture and 'the social, political and organisational context of policing, in which it takes place' (1997: 32) appears to open up a more than merely gestural analysis of the networks, the links between police culture and legal and judicial cultures. Certainly glimpses are provided, as in the discussion of process corruption, which it is noted 'is compounded by ambiguities within the legal and regulatory environment in which police work, and by senior police and members of the judiciary apparently condoning it' (1997: 36). The problem is that whenever such an object appears it does so elusively, only to disappear again. A few pages later under the 'Policing Environment' it rates not a mention (1997: 38–45).

A glimpse of (some) prosecutors

In Chapter 4, 'Corruption Found by the Royal Commission', under the heading 'Prosecutions – Compromise or Favourable Treatment' it is noted that 'evidence was called of various ways in which police interfered with prosecutions, or provided favourable treatment to persons brought before the criminal justice system' (1997: 109). However, the brief discussion is rather partial in that it seems to assume that interference runs only in the direction of *favourable* treatment, summarised as 'watering down of the available criminality', 'withholding material facts', the '"loss" of physical evidence or witnesses', creation of '"loopholes" in records of interview' and the 'provision of letters of comfort'. There was clearly evidence of such practices before the Commission but are we to believe that all police interference with prosecutions is favourable to suspects? The Commission compounds its partial view when it continues:

> Without making findings as to the involvement of police prosecutors in these practices, the problem seemed confined, at least on any direct basis of complicity, to police concerned at the arrest, bail and brief preparation stages. In many instances, however, an astute and fair-minded prosecutor might well have been expected to entertain a suspicion that all was not above board, to the point of initiating an internal investigation. (at 109)

Notice the crucial words of limitation '*police* prosecutors' as if such practices only occur prior to committals or in summary matters. But we know from previous inquiries that major problems of this sort, especially those in relation to favourable treatment of informers, occur in the higher courts where the cases are prosecuted by the DPP and by Crown Prosecutors (see, for example, Vol. 1, 1997: 113). It is in these forums, for example in applications for sentence discounts, that we have seen some of the most dubious 'letters of comfort' submitted, and some of the most partial recitations of the motives and past records of the applicant for a sentence discount, put forward by senior Crown Prosecutors and accepted by judges. Indeed the Royal Commissioner, Justice James Wood, sat on the sentence redetermination of Ray Denning's life sentence which had the effect of Denning being released within three years of a major prison escape and commission of armed robbery and other crimes, in circumstances involving a very selective and favourable interpretation of Denning's motives and history (Brook 1991; Brown and Duffy 1991: 185–90).

Where such practices are actually acknowledged a version of the 'we was duped' defence is brought into play, so that 'informants ... are spared prosecution for offences which they are known to have committed, or are given favourable treatment in relation to custodial arrangements or sentencing in return for giving evidence against others, without sufficient disclosure of their true position to senior officers, the DPP and the courts' (1997: 113). The 'some officers' solely responsible for this state of affairs are undoubtedly devilishly clever at concealing their corrupt arrangements from 'senior officers, the DPP and the courts' who apparently bear no responsibility for the cases they are supervising, managing, arguing and hearing. It is as if the cases proceed without agency, save for that of the original investigator.

Legal practitioners obtain absolution

If prosecutors and judges are absolved of any responsibility (save of course for police prosecutors) the legal profession similarly receives brief mention and then disappears from sight. While evidence suggested that some lawyers had colluded in the production of 'less than honest' expert reports and character references, 'the proof of unethical or improper practices on the part of lawyers is very difficult, because of the difficulties in penetrating legal professional privilege and in maintaining the kind of electronic surveillance required for affirmative proof' (1997: 111).

This is undoubtedly correct; there are technical impediments to such investigations. But there are no impediments to a discussion in a royal commission report of the reluctance of legal disciplinary bodies to pursue complaints against lawyers, nor of the development of mechanisms through which lawyers might take greater ethical responsibility for material presented in court. Police do not operate in a vacuum, and they are not the sole agents responsible for the ethical operation of the criminal justice system. Some rather fuller treatment of the roles and responsibilities of others and the extent to which these could be enhanced in the interests of integrity might have been expected.

Reflexivity starts at home

What is missing in a sustained way is any sense of reflexivity in the Royal Commission Report directed at any agencies other than police. As is clear from some of the individual case studies, prosecutors having ethical duties of 'fairness and impartiality' have colluded in the presentation of clearly suspect evidence. When very occasional complaints about such behaviour have been made, the disciplinary bodies of the Law Society and Bar have been reluctant in the extreme to pursue them. Magistrates and judges have often been at best gullible in their acceptance of police testimony and hostile to challenges to it. Appeal courts have lacked the necessary scepticism and nose for miscarriages of justice, or have been tardy in identifying practices productive of injustice such as police verbal or the use of informers.

When issues such as corruption are found to be reasonably commonplace in complex institutions like the criminal justice system, we cannot lay the blame for this state of affairs solely at the feet of one particular agency, and within this to an identifiable coterie of rogues and rascals. Rogues and rascals might have considerable power and influence but they do not preside over the criminal justice system. That task is carried out in the main by well intentioned people of professed integrity such as judges, prosecutors and lawyers, professionals who tend to inhabit the upper reaches of society. It ill behoves such people to minimise their agency and responsibility for their own role, performance and outcomes. Yet this is exactly one of the chief accomplishments of the Wood Royal Commission Report.

Reflexivity starts at home. The Royal Commissioner, Justice James Wood, who recommended the abolition of NSW Special Branch in the Wood Royal Commission, also sat on an inquiry into the convictions of Alister, Dunn and Anderson in 1984–85 (Wood 1985). This inquiry resulted in a pardon for the three on the basis that their convictions were unsafe. But the inquiry also revealed some of the dubious practices of Special Branch at that time, practices similar to those which horrified the same Justice Wood some 12 years later. A more sceptical, less 'idealised' (Findlay 1991), more rigorous and searching analysis of the material revealed in 1985 might have resulted in Special Branch being exposed 12 years earlier.

As mentioned earlier, Justice Wood also sat on the Denning sentence re-determination, so the dangers of compromised Crown cases should scarcely be novel. He also presided over the Leigh Leigh rape/murder case at Stockton in 1990 (*R v Webster*, unreported 24 October 1990, SC of NSW No. 70112/90) and in the process commended the police in the case: 'The police involved, working under the direction of Detective Sergeant

Chaffey, should in my view, be highly commended for the care, dedication and professionalism with which they went about the task and for bringing the offender to book' (at 11). The Webster investigation was subsequently referred to the Royal Commission as an example of a partial investigation that operated to protect a number of boys present at the events from prosecution on assault charges, some from sexual assault charges, and the possible complicity of two of the boys in the murder itself. The Commission declined to pursue the complaint further after some preliminary investigations and the matter was subsequently investigated by the NSW Crimes Commission and the Police Integrity Commission.

'The risk of naming violence: an unpleasant encounter'

Dr Kerry Carrington is a well published and award winning Australian feminist criminologist who through her research and writing of a book, *Who Killed Leigh Leigh* (1998) and several journal articles (Carrington and Johnson 1994; Carrington 1995; Carrington and Johnson 1995) probably did more than any other person to bring critical questions about the adequacy of the Leigh Leigh murder investigation and the trial and sentencing of Webster to public attention. Leigh Leigh was a 14-year-old girl attending her first beach party at Stockton, Newcastle, when she was subject to a running series of collective assaults and sexual assaults culminating in her brutal murder. After an investigation the NSW Crimes Commission came to the conclusion that 'Mathew Webster acted alone when he committed the murder and the assault which immediately preceded it; and...police did not act inappropriately in relation to the charging of other persons' (NSW Crimes Commission 1998: 1–2). Subsequently the NSW Police Integrity Commission (PIC) conducted an inquiry and hearing into certain matters surrounding the case, essentially allegations that police had mistreated suspects and witnesses. The PIC is a standing investigative body possessing similar powers to a royal commission, including powers to conduct public hearings, summons witnesses and compel answers. Dr Carrington was summonsed to appear before the PIC inquiry in January 1999 at the request of counsel representing a police officer.

And so it was that Kerry Carrington was subjected to what five colleagues who observed the PIC proceedings described in a subsequent article as an 'unpleasant encounter' (Byrne-Armstrong *et al.* 1999: 13). She was treated throughout the hearing as being responsible for putting certain unsubstantiated allegations about police sexual misconduct in the public realm when in fact they were first raised in an article that appeared in the *Sydney Morning Herald* (*SMH*) on 12 September 1998 when she was out of the country. One source for the *SMH* article was actually a leak from within the PIC itself. The *SMH* journalist was not called and all the sources for the story were not resolved. The counsel assisting had already stated that the inquiry was not going to reopen matters decided by the Crimes Commission and no cross examination of other witnesses had been permitted on these matters, so that any evidence Kerry Carrington could give relevant to the inquiry into how police treated suspects was marginal in the extreme. 'Thus the only purpose served by most of this cross examination was to afford counsel for the police (and the PIC) the opportunity to attack Kerry Carrington's credibility in respect of the matters the PIC had no intention of investigating' (Byrne-Armstrong *et al.* 1999: 23).

The only apparent purpose of this exercise 'was to denigrate academic criticism of police and law and send a message to would-be critics' (1999: 24). Cross-examined for three days by six counsel including one appearing for the Commissioner of Police, Dr Carrington was accused of being motivated by financial gain, being an ideologue, a hypocrite, incompetent and emotional. Counsel attempted to force her to accept a definition of criminology as 'the scientific study of crime'. She was closely questioned about the meaning of legal terms and her qualifications as a non-lawyer to criticise the legal process questioned. Attempts were made, with the backing of the Commissioner, to force her into yes/no responses to cross examination. This is despite the PIC being required by its own legislation 'to exercise its functions with as little formality and technicality as is possible ...' and to ensure 'hearings are conducted with as little emphasis on an adversarial approach as is possible' (Police Integrity Act 1996, NSW, section 32).

This disciplining of witnesses in cross examination is a familiar practice in criminal courts and one which skilful counsel can exploit to construct a monologic narrative through the questions themselves. It is the questions which become the operative account, irrespective of the answers actually given by the witness, which are treated as largely irrelevant. 'It is a technique for turning a witness into a ventriloquist's dummy, effacing her ... voice, knowledge and experience and replacing it with another narrative which represents her and her actions as dubious, in a form that then has the authority of a court record' (Byrne-Armstrong *et al.* 1999: 31). It is a standard feature of criminal trials and as Alison Young has shown in studies of transcripts of rape trials in Victoria, becomes a strategy for clothing the victim with 'rich signifiers of insinuation' suggestive of provocative conduct, intoxication, foolhardiness, desire, enjoyment, consent and regret, 'culminating in the excising of women's words, rendering her story "unheard"' (Young, 1998: 444). Allied strategies include 'asking leading questions; bundling up three or four questions into one; using questions beginning with "and", and completely ignoring the previous answer assuming it to be as the questioner wishes; demanding yes or no answers to a barrage of lengthy "brisk and authoritative" accusations drummed up by the defence' (Byrne-Armstrong *et al.* 1999: 33).

The irony, or perhaps a better word would be symmetry, was not lost on observers. Here we had a feminist academic criminologist who had done more than anyone else to give a voice to the dead victim, Leigh Leigh, by seeking through research and writing to 'name' the sexual violence and collective degradation Leigh Leigh had been subjected to, which, save for the killing itself, had largely been expunged in the course of the legal process, herself subjected at the PIC to a gratuitous attempted public humiliation which sought to destroy her credibility, to silence her and in the process to give a warning to non-lawyers of the dangers of criticising the legal system. 'By naming the sexual violence, it is an attempt to recover what was erased by the legal process. In a moment of double irony the PIC inquiry assumed a form of an attempt at a second order disqualification of the sexual violence utilising the very discursive and institutional devices that attracted critical analysis in the first place' (Byrne-Armstrong *et al* 1999: p. 37).

Conclusion

Here then are three stories from three varieties of inquiry: a single miscarriage case, a wide-ranging royal commission and a spin-off inquiry by one of the new standing investigative bodies akin to a royal commission. Clearly there are dangers of generalising from only three examples and the differences between both the form of the inquiries and their content should not be glossed over. Among the differences of approach between a miscarriage inquiry and the 'inquisitorial' practice of standing bodies like the PIC and to some extent some formal royal commissions such as Wood is that the latter have become active players in framing the issues, conducting the investigations and in securing the most favourable public, political and media context for their inquiries and recommendations. The key here is media management through advance briefings, selective leaking and the release of evidence such as surveillance videos, in some cases even before hearings have started. A key concern becomes the promotion of the commission's own success rate as measured in media interest and subsequent successful prosecutions, and the protection and promotion of the commission's own reputation and standing, rather than any general legitimation repair function carried out on behalf of 'the state'.

On the eve of hearings in a 2000 PIC inquiry into police corruption in the Manly drug squad, the prestigious ABC documentary programme *Four Corners* ran an exposé which included dramatic surveillance footage which could only have come from the PIC, showing police stealing drugs and money in searches of premises and receiving substantial bribes from drug dealers. Such selective leaking of surveillance material is undoubtedly successful in encouraging suspects to 'roll over' and make early admissions and engage in forms of bargaining over indemnities in exchange for evidence against colleagues and in creating a climate of media and public pressure to 'clean-up' corruption and secure convictions. Criminal prosecutions were subsequently successful against at least three police officers who received lengthy prison sentences. But in such examples selected media are effectively being used as an extension of the investigation, an arm of the inquiry, rather than reporting or commenting on evidence as it emerges in the hearing process. While perhaps productive of successful outcomes such blurring and intermeshing of roles presents real dangers, not only in relation to the rights of suspects but also in enlisting sections of the media into promoting the Commission's particular version of events.

In Burton and Carlen's terms of the (Althusserian) times, royal commissions were part of the 'ideological state apparatuses'. Two decades later with the substantial demise of such marxisante analyses and the substantial restructuring and destructuring of the state, some of the new aggressive hybrid commissions in the criminal justice sphere exhibit somewhat divergent and at times contradictory tendencies: towards becoming simultaneously more 'governmental', more enmeshed in the 'logics' and 'programmes' of neo-liberal 'government-at-a-distance', shaping and guiding specific populations in the lessons of efficient, ethical and accountable operations and the potential exposure that awaits wrongdoers; yet also more autonomous, independent and self-directed as they engage in the intrigues of media and political management in an attempt to influence the popular discursive context in which they conduct their inquiries, release their reports, measure their success, justify their own existence and defend their own practices. Sometimes, as we have seen with the PIC example, the second tendency undermines the first.

Acknowledging the limits of only three examples and the differences between them, certain similarities have also emerged. All three inquiries exhibited a striking inability to be reflexive about the everyday routines, structures, practices and assumptions of the criminal justice system, other than where overt corruption or misconduct was present. In the Pohl inquiry it seemed to be beyond the inquiring judge to even feel the necessity to account for a shocking miscarriage of justice, produced it seemed by the entirely unexceptional and 'faultless' operation of the system. Confronted with a negation of ideal justice in dramatic form, the alternative, recognition of the fallibility of everyday criminal justice, remained 'unspeakable' (Burton and Carlen 1979: 70). In the Wood Commission the critical analysis of police practice and culture contrasted with a systematic failure to scrutinise other agencies and cultures constituting part of the policing context, in particular prosecutors, lawyers and the judiciary. In the PIC example an attempt was made to denigrate and silence an academic critic of the way sexual violence and collective and public assault and humiliation had been expunged through the legal process in the Leigh Leigh rape/murder case.

Which brings us back to Burton and Carlen's observation that:

> Official Discourse on law and order confronts legitimation deficits and seeks discursively to redeem them by denial of their material geneses. Such a denial establishes an absence in the discourse. This absence, the Other, is the silence of a world constituted by social relations the reality of which cannot be appropriated by a mode of normative argument which speaks to and from its own self image via an idealised conception of justice. (1979: 138)

My argument has not been that the absence or denial of alternative accounts is a function of official inquiries nor that it is a necessity. But the particular inquiries have certainly shown a tendency to speak to and from an 'idealised conception of justice' and to avoid, downplay, ignore or defend its absence or patent denial, especially in relation to the routine workings of the criminal justice system. But the 'discursive closure' sought (Burton and Carlen 1979: 138) has indeed been partial only; any discursive curtains drawn, have been decidedly flimsy. The aim of this chapter has been to show just how flimsy and thereby to reveal a little of what is going on in the everyday realm of criminal justice behind the ideal.

References

Brook, R. (1991) Raymond Denning's best planned escape. In K. Carrington *et al.* (eds) *Travesty! Miscarriages of Justice*. Sydney: Pluto Press, pp. 102–28.

Brown, D. (1997) Breaking the code of silence. *Alternative Law Journal*, 22(5): 220–7.

Brown, D. (1998) The Royal Commission into the NSW Police Service: process corruption and the limits of judicial reflexivity. *Current Issues in Criminal Justice*, 9(3): 228–40.

Brown, D. and Duffy, B. (1991) Privatising police verbals: the growth industry in prison informants. In K. Carrington *et al.* (eds) *Travesty! Miscarriages of Justice.* Sydney: Pluto Press, pp. 181–231.

Brown, D., Farrier, D., Egger, S. and McNamara, L. (2001) *Criminal Laws*, 3rd edn. Sydney: Federation Press.

Burton, F. and Carlen, P. (1979) *Official Discourse.* London: Routledge & Kegan Paul.

Byrne-Armstrong, H., Carmody, M., Hodge, B., Hogg, R. and Lee, M. (1999) The risk of naming violence: an unpleasant encounter between legal culture and feminist criminology. *Australian Feminist Law Journal*, 13: 13–37.

Carrington, K. (1995) No justice for Leigh Leigh. *Australian Feminist Law Journal*, 4: 135–40.

Carrington, K. (1998) *Who Killed Leigh Leigh?* Sydney: Random House.

Carrington, K. and Johnson, A. (1994) Representations of crime, guilt and sexuality in the Leigh Leigh rape/murder case. *Australian Feminist Law Journal*, 3: 3–29.

Carrington, K. and Johnson, A. (1995) Some justice for Leigh Leigh. *Australian Feminist Law Journal*, 5: 126–32.

Carrington, K., Dever, M., Hogg, R., Bargen, J. and Lohrey, A. (eds) (1991) *Travesty! Miscarriages of Justice.* Sydney: Pluto Press.

Costigan, F. (1984) *Royal Commission on the Activities of the Federated Ship Painters and Dockers Union, Final Report*, Vols 1–5. Canberra: AGPS.

Devlin, J. (1976) *The Report of the Secretary of State for the Home Department of the Departmental Committee of Evidence of Identification in Criminal Cases*, HC 338. London: HMSO.

Diplock, J. (1972) *Report of the Commission to Consider Legal Procedures to Deal with Terrorist Activities in Northern Ireland*, Cmnd 5185. London: HMSO.

Dixon, D. (ed.) (1999) *A Culture of Corruption.* Sydney: Hawkins Press.

Findlay, M. (1991) The Justice Wood Inquiry: the role of Special Branch in the Cameron conspiracy. In K. Carrington *et al.* (eds) *Travesty! Miscarriages of Justice.* Sydney: Pluto Press, pp. 31–49.

Gilligan, G. (2002) Royal commissions of inquiry. *Australian and New Zealand Journal of Criminology*, 35(3): 289–307.

Hall, S., Critcher, C., Jefferson, T., Clarke, J. and Roberts, B. (1978) *Policing the Crisis.* London: Macmillan.

Hindess, B. and Hirst, P. (1977) *Mode of Production and Social Formation.* London: Macmillan.

Hogg, R. (2001) Law and order and the fallibility of the justice system. In D. Brown *et al.*, *Criminal Laws*, 3rd edn. Sydney: Federation Press, pp. 337–43.

James, E.A. (1965) *Report of the Inquiry by Mr E.A. James, QC into the Circumstances in which it was possible for Detective Sergeant Harold Gordon Challenor of the Metropolitan Police to continue on duty at a time when he appears to have been affected by the onset of mental illness*, Cmnd 2735. London: HMSO.

McInerney, J. (1992) *Report of the Inquiry Held under Section 475 of the Crimes Act 1900 into the Convicion of Johann Ernst Siegfried Pohl at Central Criminal Court Sydney on 2 November 1973.* Sydney: NSWGP.

NSW Crime Commission (1998) *Hexam References Report: Investigation into the circumstances surrounding the murder of Leigh Leigh on 3 November and other offences,* Vol. 1. Sydney: NSWGP.

Scarman, J. (1972) *The Report of the Tribunal of Inquiry into Violence and Civil Disturbance in Northern Ireland in 1969,* Cmnd 566. London: HMSO.

Scarman, J. (1977) *Report of A Court of Enquiry under Rt. Hon. Lord Justice Scarman, OBE, into a dispute between Grunwick Processing Laboratories Ltd. and Members of the Association of Professional, Executive and Clerical and Computer Staff,* Cmnd 6922. London: HMSO.

Wood, J. (1985) *Report of the Inquiry held under s. 475 of the Crimes Act 1900 into the Convictions of Timothy Edward Anderson, Paul Shawn Alister and Ross Anthony Dunn at Central Criminal Court, Sydney on 1st August, 1979,* 3 vols. Sydney: NSWGP.

Wood, J. (1996) *Royal Commission into the NSW Police Service: Interim Report.* Sydney: NSWGP.

Wood, J. (1997) *Royal Commission into the NSW Police Service: Final Report,* 3 vols. Sydney: NSWGP.

Young, A. (1998) The waste land of the law: the wordless song of the rape victim. *Melbourne University Law Review,* 22(2): 444–64.

Chapter 3

From deceit to disclosure: the politics of official inquiries in the United Kingdom

Phil Scraton

Introduction

> On a visit to my MP to try and enlist his support for an independent inquiry into the [Lockerbie] disaster his main suggestion was that I should write to the Prime Minister. I cried with frustration as I walked home. And as I sat looking at the photographs of the ground where Peter made his last mark when he fell six miles from PanAm 103, I was filled with the sense that above all I owe it to him to find out the truth. (Pamela Dix, *The Guardian*, 25 July 1998)

Pamela Dix's brother, Peter, was one of the 269 passengers on Flight PanAm 103 blown up over Lockerbie, Scotland on 21 December 1988. What followed was a decade's controversy concerning the involvement of US military and drugs agencies, a rogue CIA agent and unspecified amounts of heroin and currency carried on the flight. With the security services handling the investigation, there was 'silence from the police and a cacophony of theories from the media and politicians' (Cox and Foster 1992: 13). An in-depth study of the circumstances concluded: 'innocent people have been blamed for the bombing and the guilty remain free' (Ashton and Ferguson 2001: 11).

The lack of a public inquiry into the Lockerbie disaster was an extraordinary political decision. Pamela Dix vividly testifies that, for the bereaved, it generated 'a burning sense of shock, anger and betrayal' as they sought the 'truth'. The international political intrigue surrounding the bombing and the public interest concerning cause, circumstances and consequences suggested that a government-sponsored inquiry would be automatic. Successive governments' rejection of an inquiry implies that such an open process risked embarrassing and politically compromising public disclosures.

Pamela Dix and the Lockerbie bereaved are not exceptions. Whenever a disaster or tragedy occurs, when people die in controversial circumstances, when miscarriages of justice are revealed and when children are neglected, abused or killed, grief-stricken relatives and survivors immediately demand a public inquiry. Rarely are such calls a display of vengeance or blaming. While responsibility, culpability and acknowledgment are significant, they rarely take precedence over 'knowing'. Of course, for those likely to be held liable there is a self-evident interest in masking, deflecting or denying the 'truth'.

Less than a year after Lockerbie, 51 people were killed on the River Thames when the *Marchioness* pleasure boat was run down and sunk by a dredger. They were refused a public inquiry and the inquests were abandoned. Eventually, through the Marchioness Action Group's persistence, the Department of Transport's Marine Investigation Branch Inquiry was exposed as partial and flawed. Six years after the disaster the inquests returned unlawfully killed verdicts yet no prosecutions followed. The Group's solicitor, Louise Christian (1996: 27), noted confusion over the legal processes available to the bereaved – with 'public misinformation' prevailing. A public inquiry would guarantee 'that all the evidence will be heard' yet 'this is the one thing to which there is absolutely no right at law'.

Finally, in 1999, the Deputy Prime Minister commissioned a public inquiry. Four reports were published including a non-statutory inquiry into concerns over the removal of the deceased's hands and the return of bodies in sealed coffins. This report revealed that hands, lungs, brains, kidneys, hearts, spleens and tonsils had been removed from the bodies and stored. It had taken families a decade to establish the facts regarding the circumstances of the disaster and the aftermath. Despite being 'deeply upset, shocked and angry' by the disclosures, the bereaved felt vindicated in their campaigning.

The *Marchioness* families' experience reinforces a broadly held faith in public inquiries which elevates their assumed status above the more cynically perceived adversarial and combative procedures of courts of liability. Inquiries are assumed to be less partisan, more independent, open, thorough and searching, unfettered by theatrical, procedural and material constraints of prosecution. Christian (2002: 19) states that while not a 'panacea', public inquiries 'can be convened speedily and concluded without undue delay or expense ensur[ing] that management failings are exposed to public scrutiny'. Usually triggered by specific events, they raise questions of profound public concern regarding the functioning of state agencies or corporate bodies. Invariably, a specific 'case' signifies a deeper institutional crisis in public confidence.

An inventory of recent significant official inquiries into the acts or omissions of UK state institutions, public bodies and their employees would include: prison security and prison protests; sexual and physical abuse of children in families and care homes; medical care and organ retention; train and underground disasters; civil and military intervention in the North of Ireland; the conduct of criminal investigations and miscarriages of justice. Before reflecting on the controversies surrounding recent well-publicised inquiries, it is important to establish the role, function and legitimacy of official inquiries and their justification within the operation of the advanced democratic state. It constitutes a democratic pluralist position not without critics.

The role of official inquiries

> The trigger for setting up an inquiry is usually the need to restore public confidence in a service or organisation, or even the government as a whole. This can only happen – if indeed it should happen – if there is public confidence in the inquiry process. (Maclean 2001: 592)

Royal commissions, departmental committees and tribunals of inquiry are discretionary, arbitrary and inconsistent responses by government ministers, in consultation with colleagues and civil servants, 'set up to investigate and report upon specific matters defined in their terms of reference' (Burton and Carlen 1979: 1). Usually chaired by judges or lawyers with the assistance of designated professional 'experts', they are often the result of alleged irregularities or failures in the administration of justice or in the aftermath of major incidents, such as disasters or tragedies, which have far-reaching consequences. They are essentially investigative and inquisitorial rather than prosecutorial and adversarial, the objectives being the identification of problems, the distribution of responsibilities, the proposal of remedies and recommendations for change and reform.

The 'great and the good', with a track record of dependable public service, are selected to chair or provide 'expert' guidance. Technically their 'independence' is beyond reproach but they are recruited from 'mainstream' public life – achievers within the status quo. Supported, serviced and resourced by government departments, they are plumbed into the ideological 'ways of seeing' and political 'ways of doing' that constitute the routine expressions of civil service practice. Their reports carry the government imprimatur of legitimacy. From the moment of commission and terms of reference, through to the written report and its recommendations for action, they are part of approved discourses of the state. In contrast to Maclean's faith in official inquiries, Burton and Carlen (*ibid*. 13) consider they are 'routine political tactic[s] directed towards the legitimacy of institutions'.

Thomas (1982: 40) further develops this scepticism, noting that, traditionally, official inquiries have been regarded as 'democratic pluralism at work'. In claiming legitimacy for its interventions, the 'neutral state operating by popular consent requires active illustrations of its commitment to heed public opinion' (*ibid*. 42). Official inquiries 'stand apart from policies and it is within the principles of democratic pluralism that their justification is found'. In airing the views of competing interests before impartial arbiters whose sole objective is to establish publicly the 'facts' through thorough investigation, commissions and inquiries are presented as exemplars of democratic conflict resolution and action.

Burton and Carlen (1979: 13) researched official inquiries 'engendered as responses to specific problems raised by contentious events in the administration of judicious control incidents of wrongful imprisonment, illegal police authority, mass rioting, confrontation picketing and administrative internment ... ' Such events produce 'crises in the popular confidence of the impartiality of legal state apparatuses'. They are 'crises of legitimacy' damaging the 'ideological social relations that reproduce dominant social conceptions of the essentially just nature of the politico-judicial structures of the state'. While Maclean considers that official inquiries are initiated to restore public confidence in a service or organisation, for Burton and Carlen they are 'routine political tactic[s] directed towards the legitimacy of institutions'.

Thus, the 'task of inquiries into particular crises is to represent failure as temporary, or no failure at all, and to re-establish the image of administrative and legal coherence and rationality' (*ibid*. 48). This locates inquiries at the heart of official discourse, essential 'for political and ideological hegemony'. Thomas (1982: 40), while accepting that commissions and inquiries are used 'to defuse and delay embarrassing situations', also identifies their use 'as a device for social control'. Burton and Carlen (1979: 51, emphases added) consider the 'pedagogic task of discursive *incorporation*' derived in the application of 'bodies of knowledge' as useful information in conceiving and implementing 'strategies of social control'. This task connects to 'discourses of *legitimacy*' through which the 'state's fractured image of administrative rationality and democratic legality' is reconstructed. In achieving these ends 'discourses of *confidence*' are employed, using 'experts' to reaffirm the competence of state officials and the efficiency of the formal systems they operate and services they deliver.

The frequency and diversity of official inquiries inhibit hard and fast conclusions regarding selective commissioning, purpose, appropriateness or effectiveness. Yet their representation and justification as independent, impartial and value-free, as apolitical antidotes to the partisanship of politics and the polarisation of the law, cannot be accepted uncritically. Burton and Carlen's critique of official inquiries as reflecting yet reproducing official discourse, serving state institutions and their interests, demonstrates clearly the centrality of incorporation, legitimacy and confidence-building. Gilligan (2002: 214) comments, however, that not all royal commissions (or official inquiries) are concerned with crisis resolution. He notes that they do have positive outcomes: information gathering and provision; a modicum of accountability; occasional excursions beyond their remit. Yet in responding to crises or profoundly controversial issues their capacity for thoroughness in evidence gathering and disclosure, for establishing responsibility and securing acknowledgment and for challenging institutional, structural determining contexts is questionable.

Thomas (1982: 50), for example, recounts the failure of the 1981 Royal Commission on Criminal Procedure to respond to deep-rooted, institutionalised discriminatory practices within Metropolitan Police interventions in black communities. Ultimately this led to black demonstrators seeking 'solutions on the street'. Further, black community groups and their leaders refused to participate in the Scarman or Hytner inquiries into the breakdown in police–community relations. Within the communities the Commission and the inquiries 'were perceived as means to legitimate state interests' rather than 'the apotheosis of democratic pluralism'. The dissenting voices, whose representation and amplification should be a key objective of independent inquiry, were silenced. Theirs was a conscious refusal to be incorporated into a politically driven process intended to reinforce and legitimate institutionalised discriminatory policy and practice.

Politicians defend and promote official inquiries as the most effective, independent and legally framed mechanisms for accessing documentary evidence and examining oral testimonies. While the potential exists for inquiries to reconcile differences and resolve serious public issues (cf. Gilligan, this volume), they are open to management and manipulation. Official inquiries into circumstances which challenge the legitimacy and authority of state institutions are often undermined by partial investigation and restricted disclosure. These limitations, institutionalised and purposeful, are explored in the following overview of several major inquiries into police and military interventions in Britain and the North of Ireland.

From Scarman to Macpherson

Over three days, 10 to 12 April 1981, major civil disturbances occurred in Brixton, London. The majority of those involved were black and, although property was damaged and destroyed, the main target was the Metropolitan Police. The violence on the streets was the culmination of persistent tension between the police and black communities. In April 1979, following the allowing of a fascist march through the predominantly Asian community of Southall, there had been fierce confrontations between the police and anti-fascist demonstrators culminating in the death of a white teacher, Blair Peach, and the destruction of an African-Caribbean community centre. The perpetrators were officers of the Metropolitan Police (NCCL 1980).

Brixton's disturbances were preceded by uncompromising street policing of black male youths under the operational codename 'Swamp'. Routine stopping and searching of black people on dubious grounds of 'suspicion' throughout Britain's black communities had brought allegations of institutionalised racism. Lord Scarman was appointed to 'inquire urgently into the serious disorder in Brixton on 10–12 April 1981 and to report, with the power to make recommendations' (Scarman 1981: 1). Scarman took oral evidence over 20 days, followed by written evidence and submissions and a seven-day hearing. Eight months after being commissioned, Scarman's recommendations spanned social conditions, policing methods and social policy reform.

In managerialist terms, involving recruitment screening, training, promotion, civilianisation and consultation, Scarman had a profound impact on policing and police–community relations. Given the well-documented experiences of black communities throughout Britain, however, his response to allegations of institutionalised racism was extraordinary. He concluded: 'The direction and policies of the Metropolitan Police are not racist. I totally and unequivocally reject the attack made upon the integrity and impartiality of the senior direction of the force' (Scarman 1981: 64). He found no evidence of 'deliberate bias or prejudice'. Extending beyond his remit, Scarman denied that 'institutional racism' existed in Britain while accepting that 'racial disadvantage and its nasty associate racial discrimination, have not yet been eliminated' (*ibid.* 135). Among Metropolitan Police officers, he found evidence of 'ill-considered, immature and racially prejudiced actions ... in their dealings on the streets with young people' (*ibid.* 64). It amounted to 'an unthinking assumption that all black people are criminals' but 'such a bias is not to be found among senior officers'.

Two years later a Metropolitan Police commissioned Policy Studies Institute (PSI) report on police–community relations exposed the extent to which Scarman's view of racism had been blinkered. The PSI report provided qualitative and quantitative evidence that linking black people to crime was an all-pervasive image within the Metropolitan Police, that racial harassment and racial violence were not taken seriously at a senior command level and that racism led to routinely aggressive and intimidatory policing. Police racism was identified as inherent within a culture of values derived in white, male respectability and manifested via a 'cult of masculinity'.

As Lee Bridges (1999: 306) records, Scarman's influence stretched well beyond the contemporary policing of black communities to 'a whole school of race criminology in Britain, which adopts a pathological approach and seeks to downplay the impact, both of police racism and racial discrimination in general on Afro-Caribbeans'. In this context, and undoubtedly bolstered by Scarman's denial of institutionalised racism, differential policing on 'race' lines continued virtually unchallenged within most UK police forces. This denial, coupled with complacency, was exposed tragically in the police response to and investigation of the racist murder of Stephen Lawrence on 22 April 1993.

The Metropolitan Police response to the killing, on the night and in the subsequent investigation, was heavily criticised by the Lawrence family and their lawyers. The failure to recognise the murder as racist and to swiftly follow up positive leads on suspects, well known in the community and to the police, enabled those guilty of the attack to cover their tracks. In 1995 a private prosecution of five local white youths went to committal. Three were tried and acquitted. In 1997 the coroner's inquest returned an unlawfully killed verdict with an added rider that Stephen Lawrence was the victim of a 'completely unprovoked racist attack by five white youths'.

Following criticisms of the initial investigation by the Police Complaints Authority inquiry, the family demanded a public inquiry. In July 1997 the Home Secretary, Jack Straw, appointed Sir William Macpherson: 'To inquire into the matters arising from the death of Stephen Lawrence ... in order particularly to identify the lessons to be learned for the investigation and prosecution of racially motivated crimes' (Macpherson 1999: 6). Macpherson was supported by Tom Cook (retired Deputy Chief Constable for West Yorkshire), Dr John Sentamu (the Bishop for Stepney) and Dr Richard Stone (Chair of the Jewish Council for Racial Equality).

The Macpherson Report was exhaustive in detailing the murder of Stephen Lawrence and its aftermath. Its conclusion was uncompromising. There were 'fundamental errors' in an investigation 'marred by a combination of professional incompetence, institutional racism and a failure of leadership by senior officers' (*ibid*. 317). The internal Metropolitan Police review of the case was 'flawed' and had 'failed to expose these inadequacies'. Despite the Metropolitan Police Commissioner persistently denying that his force was institutionally racist, Macpherson found to the contrary. He defined 'institutional racism' as a 'collective failure of an organisation to provide an appropriate and professional service to people because of their colour, culture or ethnic origin'. Its presence 'can be seen or detected in processes, attitudes and behaviour which amount to discrimination through unwitting prejudice, ignorance, thoughtlessness, and racist stereotyping which disadvantage minority ethnic people' (*ibid*. 321).

Macpherson made 70 recommendations encompassing: openness, accountability and the restoration of confidence; definition of racist incident reporting and recording of racist incidents and crimes; police practice and investigation of racist crime; family liaison (by police); the handling of victims and witnesses; prosecution of racist crimes; police training (first aid, race awareness); employment, discipline and complaints; stop and search; recruitment and retention; prevention and the role of education. The impact was instant and far-reaching. Although rooted in the police handling of a single racist murder the recommendations had implications for all organisations. As Jenny Bourne (2001: 13) observes, 'the Scarman report spoke mainly to areas of government concerned about maintaining law and order and protecting property' but Macpherson raised the profile of 'the extent of racist violence in Britain, the way miscarriages of justice could take place and the incompetence and racism of the police force'.

The Taylor Inquiry into the Hillsborough disaster

On 15 April 1989 at the Hillsborough Stadium in Sheffield a fatal crush occurred on the terraces at an FA Cup semi-final match between Liverpool and Nottingham Forest. Ninety-six men, women and children were killed, hundreds injured and thousands traumatised. It was a sold-out, all-ticket match, coincidentally a repeat of the previous year's semi-final. Fans arriving in Sheffield were searched, briefed and directed to the stadium under police supervision. Most arrived in the hour before kick-off. Soon the congestion at the malfunctioning turnstiles overwhelmed the police. Lack of stewarding and no filtering made a serious crush in a confined space inevitable. The Match Commander, Chief Superintendent Duckenfield, in the police control box inside the stadium agreed to open an exit gate – bypassing the turnstiles and relieving the congestion.

Fans, four or five abreast, walked unstewarded and without police direction through the exit gate into the stadium and down a 1 in 6 gradient tunnel into two pens at the centre of the terrace – pens like cattle pens, fences to the side and front, and no way back. What the fans did not realise, but which was evident from the police control box, was that the centre pens were already full. The tunnel should have been closed and the fans directed to the near-empty side pens. With over 2,000 people packed into already full pens the crush on the steps was vice-like. Faces were jammed against the perimeter fence, people went down underfoot and then, low to the front of Pen 3, a barrier collapsed resulting in a tangled mass of bodies.

Police on the perimeter track failed to respond and those at a distance misread the struggle for life as crowd disturbance. In full view of the unfolding tragedy, Duckenfield failed to identify the consequences of his decision to open the exit gate. As bodies were dragged through the two narrow perimeter fence gates and laid on the pitch, fans ripped down advertising hoardings as makeshift stretchers. Only 14 of the 96 who died were taken to hospital. While the pens were being evacuated Duckenfield told senior Football Association officials that fans had forced the exit gate causing an inrush into already packed pens. Within minutes his lie was broadcast. As the disaster was in progress the fans were blamed.

The dead were laid out in body bags on the floor of the stadium gymnasium. Each body was numbered and allocated a police officer. Given buckets of water and cloths, officers were instructed to clean the faces of the dead. Dark and barely distinguishable Polaroid photographs were posted in the gymnasium foyer and eventually the bereaved were led to the photographs. As each was recognised the number was called and the corresponding body wheeled on a trolley to the gymnasium door. The bag was unzipped, the identification made and no touching or caressing was permitted. Grieving relatives were then taken to tables where investigating officers questioned them about their loved ones' drinking habits, criminal convictions and other 'indiscretions'. Meanwhile the coroner ordered that blood samples be taken from each body, including the children, to determine blood alcohol levels. Duckenfield's deceit, the treatment of the bereaved and the coroner's unprecedented decision illustrated a consolidating official perspective: the disaster was caused by violent and drunken fans.

The following day Prime Minister Margaret Thatcher and her Home Secretary, Douglas Hurd, visited the stadium to be briefed by the Chief Constable of South Yorkshire Police. Writing years later the Prime Minister's Press Secretary, Sir Bernard Ingham, revealed the content of that briefing: 'I visited Hillsborough on the morning after the disaster. I know what I learned on the spot. There would have been no Hillsborough if a mob, who were clearly tanked up, had not tried to force their way into the ground' (correspondence, 13 July 1994). As the UEFA President Jacques Georges described the 'frenzy' of the fans – 'beasts waiting to charge into the arena' (*Liverpool Echo*, 17 April 1989) – the Home Secretary commissioned a public inquiry headed by Lord Justice Taylor.

Lord Justice Taylor's Inquiry, the criminal investigation and the coroner's inquiry were considered 'independent'. Yet each was serviced by the West Midlands police force. Two assessors assisted the Inquiry: Brian Johnson, Chief Constable of Lancashire, and Leonard Maunder, Professor of Mechanical Engineering at Newcastle University. The Inquiry's terms of reference were brief but broad: 'To inquire into the events at Sheffield Wednesday Football Ground on 15 April 1989 and to make recommendations about the needs of crowd control and safety at sports events'. The team received and processed 2,666 telephone calls, 3,776 written statements and 1,550 letters. Oral evidence was taken on 31 days from 174 witnesses; a 'small fraction' from the pool of thousands, yet 'sufficient in number and reliability to enable me to reach the necessary conclusions' (Taylor 1989: 2). Evidence was not taken under oath.

Lord Justice Taylor published two reports. The Interim Report was published within four months, responding to 'urgent questions of safety, especially at football grounds' (*ibid.*). Five months later his generic Final Report addressed the 'future of football', safety at sports grounds, crowd control and hooliganism and the 1989 Football Spectators Act. The Interim Report concluded that the 'main cause' of the disaster was 'overcrowding' in the central pens. The 'main reason' for the overcrowding was 'failure of police control'. He criticised Sheffield Wednesday Football Club (the stadium owners), their safety engineers and the local authority but directed his most damning conclusions towards the South Yorkshire Police.

Senior officers had been 'defensive' and 'evasive' in giving evidence. Their 'handling of problems on the day' and 'their account of it in evidence' did not demonstrate 'the qualities of leadership to be expected of their

55

rank'. It was, he noted, 'a matter of regret that the South Yorkshire Police were not prepared to concede that they were in any way at fault for what had occurred' (*ibid.* 50). Duckenfield's 'capacity to take decisions and give orders [had] seemed to collapse'. He had failed to give 'necessary consequential orders' once he had sanctioned the opening of the exit gate and had lost control of the situation. His 'lack of candour' in responding to the FA representatives had 'set off a widely reported allegation'.

Years later, research uncovered confidential documents revealing the prevailing climate within the South Yorkshire Police in the immediate aftermath of the disaster. The then Head of Management Services stated that the police 'had their backs to the wall ... it was absolutely natural for them to concern themselves with defending themselves' (in Scraton 2000: 192). A former South Yorkshire Officer recalled that a 'certain chief superintendent' told him and his colleagues that 'unless we all get our heads together and straighten it out, there are heads going to roll' (*ibid*: 187).

Within hours of the disaster the 'straightening out' process was well under way. Contrary to their training, officers were instructed by their managers not to record the events of the day in their pocket-books. Instead, they submitted handwritten 'recollections' containing comment, opinion and feelings, as well as fact, solely for the 'information of legal advisers'. 'Privileged' and not subject to disclosure, these recollections were collected by senior officers, submitted to the Force solicitors and returned to the Head of Management Services as part of a systematic process of 'review and alteration' (internal correspondence, 15 May 1989). This process amounted to an institutionalised, behind-the-scenes reconstruction of police evidence intended to eliminate any criticism of senior officers and their decisions.

Technically within the law, the review and alteration of police officers' accounts raises significant questions regarding the veracity of the police evidence to Taylor, the inquests and the criminal investigation. Lord Justice Taylor's Interim Report did not record that he was aware of and endorsed the process. In fact the West Midlands police investigators, the Treasury solicitors, the Coroner and Home Office officials all knew that the police statements in their possession had been written initially as personal recollections under the guarantee of non-disclosure and had been scrutinised, reviewed and altered. While condemning senior officers for their incompetence on the day and their evasiveness at the Inquiry, Taylor failed to acknowledge that the South Yorkshire Police and their solicitors used their privileged access to the investigations and inquiries to reconstitute and register the 'facts' to their best advantage.

In 1997, following these and other revelations, the newly elected

Labour Home Secretary, Jack Straw, stated his concern as to 'whether the full facts have emerged' and his commitment to 'get to the bottom of this once and for all' (*The Guardian*, 1 July 1997). He set up an unprecedented 'judicial scrutiny' under former MI6 commissioner, Lord Justice Stuart-Smith. Widely reported as 'another public inquiry' it was, in fact, confined by its terms of reference to a review of evidence 'not available' to previous investigations and inquiries. Stuart-Smith visited the South Yorkshire Police and, amid much controversy, took evidence from 18 bereaved families. He received submissions from the Hillsborough Family Support Group and other concerned parties.

The Home Secretary welcomed Stuart-Smith's 'comprehensive report' as the 'latest in a series of lengthy and detailed examinations' into Hillsborough (*Hansard*, 18 February 1998). Jack Straw announced that neither Lord Justice Taylor's inquiry nor the inquest had been at fault and the evidence submitted to the Scrutiny had not 'added anything significant'. He trusted 'that the families will recognise that [Stuart-Smith's] report represents – as I promised – an independent, thorough and detailed scrutiny of all the evidence ...'. Stuart-Smith considered the review and alteration of police statements irrelevant to the outcome of the inquiries and investigations. Consequently, no one was held to account for the initiation and realisation of this process.

The level and intensity of official inquiry into the Hillsborough disaster, from the Taylor Inquiry through to the Stuart-Smith Scrutiny, was unprecedented. It included the longest inquests in English legal history. Despite this there remained widespread dissatisfaction regarding the focus of the official inquiries. This was ironic given the broad scope of the Taylor Inquiry as evidenced by his Final Report. Taylor adopted an inquiry framework used previously by Mr Justice Popplewell following the 1985 Valley Parade Stadium fire in Bradford, which claimed 56 lives and injured 400 (Popplewell 1985). Both inquiries produced Interim Reports on the disasters followed months later by Final Reports on broader issues. Structuring and delivering inquiries in two phases runs the risk of burying the findings and recommendations of the interim report beneath the broader issues identified in the final report. In the public mind there is also greater status afforded to a 'final' report.

Despite making a major contribution to stadium safety and crowd management, the Taylor Inquiry was found wanting by those most closely associated with the disaster. Taylor denied that the slow arrival of ambulances, inadequate medical equipment and lack of triage had contributed to the high loss of life. He paid minimal attention to the chaos in the gymnasium. He failed to consider the appropriateness of the decisions to designate the gymnasium a temporary mortuary, to take blood alcohol levels from the deceased or to present the dead in body-bags to waiting relatives. However thorough the Interim Report appeared, these were considerable oversights and drew criticism from the bereaved, survivors, social workers and senior ambulance workers. Worse still, Taylor knew of and condoned the review and alteration of police statements. Stuart-Smith's Judicial Scrutiny failed to resolve the unanswered questions or to deal with the wider issues. It was a device derived in political expediency rather than evidence of a commitment to the truth.

The Cullen Inquiry into the Dunblane primary school shootings

Early in the school day on 13 March 1996 Thomas Hamilton, licensed by the Central Scotland Police to own four handguns, two rifles and over 3,000 rounds of ammunition, walked calmly into the gymnasium of Dunblane primary school. Firing 105 rounds in just over three minutes he shot dead 16 five and six year olds and their teacher, Gwen Mayor. He wounded a further ten children and three teachers. He then killed himself. Within half an hour police officers, including the Chief Constable, were at the school. From the moment they arrived at the school the police knew the gunman's identity.

For 15 years Thomas Hamilton had been the focus of rumour, innuendo and allegations regarding his self-appointed boys' club activities. From 1981 to 1996 he had organised evening activities at secondary schools and camping trips. Following two formal allegations of indecency, opinion polarised concerning his authoritarian style. As complaints mounted, the local authority, the Scottish Commissioner for Local Administration and Members of Parliament became embroiled in the controversy. It was decided that Hamilton had been subjected to malicious and unfounded allegations and his activities continued.

In 1991 a second Central Scotland Police investigation of his summer camps resulted in a substantial report. It was critical of Hamilton's behaviour. More specifically the investigating officer was deeply concerned to learn that Hamilton held gun licences. Judging him as 'an unsavoury character' with an 'unstable personality' the officer wrote an internal memorandum recommending the withdrawal of his licences. This was rejected by a Deputy Chief Constable. In fact, Hamilton's licence was extended.

Following the 1991 investigation, Hamilton wrote letters and telephoned head teachers, local politicians and Members of Parliament claiming victimisation. The controversy continued and mounted. It was in this context that the killings occurred, making him instantly recognisable to the first police officers at the scene. It is also against this backdrop that parents were treated insensitively when they arrived at the school. Those whose children had died were held without information or appropriate facilities in the staff room until mid-afternoon. Only then were they told of their loss. Local doctors and clergy, entering the staff room throughout the day to comfort parents, were forbidden to disclose why they were there.

Eight days after the tragedy a public inquiry was established by the Secretary of State for Scotland, chaired by Lord Cullen. Its terms of reference were: 'To inquire into the circumstances leading up to and surrounding the events at Dunblane Primary School ... which resulted in the deaths of 18 people; to consider the issues arising therefrom; to make recommendations as may seem appropriate; and to report as soon as practicable' (Cullen 1996: iii). Cullen received over 1,600 letters, petitions supported by 33,379 signatures, 123 written submissions, and numerous published documents and academic papers. He made 23 recommendations regarding the certification system for holding firearms, one on firearms availability, two on school security and two on the vetting and supervision of adults working with children and young people. He noted that of 'most concern to the families in the present case were delays in being informed of the fate of their children' (ibid. 17). The delays 'were entirely unacceptable, especially when combined with the distressing lack of any information ...'.

Cullen, however, accepted the police explanation that delays were caused by ensuring accuracy of information and the briefing of family liaison teams. In fact, he praised the 'general quality of work which was done by the Central Scotland Police' (ibid. 18). He gave the impression that the families were satisfied with his inquiry, its scope and its conduct, noting: 'Shortly before opening the Inquiry I and the Lord Advocate had a meeting with the relatives ... in order to discuss any concern or anxiety which they had in regard to the taking of evidence at the Inquiry' (ibid. 7). For the families, the key issues were how Hamilton, given his known personal history, could legitimately acquire an armoury and what had caused the families to endure such appalling treatment in the immediate aftermath. As the inquiry progressed further issues of concern emerged.

Mick North (2000: 137) notes that, after hearing three weeks of evidence to the Cullen Inquiry, there 'no longer appeared to be an obvious structure to the proceedings'. 'Naively', he continues, 'I'd expected that a Public Inquiry would be conducted in a way that would help the public to understand'. Much of the Inquiry dialogue 'was almost impossible to follow, the arguments couched in legal language with examples drawn from cases no lay person would know'. As the Inquiry neared its end it became clear that the prosecuting agency in Scotland, the Procurators Fiscal, would not be questioned about why they had never taken a case against Hamilton. For the families, 'who wanted to believe that all relevant evidence would be heard', this issue was 'crucial'. North concludes, '[e]xamining the prosecution service in depth was not possible; this was one boundary that the Scottish judicial system would not or could not cross' (*ibid.* 138).

The Dunblane families were profoundly disappointed by the conduct and outcome of the Cullen Inquiry. Criticism was not confined to Cullen's limited analysis and recommendations regarding firearms control. Families were given no detailed information or explanation concerning the status of the Inquiry or their entitlement to legal representation. Cullen's preliminary meeting with families 'provided an expectation of openness that wasn't fulfilled' (*ibid.* 194). In the selection of evidence there was 'no clear overview of the strategy being adopted by the Crown ... there to represent the public interest'. The legal procedures adopted and the language of the Inquiry represented 'an alien world to many of the families', denying their 'full participation in a supposedly public process'.

For grief-stricken families there was no time to prepare, to gain advice and information or to grasp fully the realities or potential of the process. As the families later argued, an official inquiry cannot deliver a detailed and thorough examination of all relevant evidence if time and opportunity have not been given for all available information to emerge. North specifies several significant 'omissions' by Cullen in setting his Inquiry's parameters: the 'link' between Hamilton and Dunblane concerning his 'problems' with the town; the failure to call witnesses to explore that link; the decision not to call successive Central Scotland Police Chief Constables; the lack of open discussion of Hamilton's suggested relationship with the Masons; the partial examination of discrepancies and deficiencies in the gun licensing process; the lack of accountability of the Procurator Fiscal; the stark discrepancies in evidence between the police and parents over their treatment.

North (*ibid.* 197) reflects strongly felt and shared feelings about these discrepancies: 'Had there been a ruthless determination to establish the truth and to demonstrate that only the whole truth was acceptable, then those police officers who'd distorted the times ought to have been recalled ... to explain the discrepancy'. According to a bereaved father police evidence to the Inquiry amounted to 'a concerted attempt to make out we had not been left waiting for news of our children as long as we had' (personal interview, June 1998). Another bereaved relative was 'stunned ... the police just stood there and lied on oath – sticking to bizarre time-scales' (personal interview, June 1998). A family's social worker 'was subjected to tougher cross-examination than most police officers in order to verify times' (personal interview, June 1998). Given little notice of being called, according to a bereaved father, the social worker 'confirmed our version of events'. Yet 'no police officer was called to explain the discrepancy between hers and their evidence' (personal interview, June 1998). Another parent concludes, 'it was us who were made to feel that we were the ones that were lying' (personal interview, June 1998). North (2000: 199) concludes that an inquiry governed by a 'pre-determined agenda' of 'damage limitation or finding a scapegoat' is reduced to 'little more than a piece of theatre'.

At the close of his inquiry, Cullen placed the crucial internal police report on Thomas Hamilton under a 100 years' secrecy order. Following a campaign by the bereaved families, the ban appeared to be lifted in March 2003 by the Lord Advocate (under pressure from the Scottish Parliament). In fact, it became evident that 106 documents had been subject to the secrecy order. The four Central Scotland Police reports released were 'edited' versions of the originals. Many of the other documents, not released and held in Scotland's National Archives, are police summaries or edited witness statements. Mick North stated that 'this raises questions about what was made available at the time of the Inquiry ... Everything was supposed to come out ... it seems the Crown Office was less than open' (*The Mail on Sunday*, 6 April 2003). The issue of non-disclosure and police editing supports North's (2000: 199) conclusion that the Cullen Inquiry 'appeared unwilling to challenge the status quo', raising the question: 'Which public do they [official inquiries] serve?'

In whose interest?

[Lord Widgery] seemed to take to heart Prime Minister Heath's extraordinary understanding of the British role in Northern Ireland – that 'we [are] in Northern Ireland fighting not only a military war but a propaganda war'. (Mullan 1997: 43)

Don Mullan recounts a meeting held at the Prime Minister's residence on 1 February 1972. It was attended by the Prime Minister, the Chancellor Lord Hailsham, and the Lord Chief Justice Lord Widgery. Two days earlier, 13 civilians had been shot dead and a further 14 injured, by British soldiers during a civil rights protest in Derry. The meeting was to confirm Lord Widgery as the chair of an official inquiry into what soon became known as Bloody Sunday. At the meeting, undisclosed until 1995, Widgery requested his inquiry be limited 'to what actually happened in those few minutes when men were shot and killed ... to confine evidence to eyewitnesses' (quoted in Winter 1997: 27). This 'confinement' of evidence 'precluded any investigation of the planning that led up to the deployment of the Paras [Parachute Regiment] against civilian demonstrators' (*ibid.*).

Widgery's report drew heavy criticism from the nationalist/republican communities throughout the North of Ireland. Today it gathers dust, discredited. It contained 'many inconsistencies: it failed to resolve conflicting evidence and to give evidence due and proper weight; it failed to recognise the complete unreliability of the forensic evidence; it incorrectly applied the law on lethal force; it failed to reach conclusions justified by the facts' (*ibid.* 26). Mullan's conclusion is that Widgery 'laundered' the truth, revealing a 'determination to shield and protect military personnel who had participated in the murder of civilians' (Mullan 1997: 43). Perhaps the most disconcerting aspect of Widgery's report was his selection of 'reliable' evidence. For example, his conclusion as fact of the precise number of shots fired at military personnel in the months preceding Bloody Sunday – and the figure for explosions – was taken without qualification from the testimony of the British Army Commander in operational control on the day. In his summary of testimony, Widgery recorded his admiration for the 'demeanour' of the soldiers giving evidence and praised their 'confidence' under the pressure of cross examination. It contrasted with his criminalisation of those who took part in the march.

Widgery's report came as no surprise to the republican/nationalist communities or human rights lawyers and campaigners. Just months earlier, Sir Edward Compton had reported on the use of internment in the North of Ireland. His inquiry, held in secret, concluded that internees had experienced 'physical ill-treatment' but that allegations of brutality had been unfounded. At his inquiry, detainees were refused legal aid and, after protesting, were granted a lawyer. Yet the police and military witnesses were legally represented. All but two detainees boycotted the inquiry. In contrast he consulted 95 army personnel, 26 police officers, 11 prison officers, 5 regimental medical officers, 2 medical staff officers and 4 civilian doctors. Compton did not recognise that hooding, forced standing on toes, 'white noise' and food and sleep deprivation amounted to torture or even inhuman and degrading treatment.

Knighted by the British state, Compton had been a Unionist government Ombudsman. Of Lord Widgery, 'who held the highest judicial office in the United Kingdom', Mullan (1997: 43) concludes that despite being 'presented as a man of impeccable integrity and scrupulous impartiality', he had a 'high-ranking military background'. The proposition that official inquiries have been used selectively 'on a terrain laid down by the State' (Sim *et al.* 1987: 32) to deflect criticism, legitimate unacceptable levels of state intervention and recover confidence regarding the abuse of power was brought into sharp relief by their use in the North of Ireland.

Twenty-seven years after Bloody Sunday, the Labour government commissioned Lord Saville to chair a new inquiry (assisted by Canadian judge Justice William Hoyt and Sir Edward Somers from New Zealand). From the outset, the Saville Inquiry was steeped in controversy regarding the location (Derry and London), the anonymity of military personnel giving evidence and the 'loss' of documents, statements, photographs and exhibits. Use by the state's lawyers of the judicial review to challenge Saville's rulings was a continuing frustration for families keen to establish the facts of the case so long after the event. Preliminary hearings were held in September 1999 and four years later the inquiry remains in session. Commissioning an inquiry to compensate for the failings of another is rare.

Official inquiries into events in the North of Ireland, invariably involving matters of state security, represent the sharp end of a continuum at which the state's interests are protected and served at the expense of those caught up in events. In winning the 'propaganda war' it was inconceivable to the government of the day, and its appointees, that the truth could be revealed. In such circumstances official inquiries have been staged, managed and manipulated to obstruct disclosure and promote accounts in keeping with a broader political agenda.

Truth, acknowledgment and 'appalling vistas'

The decision to commission an inquiry, its status and terms of reference, are political. There is no public debate or transparency regarding the advice sought and given within or between government departments and other agencies. Who is appointed as chair, assessors and advisors forms part of a hidden discretionary process. Once appointed, chairs exercise broad discretion in gathering evidence and information, the conduct and progress of the inquiry, the selection of witnesses and disclosure of documents, the significance attached to evidence and its influence on findings and recommendations. There is no opportunity to challenge, and no accountability with regard to the decisions through which evidence has credibility ascribed or denied. It is not surprising that lawyers reflect that those who chair inquiries rely on evidence that suits their perception of what happened.

Given the potential for, and reality of, information management and procedural manipulation embedded in a process so heavily imbued with discretion, official inquiries of various forms have been used politically to deflect criticism and strengthen public confidence. As Cohen (1993) argues, the unwillingness to confront anomalous or disturbing information extends to democratic societies. A 'complex discourse of official denial' harnesses processes and procedures of state inquiry and investigation to promote an effective and authoritative legal defence (Cohen 1996: 521). 'Historical skeletons', he states, 'are put in cupboards because of the political need to be innocent of a troubling recognition' (Cohen 2001: 139). Such a political imperative creates a purposeful inhibition on disclosure, selection, examination and presentation of information as evidence. As the Widgery Inquiry demonstrated, those official inquiries that focus on unreasonable force, negligent acts or omissions, or miscarriages of justice perpetrated by state institutions are under considerable pressure to receive and effectively incorporate criticism while guaranteeing legitimacy and renewing authority.

In his definitive critique of the 'sociology of knowledge', Becker (1967: 240) makes the obvious contextualising point – that it is essential to 'distinguish between the truth of a statement and an assessment of the circumstances under which that statement is made'. For Becker, deceit is built into the fabric of state institutions. Prisons, schools, hospitals, police and so on, despite target-setting, performance indicators and mission statements, regularly fail to deliver an appropriate and effective service. They also place at risk those to whom they have a 'duty of care'. In this context 'officials develop ways of denying the failure of the institution to perform as it should and explaining those failures that cannot be hidden' (*ibid.* 243).

Becker was commenting on 1960s USA state institutions, yet his analysis remains pertinent. In questioning the circumstances in which state institutions, through their employees, intervene and act, concern extends beyond 'the moment'. Contextualisation, regarding operational policies, professional judgments, custom and practice, lifts the focus of the inquiry from the specific to the generic, from the individual to the institution. As Scarman's denial of institutionalised racism shows, what can be at stake amounts to more than individual culpability for an act or omission; it is the legitimacy of an agency in the administration of its authority. This was the deeply ingrained fear that led Lord Denning, as Lord Chief Justice, to urge that six wrongfully imprisoned men should not be released. Why? Because their release would constitute, 'an appalling vista ... it will mean that the police were guilty of perjury ... of violence and threats, that the confessions were involuntary and improperly admitted in evidence and that the convictions were erroneous ...' (quoted in Gilligan 1990: 227).

Denning's contemptible rationale suggested that truth was the first casualty in protecting the tarnished image of English justice. The second casualty, of course, was the liberty of the Birmingham Six. This is a dramatic, contemporary example of Becker's notion of institutionalised deceit. It contributed to the setting up of the 1993 Royal Commission on Criminal Justice chaired by Viscount Runciman. Given the extent of miscarriages of justice, particularly but not exclusively the Irish cases, it was ironic that Runciman (1993: 2) opened his report with the following unsubstantiated comment: 'It is widely assumed – and we are in no position to contradict it – that the guilty are more often acquitted than the innocent convicted'. From the outset, then, he employed two 'guiding principles the first being "balance" (wrongful convictions set against wrongful acquittals) and the second that miscarriages of justice were an aberration' (Scraton 1994: 102).

Restricted disclosure, privileged access to evidence and, as in Runciman, the realignment of terms of reference do not occur in a vacuum. As Foucault argues, 'truth' is derived and sustained within the dominant, structural relations of power. However apparently diverse are the 'relations of power which permeate, characterise and constitute the social body', their influence and effectiveness depends on the 'production, accumulation, circulation and functioning of a discourse' itself closely associated with the 'production of truth' (Foucault 1980: 93). Thus '[p]ower never ceases its interrogation, inquisition, its registration of truth: it institutionalises, professionalises and rewards its pursuit ...' (*ibid.* 94). What is produced is a 'régime of truth'.

Foucault (*ibid.* 131) considers the material reality of societal régimes of truth as comprising: 'types of disclosure which it [society] accepts and makes function as true; the mechanisms and instances which enable one to distinguish true and false statements; the techniques and procedures accorded value in the acquisition of truth; the status of those who are charged with saying what counts as true'. The mechanisms, techniques, procedures and ascribed statuses constituting the operational practice of official inquiries are not value-free. Nor are they independent of the powerful, defining state institutions whose authority they seek to reaffirm. As they set out to reconstruct public confidence, official inquiries more often than not become part of 'official discourse, institutional processes and professional processes' which, within advanced democratic states, 'are expressions of power which construct and legitimate self-serving versions of truth' (Scraton 2002: 116).

While this analysis is sceptical regarding the political agendas that contextualise the commissioning, delivery and outcomes of UK official inquiries, it also suggests that there is potential for disclosure and rigorous testing of evidence. Official inquiries can provide a public forum for knowing, for understanding and for acknowledgment in circumstances where the bereaved and survivors seek 'truth' (Maclean 2001). Equally, however, when institutional, discretionary powers of state institutions have been abused with impunity, official inquiries can add to the pain of grief through inadequate and partial investigation and disclosure, through the disqualification of alternative accounts and the vilification of those who make them. Official inquiries concerned with responsibility and accountability are also overshadowed by culpability and liability. It is at this point that the commitment to 'truth' and 'acknowledgment' becomes Denning's 'appalling vista' and, rather than functioning as an expression of 'democratic pluralism', they present a barely disguised veneer to deep-rooted authoritarianism.

Acknowledgments

With many thanks to Deena Haydon and to my co-workers at the Centre for Studies in Crime and Social Justice, particularly Barbara Houghton. Much appreciation to the ESRC-funded Disasters Research Seminar Group and the participants in the Public Inquiries and Inquests seminar. Finally, deepest respect to the bereaved and survivors whom I have been privileged to know and work with over the last two decades.

References

Ashton, J. and Ferguson, I. (2001) *Cover-Up of Convenience: The Hidden Scandal of Lockerbie*. Edinburgh: Mainstream Publications.
Becker, H. (1967) Whose side are we on? *Social Problems*, 14, Winter: 239–47.
Bourne, J. (2001) The life and times of institutional racism. *Race and Class*, 43(2): 7–22.
Bridges, L. (1999) The Lawrence Inquiry – incompetence, corruption and institutional racism. *Journal of Law and Society*, 26(3): 298–322.
Burton, F. and Carlen, P. (1979) *Official Discourse. On Discourse Analysis, Government Publications, Ideology and the State*. London: Routledge & Kegan Paul.
Christian, L. (1996) The seven year history of the Marchioness disaster: lessons for the handling of other incidents involving mass deaths requiring investigation. Unpublished paper, presented to the European Group for the Study of Deviance

and Social Control Conference, Bangor, Wales, September.

Christian, L. (2002) The battle of Potters Bar. *Guardian,* Comment and Analysis, p. 19.

Clarke, L.J. (2001) *Public Inquiry into the Identification of Victims following Major Transport Accidents,* Vols 1 and 2, Cmnd 5012. London: HMSO.

Cohen, S. (1993) Human rights and crimes of the state: the culture of denial. *Australian and New Zealand Journal of Criminology,* 26(2): 97–115.

Cohen, S. (1996) Government responses to human rights reports: claims, denials and counter claims. *Human Rights Quarterly,* 18.

Cohen, S. (2001) *States of Denial: Knowing about Atrocities and Suffering.* Cambridge: Polity Press.

Cox, M. and Foster, T. (1992) *Their Darkest Day: The Tragedy of PanAm 103 and Its Legacy of Hope.* New York: Grove Weidenfeld.

Cullen, The Hon. Lord (1996) *The Public Inquiry into the Shootings at Dunblane Primary School on 13 March 1996,* Cmnd 3386. London: HMSO.

Foucault, M. (1980) *Power/Knowledge. Selected Interviews and Other Writings 1972–1977,* ed. C. Gordon. Brighton: Harvester Wheatsheaf.

Gilligan, G. (2002) Royal commissions of inquiry. *Australia and New Zealand Journal of Criminology,* 35(3): 269–88.

Gilligan, O. (ed.) (1990) *The Birmingham Six: An Appalling Vista.* Dublin: Litéreire Publishers.

Maclean, M. (2001) How does an inquiry inquire? A brief note on the working methods of the Bristol Royal Infirmary Inquiry. *Journal of Law and Society,* 28(4): 590–601.

Macpherson, Sir W. (1999) *The Stephen Lawrence Inquiry – Report,* Cm 4262-I. London: Stationery Office.

Mullan, D. (ed.) (1997) *Eyewitness Bloody Sunday: The Truth.* Dublin: Wolfhound Press.

NCCL (1980) *Southall: 23 April 1979 Unofficial Committee of Enquiry Report.* London: National Council for Civil Liberties.

North, M. (2000) *Dunblane. Never Forget.* Edinburgh: Mainstream Publications.

Popplewell, Mr Justice (1985) *Committee of Inquiry into Crowd Safety and Control at Sports Grounds. Interim Report,* Cmnd 9585. London: HMSO.

Rolston, B. (2000) *Unfinished Business: State Killings and the Quest for Truth.* Belfast: Beyond the Pale.

Runciman, Viscount (1993) *The Royal Commission on Criminal Justice. Report,* Cmnd 2263. London: HMSO.

Scarman, Rt Hon. Lord (1981) *The Brixton Disorders 10–12 April 1981,* Cmnd 8427. London: HMSO.

Scraton, P. (1994) Denial, neutralisation and disqualification: the Royal Commission on Criminal Justice in context. In M. McConville and L. Bridges (eds) *Criminal Justice In Crisis.* Aldershot: Edward Elgar, pp. 98–112.

Scraton, P. (1999) Policing with contempt: the degrading of truth and denial of justice in the aftermath of the Hillsborough disaster. *Journal of Law and Society,* 26(3): 273–97.

Scraton, P. (2000) *Hillsborough: The Truth,* 2nd edn. Edinburgh: Mainstream Publications.

Scraton, P. (2002) Lost lives, hidden voices: 'truth' and controversial deaths. *Race and Class,* 44(1): 109–18.

Sim, J., Scraton, P. and Gordon, P. (1987) Introduction: crime, the state and critical analysis. In P. Scraton (ed.) *Law, Order and the Authoritarian State*. Buckingham: Open University Press, pp. 1–70.

Smith, D.J. and Gray, J. (1983) *Police and People in London: IV The Police in Action*. London: Policy Studies Institute.

Stuart-Smith, Rt Hon. LJ (1998) *Scrutiny of Evidence relating to the Hillsborough Football Stadium Disaster*, Cmnd 3878. London: HMSO.

Taylor LJ (1989) *The Hillsborough Stadium Disaster: 15 April 1989. Interim Report*, Cm 765. London: HMSO.

Thomas, P.A. (1982) Royal commissions. *Statute Law Review*, Spring: 40–50.

Winter, J. (1997) Preface. In D. Mullan (ed.) *Eyewitness Bloody Sunday: The Truth*. Dublin: Wolfhound Press.

Part 2
Official discourse, legitimation and delegitimation

Chapter 4

The acceptable prison: official discourse, truth and legitimacy in the nineteenth century

John Pratt

We have come to assume that prisons are places of secrecy, cloaked by an impenetrable bureaucratic shroud. However, while this may be the case today, it has not always been so. In the second half of the nineteenth century in England, there was, in fact, an explosion of prison discourses: that of prison governors, chaplains and doctors in their memoirs and competing blueprints for the future development of prisons; that of journalists and social commentators who in the mid-nineteenth century still had reasonable access to prisons and were able to report on their findings without any official interference; there was an official prison discourse set out in the annual reports of the prison inspectors; and there were competing critical discourses – one from essayists, literati, penal reform groups and so on who claimed that prison was not severe enough, and one from prisoners, ex-prisoners and their various supporters who proclaimed that prison was much too severe. In addition, there was a succession of formal inquiries into prisons between 1850 and 1895 (three Royal Commissions, six Select Committee Reports, three Departmental Committees of Inquiry and three Commissions appointed by the Secretary of State).

All this discourse and debate, then, in a period when it might be thought that 'the birth of the prison' would effectively end all such discussion. The opening of Pentonville model prison in 1842 marked this point in England. Its influence on subsequent prison building and design during the rest of the nineteenth century was considerable (see Markus 1993). Its internal regime – 18 months' solitary confinement for penal servitude prisoners followed by hard labour on public works – seemingly resolved the debate about the merits of the respective separate and silent systems (Crawford 1835). It became well known for its advanced technological and mechanical arrangements (Dixon 1850; Mayhew and Binny 1862) and the absence within it of all the squalid and chaotic premodern prison trappings. Instead, it provided its inmates with uniforms, masks (to avoid recognition), their own cells and then further separation while at chapel and exercise. Completing these internal disciplinary arrangements, slippered guards silently patrolled the corridors, keeping surveillance through the spyhole in each cell door (cf. Foucault 1978). Outside, its boundary wall provided the separation between the institution and the public that became another characteristic of modern penality. And yet, rather than ending debate about prisons, Pentonville helped only to further stimulate it. What, then, was the significance of all this 'garrulous discourse' (Foucault 1980) on prisons in the second half of the nineteenth century? What I want to suggest is that the birth of the prison and its subsequent embeddedness in modern society has been taken too much for granted. During this period, there was no inevitability to this, no certainty as to the nature of prison development, no taken-for-granted assumptions about its role and place in modern society. In contrast, for most of the nineteenth century, prison was still a highly contested site – it was not then the exclusive secretive property of the penal bureaucracies that we recognise it as today. At that time, official discourse was only one of a range of competing voices proclaiming their own version of 'the truth' about prisons.

In these respects, the succession of formal inquiries of this period – regarded as 'impartial, expert and representative' (Cartwright 1975) – had become the way to resolve such competing and contestable accounts of prison truth. However, the Report of the Gladstone Committee (1895) marked the end of this period of inquiry and investigation, with a gap of more than half a century between it and its successor. In these respects, the significance of Gladstone was not that it put an end to criticism of the prison; instead, its significance lay in the fact that it marked the end of the battle for truth. Ultimately, these very processes of inquiry had not only confirmed that official discourse was 'the truth' about prisons but had effectively disqualified or nullified any alternative truth accounts. There would be no need for any further inquiries for another half century because official discourse had become acceptable and uncontestable, precluding the need for any investigation or examination – thus drawing across the prisons that curtain of bureaucratic secrecy that we have become so familiar with today, and finally establishing prison and all that we now associate with this concept in modern society.

The unacceptability of palace prisons

Of the period that Pentonville was opened, Griffiths (1875: 140) subsequently wrote that 'prison discipline filled the public prints and men's mouths whenever they talked, whether in the Houses of Parliament, or in the world at large.' Essentially, then, at this juncture, there was no central, unified prison establishment: instead, we find a range of competing voices, with no set hierarchy of credibility to order them, attempting to pull prison development in a variety of ways. While, under the terms of the 1835 Prisons Act, central government now controlled convict prisons and had the power to inspect and make regulations for local gaols, these were still under day-to-day control and management of local justice and their own authorities. As such, a variety of prison governors, chaplains and doctors were keen to advertise what they saw as their own successes in their particular adaptations of the separate/silent system and attendant issues (see, variously, Field 1848; Burt 1852; Hill 1853; Kingsmill 1854; Chesterton 1856; Clay 1861). They were able to do so at this stage because they were not yet bound into a central, unified prison system. They could put forward their own views independently of the official discourse that was now to be found in the annual prison reports – at this stage, one from the Director of Convict Prisons and one from the three Inspectors of Local Prisons.

These in their own turn were highly critical of the premodern excesses that they still found in place in many local prisons on their visits, since it was their task to attempt to standardise prison régimes so that these might be developed 'with advantage to the discipline and health of the prisoners' (Report of the Inspector of Prisons (Home District) 1844: 13). There was thus a complaint after a visit to Newgate of 'defective and unsatisfactory arrangements regarding clothing. Many even of the convicted prisoners generally wear a portion at least of their own clothing, and few of the untried are clad in prison dress ... the use of party-coloured (sic) clothing also continues in many English prisons, carrying with it a degrading badge as opposed to the feeling of self-respect we wish to encourage' (Report of the Inspectors of Prisons (Home District) 1836: 32). Again, building design had an important role to play in both reforming prisoners and generating a humane atmosphere. At Armley Gaol, Leeds, for example, it was noted that 'the glass of cell windows is fluted, which diminishes the light and prevents the inmate of the cell from even seeing the sky. This I consider objectionable, partly because it must tend to produce that depression of spirits which has to be peculiarly guarded against and partly because an abundant supply of light is of importance in a medical point of view' (Report of the Inspectors of Prisons (Eastern and Northern District) 1847–8: 428).

At the same time, the commitment to dietary arrangements designed to ensure the health of the prisoners led to vigilance on the part of prison doctors who then had few qualms in speaking out and exposing inadequacies in their own reports which were supplementary to those of the inspector of their district, and at the same time pose their own remedies for dietary deficiencies. Thus: 'I would strongly advise that 2 oz bread should be added to the supper and breakfast of the men, making the quantity of each of these meals 8 oz. If this change were made ... there would remain, I think, no further complaint and the strength of the sentenced prisoners, which is now decidedly below the healthy average, would be greatly improved' (Report of the Inspectors of Prisons (Southern District) 1858: 53). In similar vein, Colonel Jebb, as Director of Convict Prisons, quickly proposed abandoning the rigid separation of prisoners at all times that had been incorporated in the Pentonville model, as well as the anonymising masks they had to wear (Report of the Director of Convict Prisons 1853).

What is absent from both sets of discourses – the governors' memoirs on the one hand, the annual prisons reports on the other – is any reference to the less eligibility incumbrances that had been enshrined in the new Poor Law of 1834 and which had become the central principle in the administration of workhouses for the poor and indigent. Thus, on reception to prison, official discourse now proclaimed that the prisoner was to be 'placed in a warm bath, and after undergoing a thorough cleansing, he is clothed in the dress appropriate to the class to which he may belong' (Report of the Inspectors of Prisons (Home District) 1839: 284). Equally, Hepworth Dixon (1850: 153) found at Pentonville that 'the diet is better, richer than in other prisons'; overall, it seemed to him that Pentonville was 'a palace prison, conducted with military precision and regularity'. Nonetheless, the effect of such reporting was to make the idea of prison of this kind unacceptable, and generated a further discourse which was highly critical of these 'palace prisons'. In relation to their physical structure, Carlyle (1850: 44) wrote of a visit to a model prison:

> ... gateway as to a fortified palace; then a spacious court, like the square of a city; broad staircases, passages to interior courts; fronts of a stately architecture all round ... surely one of the most perfect buildings, within the compass of London. We looked at the apartments, sleeping cells, dining rooms, working rooms, general courts or special and private: excellent all, the ne-plus-ultra of human care and ingenuity; in my life I never saw so clean a building; probably no Duke in England lives in a mansion of such perfect and thorough cleanness.

At the same time, it was made abundantly clear that the dietary arrangements ('the bread, the cocoa, soup, meat, all the various sorts of food, in their respective cooking places we tasted: found them of excellence superlative', Carlyle 1850: 45) in the model prisons were unacceptable because of their superiority not just to workhouse residents but to non-dependent worthy citizens as well. For example, Charles Dickens who had famously highlighted the hunger of workhouse children in *Oliver Twist* (Dickens 1838) wrote, in contrast, of mealtime in the prisons as follows in *David Copperfield* (Dickens 1850: 714): 'I wondered whether it occurred to anybody that there was a striking contrast between these plentiful repasts of choice quality and the dinners, not to say, of paupers, but of soldiers, sailors, labourers, the great bulk of the honest, working class community; of whom not one man in five hundred ever dined so well.' There seems no doubt that, during the 1840s at least, prisoners in the new jails were indeed better fed than many sections of the working classes at that time (Burnett 1966). There were also anecdotal reports of paupers committing crimes for the specific purpose of being sent to prison rather than face the greater severity of the workhouse (Field 1848; Delacy 1986).

There were thus insistent challenges to the validity of the official prison discourse and demands that its seemingly liberal prison policy be reversed: 'we have had the mockery and mischief of lenity for too long already, and the prisoners themselves, of the last ten years, have suffered even more from it than the innocent portion of society, whose lives and property have paid the penalty of our foolish favour to crime' (Symons 1849: 150). Indeed, it seemed at times that there was no control at all over the prisoners, one observer of the 1858 Portland prison riot noting that:

> 30–40 men rushed to a central point in the quarry. The authorities were prepared. They charged with level bayonets on the rioters who took flight. The convicts burst out in jets of violence throughout the day... They do not seem to have rebelled against confinement or any regulations – their treatment could not furnish complaint. It was just a civil protest. We should consider the result had they succeeded. (*The Times*, 23 September 1858)

And when sighted performing their hard labour tasks, it seemed that they still enjoyed superior working conditions to free labourers: 'Convicts are entirely idle on wet days and some (carefully nursed) are excused of work altogether. It is high feeding and low work... convicts do not dread the labour – it is imaginary hard labour' (*The Times*, 16 December 1862).

The then embryonic prison bureaucracy was insufficiently embedded in the structure of modern society to be able to ignore and disregard this critique and was instead placed on the defensive, Jebb (Report of the Director of Convict Prisons 1852: 55) contending that 'a healthy diet and good order are not the result of any undue desire to administer to the *comfort* of a prisoner, but the whole bearing of the daily routine by which they are secured, is calculated to thwart the natural tastes and habits of most criminals, and to direct them into new and improved channels.' Again, in the early 1850s, dietary provisions for some categories of prisoners were reduced to a level below those of workhouse residents, and Jebb's own suggestions for the abolition of prison masks and unnecessary separation were put on hold. Nonetheless, the power of this alternative prison discourse had, by this time, been able to recast the convicts as a different species of humanity altogether. On their visit to Pentonville, Mayhew and Binny (1862: 141) noted that

> each of the prisoners is not only clad alike – and brown as so many bees pouring from the countless cells of a hive – but every one bears a peculiar brown cloth cap, and the peak of this...hangs so low down as to cover the face like a mask, the eyes alone of the individual appearing through the holes cut in the front, and seeming almost like phosphoric lights shining through the sockets of a scull.

They had thus become feared and shunned, to be kept out of the way for fear of the menace they were thought to constitute, and starved of any residual pity or sympathy (see Dickens 1860; Carpenter 1864).

Official prison discourse which had spoken of the need for cleanliness and good hygiene, a diet sufficient to maintain health, the importance of disciplinary training as a reformative influence and so on was outweighed by this critical discourse which saw the prisoners as privileged citizens of the palace prisons: it was the latter which had greater acceptability at this time. As a result, there was a succession of formal prison inquiries (which incorporated what was then thought to be the most advanced scientific knowledge on nutrition and hygiene) in the early 1860s designed to reduce the luxuries of these palaces. For example, the link that had been established between diet and health was now broken:

> I think that by a system in which the food is only just sufficient to meet the wants of the human frame, and where it is of a very simple

kind, and where the system is rather one of punishment, you will deter a person from crime much more than you do under present circumstances. (Report from the Select Committee of the House of Lords on Prison Discipline 1863: 120)

Similarly, hard labour was to be made deliberately punitive, abandoning any attempts to foster industrious habits through its performance, and was also to be conducted within the prison: '[it] shall consist of nothing else but the treadwheel, crank and shot drill' (*ibid.* vii). These provisions alongside other changes to prison policy that were recommended at this time (abandonment of schooling, extra provisions for the infliction of corporal punishment and so on) were characteristic of the 'hard bed, hard labour, hard fare' era of prison policy in the second half of the nineteenth century. As such, the former palace prisons had become institutions to be dreaded. Now indeed it could truthfully – and acceptably – be proclaimed that

the life of prisoners is extremely monotonous. Having been used in most cases to constant change and excitement, they are debarred from all pleasures and amusements, they are compelled to pass their time in a dull, unvarying routine of distasteful labour, and at the close of each day's work they return to the cheerless solitude of their cells. (Report of the Commissioners Appointed to Inquire into the Operation of the Acts Relating to Transportation and Penal Servitude 1863: 41)

The growth of bureaucratic control

Nonetheless, to ensure that this became the only acceptable way to speak about prison, this reformulation also needed a significant growth in central bureaucratic management to restrict any departures from this new standard – as had been recognised in the Report from the Select Committee of the House of Lords on Prison Discipline (1863: 10): 'The Committee are of the opinion that it is desirable to establish without delay a system approaching as nearly as may be practicable to a uniformity of labour, diet and treatment.' Inevitably, this would be at the expense of local prison governance by visiting justices. This latter group had anyway come to be regarded by the central authorities as ineffectual and inadequate, ultimately responsible for scandals such as that which emerged at Birmingham prison[1] in 1854, of which *The Times* (29 July 1854) subsequently wrote:

It is not less than a twelvemonth since a very painful sensation was made in this country by the discovery that in one prison... constructed on the best plan, visited by magistrates, and managed by officers of reputation and experience, there was a systematic practice of atrocities that brought one back to the days before Howard.

The affair was then satirised in Reade's (1856) *It's Never Too Late to Mend* which, essentially, was a strong plea for the professional administration of prisons rather than amateur inefficiency. While it was now entirely acceptable for prisons to be 'dreaded', what had become unacceptable was any return to gratuitous, arbitrary abuses (whether of too much or too little punishment) that the localised system of prison governance had made possible.

As such, the Prisons Act 1865 deprived the local bodies of their previous autonomy by standardising conditions throughout the whole prison system: for example, cells would have to be certified by the respective Inspector of Prisons; dietaries would have to be framed in accordance with instructions from the Secretary of State who had the power to withhold financial support from the prison in the event of departures from these standards (changeable only by a further Act of Parliament). The consequence of this administrative reorganisation was to draw a bureaucratic veil across the prison, thereby restricting knowledge of and debate on prison policy. These curbs on local discretion and initiative led to what Webb and Webb (1922: 188) referred to as 'a falling off in the output of books on prisons in the 1860s'. There is little surprise that the discourse of the prison governors and so on expressing their own views on prisons should now fall into decline. There was no longer any place for their views as individuals since the Prisons Act had already determined what prison had to be like – and had set in place the bureaucratic machinery to enforce this throughout the entire prison system.

At the same time, the potential for (formal) rivalry among the different sections of the prison establishment was brought to an end, as their respective roles and status were redefined by Act of Parliament rather than fitted to and shaped by local contingencies. Thus, as regards the chaplains, they were now downgraded and given lesser status than their Chief Prison Officer, to whom they were to report 'any abuse or impropriety' (Prisons Act 1865: Rule 49) – their autonomy within the prison thus being stripped away. As for the doctors, their discretionary power to provide dietary adjustments was removed and instead they themselves would be subjected to checks and controls. Any decisions to provide extra food would have to be recorded and 'framed in such a way as to afford the means of judging his mode of proceeding. This record will be particularly useful in enabling a comparison to be made between the practice of different medical officers, [and] will afford a very useful check on the abuse of discretion in this regard' (Report from the Select Committee of the House of Lords on Prison Discipline 1863: xii). In addition, while the previous annual reports from prison chaplains would be dispensed with altogether, those of the doctors, instead of expressing concerns, making suggestions and so on, would now be summarised with the stock phrase 'provisions are good quality and the general diet is sufficient but not more than necessary for maintaining the health and strength of the prisoners' (Report of the Inspectors of Prisons (Southern District) 1870: 28).

Similar bland phraseology would also be used to encompass the prison officers ('the subordinate officers have performed their duties with intelligence, zeal and fidelity and to my entire satisfaction', Report of the Directors of Convict Prisons 1872: xiv). In other words, the growth of central bureaucratic control began to have the effect of closing down debate and discussion of prison policy. There would be no more reports of wavering priests giving unnecessary pity and comfort to prisoners, no more reports of doctors allowing their Hippocratic Oath to come between them and the role now prescribed for them in prison, no more reports of prison officers unable to control their own prisoners. Instead of being only one of a fragmented range of voices representing the prison authorities, official prison discourse would now be the only such voice, and with this power to control knowledge, be able to proclaim that all was as it should be in the prisons.

The trend towards centralisation and the unification of the prison establishment came to fruition in the Prisons Act 1877. Now, ownership of all prisons was to be vested in the Secretary of State, with a body of Commissioners (maximum five), appointed by and accountable to the Secretary of State, overseeing them. In addition, the previously separate convict and local prisons were fused into a single administration, headed by Colonel (later Sir) Edmund Du Cane (former Chairman of the Board of Directors of Convict Prisons) which came into existence in April 1878, with the immediate closure of 38 local prisons. Official discourse would thus become both more restricted and more unchallengeable. As Webb and Webb (1922: 216) were to put the matter:

When the Inspectors expressed themselves freely upon particular abuses, it was deemed inconvenient to make their strictures known to the public ... nothing was therefore published that was likely to give rise to Parliamentary complaint, or afford a handle to newspaper criticism. The visits of non-official persons to the prisoners were severely discouraged.

Indeed, there was to be no more gratuitous prison visiting by curious social commentators such as Hepworth Dixon (1850) and Mayhew and Binny (1862).[2] The latters' *Criminal Prisons of London* was the last such work for another sixty years.[3] What the public knew about prisons would increasingly have to come from official discourse itself.

At the same time, the authorities became increasingly aware of the power of scandal to prise the prisons open again. As Home Secretary Cross put the matter in 1878, 'while it is commonly admitted that it is better that 99 persons should escape conviction than one innocent man should suffer, it may also be fairly said that it is better that any number of prisoners should be somewhat more favourably treated than they deserve to be, than one man, through any unnecessary prison treatment, or want of early care, should fall sick or die' (McConville 1995: 309). Thus after claims by noted ex-prisoners that bedclothes were sometimes soiled with faeces and that blankets and rugs were never washed,[4] laundry facilities and arrangements for personal cleanliness were somewhat improved (Report of the Prison Commissioners 1883), and the potential of this alternative discourse from ex-prisoners to disrupt the 'truth' proclaimed by the authorities thereby nullified: it was not true, it does not happen now, could be their response.

New voices of opposition

This did not mean, however, that all such scandal could be defused or suppressed so surreptitiously. And it did not mean that there were no other voices at all to be heard on the subject of prisons and prison policy. If the unified prison establishment that had now come into existence was responsible for the decline in the publication of books written by prison officials, the austere regime it now presided over helped to generate a new critical prison literature: not about the luxuries of palace prisons anymore, but, instead, about the unremitting inhumanity of their successors. This was to be found in the memoirs of ex-prisoners (as in the above example of soiled bedclothes and unhygienic bedding), particularly those who enjoyed some sort of celebrity status, as well as Irish political prisoners and their influential supports beyond the prison.[5] These complaints were sufficiently forceful in their own right to be able to break through the administrative curtain that the prison authorities had begun to draw but had not yet closed. Questions were again raised about the acceptability of prison: now, in relation to its severity rather than its leniency. As a result, a further series of inquiries adjudicated on whether or not the new prison régimes were acceptable. In such settings, more experts could give their views on nutrition, hygiene and so on, but, in accordance with the credentials of neutrality and impartiality that had come to be associated with them, they also heard evidence, on a number of occasions at least, from prisoners themselves, alongside luminaries from the prison establishment, including Sir Edmund Du Cane.[6] Alternatively, their memoirs might be treated as authoritative texts, the claims of which Du Cane or other members of the prison establishment would be challenged on.

The Report of the Commission of Inquiry into the Treatment of Certain Treason-Felony Convicts in English Convict Prisons (1867) was the first in this new sequence. However, after hearing evidence of ill-treatment from 17 prisoners, it then refuted this on a step-by-step basis, concluding that

A convict's bread is bitter food at best ... the terrible monotony of the life; the stern order, and the instant obedience, constitute a very terrible punishment. We know that these men have a better diet, sleep in better beds, are more cared for in sickness, have lighter labour than the bulk of the labouring classes ... and that the stories of their ill-treatment are simple falsehoods; but the meanest and poorest labourer in the empire would scarcely change places with them. (ibid. 23)

And most certainly not if the prisoners' refutation of every one of these assurances had been believed and accepted as the new prison truth. Thus, notwithstanding the impartiality of the inquiry process, the growing credibility of the prison establishment as custodians of good order and discipline, and the growing incredibility of the prisoners as creatures to be feared, led to some inevitable conclusions. At the same time, these formal conclusions themselves only further vindicated and validated the official discourse of the prison authorities, as Du Cane recognised in the next annual report which he authored: 'Grave complaints were made during the year of the treatment of the [Irish] convicts ... the [subsequent] report went fully into the whole question of convict management, was submitted to Parliament and entirely set at rest any doubts as to the treatment of those prisoners' (Report of the Directors of Convict Prisons 1867: 8).

We see the same effects and consequences in relation to the Report of the Commissioners on the Treatment of Treason-Felony Convicts in

English Prisons (1871). Here, some minor points in favour of the prisoners were actually conceded. However, these were then seen as the product of aberrations rather than anything systemic. Indeed, problems were recognised as occurring precisely because of departures from uniformity and standardisation, rather than because of it – and which lay at the heart of prisoner grievances. For example, 'the tea supplied to certain classes of the prisoners attracted our attention; it appeared to us to be of inferior character, owing to its being kept in the cauldron before use' (ibid. 8); and 'in one instance the Commission detected portions of meat unfit for human use in the supply sent in for the infirmary ... when three pieces of mutton of greenish colour in parts and of a very bad smell were pointed out' (*ibid.* 13). Overall, however, as regards diet, 'we see no reason to doubt that, in the vast majority of instances, the food is wholesome and good of its kind. We have carefully inspected the bread in all stages in most of the prisons we have visited. It is made of the best seconds flour which, when, examined, appeared good and wholesome' (*ibid.* 8).

Again, the Report of the Committee Appointed to Consider and Report upon Dietaries of Local Prisons (1878: 12) confirmed the validity of existing prison arrangements:

> In the course of our numerous visits to local gaols, we have conversed with many prisoners; we have watched them at all hours of the day; and we cannot avoid the conclusion that, in a large number of cases, imprisonment as now generally conducted, is a condition more or less akin to that of physiological rest ... the struggle for survival is suspended; and the prisoner appears to feel that the prayer for daily bread is rendered unnecessary by the solicitude of his custodians. Tranquillity of mind and freedom from anxiety are leading characteristics of his life.

Similarly, the Report of the Commissioners Appointed to Inquire into the Working of the Penal Servitude Acts (1879: xxi) states: 'After examining a variety of witnesses, we have come to the conclusion that the system of penal servitude as at present administered is, on the whole, satisfactory: that it is effective as a punishment, and free from serious abuses.' In respect of these particular findings, Du Cane (now in his new position as Chairman of the Prison Commissioners) again took the trouble to point out this was tantamount to a vindication of the prison system:

> We have awaited the result of this inquiry with perfect confidence for, though we were aware of course, that statements had been made which produced an unfavourable impression on those who

accepted them without inquiry, we were equally aware that they could not stand the test of investigation' (1879–80: v–vi).

In these respects, Du Cane was to all intents and purposes correct. The processes of inquiry that had been invoked to investigate abuses, cruelties and ill-treatment had the effect, when finding them by and large unsustained, of strengthening the prison establishment while discrediting the prisoners. By the same token, as the processes of inquiry had the effect of embedding the central penal bureaucracy in the social structure of the modern state, so its own bureaucratic requirements in relation to prison management began to override concerns about otherwise shameful and degrading practices. Thus in relation to prison uniform, the Report of the Committee of Inquiry on Press Rules and Prison Dress (1889: 44) recognised that '[prison clothing] has too long been associated with all that is vile and shameful to be assumed by the lesser offenders without a sense of degradation and a shock to self-respect which should never be unnecessarily inflicted.' Nonetheless, the prison uniform had by now become a 'necessary incident to imprisonment', and to relax the rules regarding the wearing of it 'would produce in the mind both of the prisoner and of the public the impression that certain classes of offenders are exceptionally favoured.' At the same time, the uniform might also serve humanitarian concerns:

> The present practice whereby prisoners of different classes are distinguished by different colours and patterns of dress, and every prisoner has on various articles of his clothing distinguished badges ... not only make it unnecessary for the warder to know or address him by his name, but avoid the necessity for making each prisoner's name known to then other prisoners with the disadvantages which might result to the prisoner therefrom. (*ibid.* 46)

The end of inquiry and the supremacy of official discourse

The growing authority of the prison establishment and its ability to control 'the truth' about prisons did not itself prevent further scandal and dissent from this version: what it did do was to affect the way in which competing accounts came to be believed. As such, the critical discourse of dissent reached a crescendo in the early 1890s, as a result of an important coalition between trade unionists with prison experience, MPs (including ex-prisoners Michael Davitt and John Burns), the rebel prison chaplain William Morrison, and sections of the popular press, particularly the

Daily Chronicle and its editor Henry Massingham. Many of their complaints continued to focus on what were seen as the unnecessary hardships and brutalities of prison life. What lay at the heart of these concerns, however, was not the over-repressive régimes themselves but the very processes of bureaucratic control which presided over this systemic privation and inhumanity, and which by its very nature had become steadily closed off from public scrutiny and accountability – and had become identified with the martinet-like personal qualities of Du Cane. Morrison (1894) in particular claimed that imprisonment destroyed the prisoner's spirit, to the point where their reform became impossible, but made their return to prisons after release inevitable (using the prison authorities' own reconviction and recidivism statistics to make his point).

From this point of view, the prison system itself was a failure and was in need of systemic reform. To bring this about, there should be a return to local control of the prisons, rather than its concentration in central government bureaucratic forces: 'The old prison administration was a system which kept the ruling classes in touch with social miseries in their acutest form...local power created local interest and a sense of local responsibility' (*ibid.* 461). Now, he argued, the only knowledge made available to the public on the subject of prisons was likely to be in the form of annual prison reports and other official discourse outlets. This, though, was the crux of the matter. There were alternative discourses – prisoner memoirs, reports of reform groups, and periodic interest and agitation in the popular press, in which Morrison himself was then an important figure.

Ultimately, however, the very processes of central government bureaucratisation had greatly weakened any vestigial public interest in local control. As early as 1871, Du Cane had noted that

> whereas before 1863 but few years went by without either Parliamentary Committee or Commissions on the subject, and it was continually discussed in one form or other in the popular press, there is now no demand for investigations of that nature, and in fact it is difficult to interest in it any but those who have some official connection with it, or have taken it up as a special study. (Report of the Directors of Convict Prisons 1871–2: 6)

If he was being a little precipitous at that time, there is no doubt that his subsequent rejoinder to Morrison was well founded:

> The truth is that when the revival of local interest in the prison is talked of, it assumes that all or more localities alike took such an

active and intelligent part in the administration of their prisons as was undoubtedly taken by a few. There were, however, certainly other samples of local supervision in those days. (Du Cane 1895: 283).

As Laslett-Brown (1895: 233) put the matter, 'outside a narrow circle ... the public believe that our prison system has been conducted with all humanity, with undoubted economy, and with a reasonable amount of success.'

There seems little doubt he was correct. The more inquiry into the administration and management of prisons reaffirmed 'the truth' of official discourse and, by so doing, discredited the alternative discourse of prisoners and their supporters, so indeed the public lost interest and were prepared to give credibility to the bland assurances of the authorities, notwithstanding the challenges to official discourse posed by its critics, as here. Now, the further claims of brutalities and privations, exacerbated by the intransigence and austerity that Du Cane brought to his position of Chairman of the Prison Commissioners, gathered enough momentum to generate another major inquiry into English prisons. On this occasion, however, and unlike the major inquiries of the late 1860s and 1870s, there was to be no evidence given from prisoners, indicative of the credibility and authority now enjoyed by the prison establishment on the one hand, and the prisoners on the other. As it was, the subsequent Report of the Gladstone Committee (1895) made a number of significant proposals for prison reform, a good many of which were subsequently put into place: the abolition of punitive labour, for example, relaxation of the rules on silence, some improvement in diet and so on. There was still, then, sufficient force to this critical discourse to be able to generate prison reform, leading to a relaxation of what had now come to be seen as its unnecessarily severe policy:

> The centralization of authority has been a complete success in the direction of uniformity, discipline and economy. On the other hand it carried with it some inevitable disadvantages ... the prisoners have been treated too much as a hopeless or worthless element of the community, and the mood as well as the legal responsibility of the prisons authorities has been held to cease when they pass outside of the prison gates. (*ibid.* 7)

Yet at the same time, the Gladstone Committee and the subsequent Prisons Act 1898 completed the administrative sequestration of prisons, finally drawing shut the bureaucratic veil that had been first set up in

1835. The new legislation vested its faith in bureaucratic management. Rather than diverting control to local, elected authorities, it increased the number of central government officials – inspectors, for example, and official prison visitors who, of course, would first have to gain accreditation from the prison authorities before being allowed to perform such duties. Furthermore, it transferred the power to make prison rules from Parliament to the Home Secretary: which meant, for all intents and purposes, that the power to make them would be vested in the central government penal bureaucracy and accordingly approved by the Home Secretary. As McConville (1995: 753) has succinctly put the matter: 'The debates on the Bill had been fought over the rules yet it was the essence of the measure that rule-making would be removed from Parliament. Once it was conceded that the rules should no longer be embodied in a statute, Parliament lost its control.'

Thus, while bringing about some prison reforms, and bringing about a periodic adjustment to the managerial balance between severity and humanitarianism, neither the Gladstone Committee nor the subsequent 1898 legislation was prepared to challenge the axis of penal power which had been gathering momentum during the second half of the nineteenth century. Instead, this was strengthened. In these respects, the battle for prison truth was over. There would be no more formal inquiries for another half century: what the authorities had to say about prisons had become the accepted and acceptable discourse on this subject. This did not mean the end of scandal; it did not mean the end of suffering and privation, as prisoner biographies continued to detail. What it did mean, however, was that for the most part whatever form such scandal took it would not be of sufficient weight to disturb the equilibrium of the prison establishment (now sufficiently powerful and embedded to be able to simply deny or dismiss such matters) nor make existing prison arrangements unduly problematic for most sections of the public: what official discourse proclaimed had become the accepted truth. In these respects, the contestable prison for much of the nineteenth century became the acceptable prison for much of the twentieth.

Notes

1. Governor Austin had introduced a brutal adaptation of Maconochie's mark system, using the crank as a gauge of labour.
2. A visitors' book had been introduced to English prisons in 1843. Even Hepworth Dixon (1850: 3) had been denied access to some prisons; see also Chesterton (1856) on restriction of public access to prisons.

3. That being Hobhouse and Brockway (1922). This had been commissioned by the Executive of the Labour Research Department in 1919 as the Prison System Inquiry Committee: 'There had been no systematic enquiry since the Prisons Departmental Committee of 1894–5, and an exceptional fund of evidence was available in the prison experiences of a large number of men and women able to observe and to record their observation ... There seemed to be, at the time, no prospect of any Government inquiry ... [our] enquiry has had to face the initial difficulty of the secrecy which surrounds the prison system. It is practically impossible for the public to obtain entrance to prisons or knowledge of what goes on inside them. The Prison Commission itself is one of the most secluded of Government departments' (v–vi).
4. See, for example, 'One who has suffered' (1882).
5. There are very few such biographies dealing with the experience of pre-1860s prisons. The genre then becomes much more extensive, one of the first being that of the Irish political prisoner Rossa (1882). See also Priestley (1985, 1989); Pratt (2002).
6. Du Cane, for example, was questioned about allegations made by 'One who has endured it' (1877). See Report of the Commissioners Appointed to Inquire into the Working of the Penal Servitude Acts (1879: 46).

Bibliography

Burnett, J. (1966) *Plenty and Want*. London: Scolar Press.
Burt, J. (1852/1969) *Results of the Separate System of Confinement*. Montclair: Paterson Smith.
Carlyle, T. (1850) *Latterday Pamphlets*. London: Chapman & Hall.
Carpenter, M. (1864/1969) *Our Convicts*. Montclair: Paterson Smith.
Cartwright, T.J. (1975) *Royal Commissions and Departmental Committees in Britain*. London: Hodder & Stoughton.
Chesterton, G. (1856) *Revelations of Prison Life*. London: Hurst & Blackett.
Clay, W. (1861/1969) *The Prison Chaplain*. Montclair: Paterson Smith.
Crawford, W. (1835/1968) *Report on the Penitentiaries of the United States*. Dublin: Dublin University Press.
Delacy, M. (1986) *Prison Reform in Lancashire 1700–1850*. Stanford, CA: Stanford University Press.
Dickens, C. (1850/1969) *David Copperfield*. London: Thames.
Dickens, C. (1860/1969) *Great Expectations*. London: Thames.
Dixon, W.H. (1850) *The London Prisons*. London: Jackson & Walford.
Du Cane, E. (1895) The Prison Committee Report, *Nineteenth Century*, 38: 278–94.
Field, J. (1848) *Prison Discipline*. London: Longmans.
Foucault, M. (1978) *Discipline and Punish*. London: Allen Lane.
Foucault, M. (1980) Prison talk. In C. Gordon (ed.) *Michel Foucault. Power/Knowledge*. Brighton: Harvester Press.
Griffiths, A. (1875) *Memorials of Millbank*. London: Chapman & Hall.
Hill, F. (1853) *Crime: Its Amount, Causes and Remedies*. London: John Murray.
Hobhouse, S. and Brockway, F. (1923) *The English Prison System*. London: Macmillan.
Kingsmill, J. (1854) *Chapters on Prisons and Prisoners*. London: Longmans.

Laslett-Browne, H. (1895) Common-sense and crime. *Fortnightly Review*, 64: 224–33.

McConville, S. (1995) *English Local Prisons 1860–1900*. London: Routledge.

Markus, T. (1993) *Buildings and Power*. London: Routledge.

Mayhew, H. and Binny, J. (1862/1968) *Criminal Prisons of London*. London: Frank Cass.

Morrison, W. (1894) Are our prisons a failure? *Fortnightly Review*, 61: 459–69.

One who has endured it (1877) *Five Years Penal Servitude by ...* London: Richard Bentley.

One who has suffered (1882) *Revelations of Prison Life by ...* London: Richard Bentley.

Pratt, J. (2002) *Punishment and Civilization*. London: Sage.

Priestley, P. (1985) *Victorian Prison Lives*. London: Routledge.

Priestley, P. (1989) *Jail Journey*. London: Routledge.

Reade, C. (1856) *It's Never Too Late to Mend*. Leipzig: Tauchnitz.

Report of a Committee Appointed to Consider and Report upon Dietaries of Local Prisons (1878) PP XLIII.

Report of the Commission of Inquiry into the Treatment of Treason-Felony Convicts (1871) PP XXXII.

Report of the Commissioners Appointed to Inquire into the Workings of the Penal Servitude Acts (1879) PP XXXVII.

Report of the Commissioners Appointed to Inquire into the Operation of the Acts Relating to Transportation and Penal Servitude (1864) PP XLIX.

Report of the Commissioners on the Treatment of the Treason-Felony Convicts in the English Convict Prisons (1867) PP XXX.

Report of the Committee of Inquiry on Prison Rules and Prison Dress (1889) PP LXI.

Report of the Directors of Convict Prisons (1852) PP LI.

Report of the Directors of Convict Prisons (1853) PP XLII.

Report of the Directors of Convict Prisons (1867) PP XXXIV.

Report of the Directors of Convict Prisons (1870) PP XXXI.

Report of the Directors of Convict Prisons (1872) PP XXXI.

Report of the Gladstone Committee (1895) London: PP LVII.

Report of the Inspectors of Prisons (Home District) (1836) PP XXXV.

Report of the Inspectors of Prisons (Home District) (1839) PP XXI.

Report of the Inspectors of Prisons (Home District) (1844) PP XXIX.

Report of the Inspectors of Prisons (Northern and Eastern District) (1847–48) PP XXXVI.

Report of the Inspectors of Prisons (Southern District) (1858) PP XXIX.

Report of the Inspectors of Prisons (Southern District) (1870) PP XXXVII.

Report of the Prison Commissioners (1879–80) PP XXXIV.

Report of the Prison Commissioners (1883) PP XXXI.

Rossa, J. (1882) *My Years in English Jails*. New York: D.J. Sadleir & Co.

Symons, C. (1849) *Tactics for the Times: As Regards the Conditions and Treatment of the Dangerous Classes*. London: John Olliver.

Webb, B. and Webb, S. (1922) *English Prisons under Local Government*. London: Longmans.

Chapter 5

Truth, independence and effectiveness in prison inquiries

Nigel Hancock and Alison Liebling[1]

We last inspected Wormwood Scrubs in February 2000. This was two years after the presentation of a dossier of allegations against staff which led to over a hundred officers being investigated, 27 suspended and three eventually convicted of violence against prisoners; and a year after the second of two damning Inspectorate reports ... Two interrelated factors seem to us to be fundamental. The first is the absence of closure in relation to allegations of violence against prisoners ... prison officers remained under investigation and suspended officers had returned to work. Yet there had been no independent and published inquiry ... All were free to make their own assumptions and draw their own conclusions about what had happened, why and how. This situation was corrosive. It undermined prisoners' confidence and the morale of good staff, gave other staff a reason, or excuse, not to engage with prisoners, and took up a large amount of management time. It led prisoners to believe that they could only expect to get redress through solicitors, not through the prison management. It also infected staff–management relationships and undermined attempts to negotiate improved régimes. (HMCIP 2001: 3–7)

During the 1970s and early 1980s, critical criminologists argued that the secretive and elitist institutional forms of working of state power required exposing and challenging via independent sociological inquiry. The key term in their argument was *independence*. Left to its own devices, the state produced its own internal version of events, often behind closed doors. These sanitised accounts of major events such as riots, deaths in custody or instances of brutality avoided exposure and thorough investigation of suspect practices, thereby legitimising the status quo. Their processes of discovery, characterised by minimum investigation and disclosure, routinely excluded 'views from below'. Prisoners had no effective means of redress and the 'day-to-day administration of the prison system' was 'shielded from wider public scrutiny' (Ryan 2003: 53). This self-legitimising set of activities existed to paper over the cracks in a flawed economy that served the interests of the powerful, often leaving those on the receiving end of state power and intransigence with a potent sense of injustice. Burton and Carlen argued, for example, that official inquiries were unlikely to produce irrefutable truths, whatever their claims. This form of official knowledge production is designed to close off further debate rather than to discover truth (Burton and Carlen 1979). They suggest that official inquiries produce only obfuscation or a veneer of truth.

The critical perspective developed by prisoners' rights organisations and pressure groups gradually precipitated some significant changes to practice, especially in the fields of deaths in custody. They hosted alternative inquiries and provided alternative explanations for the abuses of power they identified (Sim *et al.* 1987; Ryan 2003: 53). A vibrant penal lobby made their presence felt and influenced policy and practice to a modest degree (Ryan 2003: 45–73).

In this chapter we revisit the question of official prison inquiries in the light of contemporary penal practices and a much changed social and political environment. How accessible is the 'truth' about a prison in our newly organised late modern society? What new forms of information are reliable? We have witnessed a 'quality revolution' in organisational life (Power 1997), as well as a sustained attempt by those managing the prison system to (re)legitimise it in the eyes of prisoners and the public after ongoing crises and failures of governance in the 1970s and 1980s (see Sparks 1994). But what is the relationship between the modern obsession with quality – or performance – and justice? Practitioners complain of official information and inquiry overload. Does this new self-reflecting and much more widely used form of imprisonment satisfy prisoners, their families and critics? We revisit some of the questions raised in a more critical (and secretive) era with contemporary practices and sensibilities in mind. Is the primary aim of a formal prison inquiry the production of a credible account, the legitimation of the institution, or the accomplishment of change – and what can be said about the relationship between these aims? We explore some specific prison inquiries, drawing selectively on an exploratory research project undertaken with these questions in mind.

First we set out briefly some early sociological roots for this important set of questions in accounts of the problem of deaths in custody and the social organisation of its investigation. We suggest, as our more critical colleagues did before us, that the insights provided by sociological inquiry in this field should be applied to all processes of official knowledge gathering, including the sociologically complex, but modernised, practice of prison inquiries.

Prisons and the social organisation of suicide

Organised knowledge about the social world is, as we know, subject to processes of production, practical reasoning, discovery and rediscovery. Sociologists of suicide argued that knowledge about sudden deaths is socially constructed (Atkinson 1982; Douglas 1967). Suicide figures tell us more about organisational processes than about suicide per se. Suicide verdicts are arrived at via a process of interpretative reasoning or 'digging' based on what suicides 'look like' (Liebling 1992: 85–8). Such 'social facts' disguise disagreement, the selective nature of the evidence heard and 'wide discretion in the telling of the tale' (Liebling 1992: 86).

It is not just the suicide statistics that require critical analysis, but the content of the categorisations that follow and the explanations of suicide generated as a result. It is after the event has occurred that 'signs' and 'warnings' are 'discovered' in reconstructions of past events (Atkinson 1982). Retrospectively formulated accounts are shaped by interpretations, some of which are shared and some of which are contested, by interactions and by the overall purpose of the inquiry, as well as by the personal qualities and professional occupation of the person leading it. The uncertainties of meaning are lost in the officially organised account, where decisions are made about 'contributory factors', about the following (rather than the appropriateness) of formal procedures and about blame. These selective procedures have important implications for our knowledge about suicide and its causes (Liebling 1994). Coroners pursue, knowingly or otherwise, conflicting and complex agendas, protecting sensitivities (and institutions), drawing on conscious and unconscious assumptions (for example, that 'it was an accident '). What counts as knowledge (Atkinson 1982: 65)? Who is invited to contribute to the account and who is left out? What assumptions operate at the taken-for-granted level?

Methods of reasoning in the production of official information, the 'ways in which members collaborate to produce sense, facticity and orderliness', should always be a topic of inquiry (Atkinson 1982: x). Yet it rarely is. We should pay far more attention to the sociologically complex *production* as well as the operation of rules, policies, structures and formal accounts, as Dixon (1997) suggested in relation to the police. Thus, in this chapter, we take some recent formal prison inquiries as our main focus. We explore notions of 'truth', 'independence' and 'effectiveness', arguing that truth and effectiveness may sometimes be related to factors beyond independence – for example, to individual qualities in the inquirer and to context. Many internal inquiries have been strongly praised by practitioners of the organisation and critics alike, but because they were conducted by internal 'knowledgeable' individuals, their conclusions have been challenged. We explore the increasing use of internal and external inquiries into prison matters in England and Wales (and selectively elsewhere),[2] asking whether the purpose of contemporary prison inquiries is to establish 'what took place' and to improve matters, or whether there are other purposes (such as legitimation and obfuscation), as suggested above. We explore the extent to which different characteristics of inquiries and inquirers accomplish these various and competing objectives.

We are concerned in this account, then, with two types of effectiveness, which should be distinguished from each other: effectiveness in the *production of knowledge* (in 'truth-seeking'), and effectiveness in *reform*, that is in bringing about change both as a result of the inquiry process, and as a direct result of the formal account or report produced.[3] There are other purposes served by inquiries, including the satisfaction of injured parties, which we shall also explore.

> Inquiries serve a wide variety of purposes. The people who have been the victims want whatever has happened to be acknowledged, to be recognised. They want to find out what happened ... What inquiries are trying to achieve is to satisfy the public that the story has been told; to make recommendations which reduce the chances that this is going to happen again; to enable the institution in which the events took place to be able to move on. (Interviewee)[4]

The lack of a public inquiry into allegations of staff brutality at HMP Wormwood Scrubs led to further management dysfunction and to continuing suspicion and conflict (see also Edwards 2002). The strongly written Preface to the unannounced inspection said:

> [T]he failure to establish, publicly and independently, what took place at Scrubs during the 1990s has severely hampered attempts to change the culture and régime there, or to establish whether there

were underlying systemic problems which may need addressing in this, and other, prisons. (HMCIP 2001: 8)

There is an assumption in this report that public and other large-scale inquiries improve organisations and social practices. But the quality and impact of inquiries differs. As one of our interviewees said:

> Where you have a really big inquiry when something goes badly wrong, such as the Brixton riots of 1981, Lord Scarman's inquiry or the Macpherson inquiry into the murder of Stephen Lawrence ...[5] I think the long term impact of those is they either begin, or consolidate ... quite fundamental changes in practice and policy. They become a watershed ... Because of the degree of interest, and the weight, and the detail that they go into, and the political pressure. There is also a history of inquiries that lie on the shelf because they are seen as too difficult ... then an inquiry is not a very powerful means of addressing a problem. (Interviewee)

Internal and external prison inquiries are conducted more frequently than they were in the 1970s and 1980s. Internal inquiries are conducted to more clearly defined guidelines. There are still influential choices made about what to investigate (and what not to), as well as when to go 'external' and, if so, to whom.

The statutory and other bases of inquiry

Sections 1 and 2 of the Tribunals of Inquiry (Evidence) Act 1921 provide for the establishment of an inquiry into a matter of 'urgent public importance' if both Houses of Parliament so resolve and if the Prime Minister approves. Such an inquiry has the powers of a High Court Judge (witness and evidence compulsion, contempt powers). There have only been 21 in 80 years but four since 1995: Dunblane 1996 (primary school shootings in Scotland), North Wales child abuse 1996, Bloody Sunday 1998 (Northern Ireland) and Shipman 2001 (mass murdering doctor).

Non-statutory ad hoc inquiries, like that into the BSE controversy (mad cattle disease) can cover the same ground as a 1921 Act inquiry but include no formal powers to compel witnesses or produce documents. Ad hoc independent inquiries proceed mostly in private (e.g. the Sierra Leone arms investigation 1998) but publish reports. Private inquiries can be controversial; for example, the original decision to hold the Shipman inquiry in private was overturned by judicial review.

Royal commissions, in more leisurely times seen as a key vehicle for addressing weighty policy issues (often to beyond the following general election), are heavyweight, independent ad hoc advisory committees, reporting to the Monarch through Parliament. They have become rare in the UK since 1979, with none since the Royal Commission on Criminal Justice in 1993. This contrasts with the profusion of royal commissions in Australia described by Gilligan (2002; and see Pratt, this volume). Committees of Privy Counsellors have looked at six 'referred issues' in 30 years, usually with a defence or security connotation (such as the spies Burgess and Maclean).

Where evidence suggests that individual accountability can be addressed through criminal proceedings, these are adversarial in nature and strictly controlled by rules of procedure, the admissibility of evidence and a standard of proof 'beyond reasonable doubt'. Similarly, civil proceedings are adversarial and are controlled by rules of evidence and procedure, with the lower standard of proof on the balance of probabilities. Authority to hold a disciplinary tribunal is usually derived from statute and is generally heard, adversarially, by a panel of members with expertise in the business or profession concerned.

Other forms of inquiry include proceedings for judicial review of administrative decisions relating to, for example, adjudications or security categorisation. Even when such applications on behalf of prisoners are unsuccessful (as they often are), the judgments often provide some critique of current practices (for example *R v. SSHD, ex p Mehmet and O'Connor* (1999) 163 JPN 755).

The Home Secretary does not require statutory powers to set up an independent inquiry into a Home Office (including Prison Service) matter but legislation is required for powers to compel witnesses. Section 5A(4) of the Prison Act 1952 allows the Home Secretary to refer 'specific matters connected with prisons in England and Wales and prisoners in them' to the Chief Inspector of Prisons and direct that (s)he report on them. Section 48(1) of the Race Relations Act 1976 recently empowered a Commission for Racial Equality investigation following issues arising at HMP Feltham.

Internally, during the period 1 April 2002 and 31 March 2003, 1,137 completed investigation reports were received by the Prison Service Investigation Support Team under the terms of Prison Service Order 1300.[6] These constitute small-scale inquiries into a variety of prison matters, including 142 assaults on prisoners by staff, 88 non-natural cause deaths and 64 allegations of a racist nature. There were 105 apparently self-inflicted deaths in custody requiring internal investigation by senior Prison Service staff. The increasing number of internal investigations led to the setting up of the Investigations Unit in 2001.

Prison inquiries in Northern Ireland have focused on The Maze, with Sir James Hennessey (1984), Martin Narey (1998) and Sir David Ramsbotham (1998) each reporting on, respectively, an escape, a murder and wider related issues. The Northern Ireland Prison Service, which accommodates about 1,000 prisoners in three locations, is now subject to periodic inspection by the Prisons Inspectorate. A range of smaller investigations address deaths in custody and other serious incidents. Major prison inquiries are rare in Scotland, which has its own Inspectorate. Deaths in custody in Scotland are subject to Fatal Accident Inquiries, which are akin to the Coroner system in England and Wales.[7]

The best known major prison inquiries in England and Wales in recent years (for rather different reasons) have been the Woolf Report, the Woodcock Report and the Learmont Report (Home Office 1991; 1994; 1995). The landmark Woolf report (which followed the 1990 Strangeways and other disturbances in local prisons) was acclaimed as an unprecedently open and wide-ranging inquiry, providing a long-term agenda for substantial change. Lord Woolf was one of the country's leading public law judges.[8] He looked in detail at the specific causes of the most serious riots, at the broader context of the style of imprisonment being imposed upon prisoners and at staff. The second part of his report addressed the underlying problems of the Service and tried to identify remedies. Woolf found tensions between staff and management, low staff morale, unsuitable buildings and a widely shared sense of injustice:

> A recurring theme in the evidence from prisoners who may have instigated, and who were involved in, the riots was that their actions were a response to the manner in which they were treated by the prison system. Although they did not always use these terms, they felt a lack of justice. (Home Office, 1991: 9.24)

The underlying problems included the lack of respect with which prisoners were treated and the lack of any independent redress for grievances. Critics stressed the independence of the report, led as it was by a high-quality inquirer (with a past chief inspector and two academic assessors to assist) who, despite being a judge, resisted the temptation to stray into sentencing territory. He vigorously pursued the 'remarkably open-ended terms of reference' (Morgan 1992: 232) set for him by the Secretary of State. Woolf's Inquiry solicited evidence from staff, prisoners, individuals and organisations with experience in prison matters. Public seminars were held on a range of wider issues of concern.[9] The methodology employed throughout this long-lasting inquiry was regarded as open, inclusive and fair. Morgan argued that Woolf's approach achieved 'the balance which has to be struck between procedural fairness and establishing broad public legitimacy for the inquiry' (Morgan 1991: 722).[10] King and McDermott noted the remarkable degree of consensus achieved both in the report and in discussions to follow from its publication (King and McDermott 1995: 38–9).[11] It 'became, in all but name, the much needed and long overdue Royal Commission into prisons in England and Wales' (Stern 1993; see also Morgan 1991: 716; 2001: 5). Some have argued, however, that its role in securing lasting change has been limited. It has not set a precedent for the conduct and methodology of later prison inquiries (which have been concerned with rather different issues, such as security and internal accountability).

How could this liberal, thorough and wide-ranging report have failed to satisfy its many audiences? The inquiry was all about justice. The radical reform agenda, and the methods used by Woolf to solicit evidence and form his understanding, represented a major departure from earlier Home Office inquiries. Some of the changes to policy and procedure that followed have been implemented more effectively than others.[12] Some have survived better than others the change of climate witnessed shortly after this period of 'liberal optimism' (Liebling 2000, 2002).[13] We might characterise the effectiveness of the Woolf inquiry as exceptionally high on truth and medium (slow burn) on change. Most commentators are agreed that a considerable portion of the Woolf agenda was knocked off course during the second half of the 1990s. (The question of what has happened more recently and of its continuing or resurgent relevance 'post-austerity' is of course another matter which we might wish to consider separately; see for example Liebling, forthcoming.) This was as a result of an already changing penal climate, a drastic set of events and two contrasting external 'independent' inquiries.

In 1994 and 1995, two sets of escapes from maximum security prisons led to calls for two rather different and swift independent inquiries. In these cases, at the early stages of a less liberal and highly politically charged penal climate, the choice of inquirers was radically different. Sir John Woodcock (a policeman) and General Sir John Learmont (a Quartermaster General) were invited to investigate events leading to the escapes and the more general problem of prison security. The tone, methods, overall approach and quality of the analysis in both reports were severely criticised. King provided a withering critique of the Woodcock Report, suggesting that it was unique among reports as 'less deserving of serious attention but more dire in its largely unnecessary consequences...' (King 1995: 63–5; and see Liebling 2002). Woodcock had 'looked at security through a close-up rather than a wide-angled lens'.

There was no evidence of understanding or any appreciation of the historical background against which the escapes had taken place. The inquiry, King suggested, was politically motivated and '... either an internal review or an Inspectorate review would have produced a better informed analysis and a better considered set of recommendations... the public inquiry into Whitemoor and the choice of a policeman to lead it owed more to political than operational needs' (King 1995: 65; Home Office 1994; 1995).

The contrast between the receptions given to the Woolf Report and to the Woodcock and Learmont Reports could not be greater. Yet the impact of the latter reports was profound and instant. Millions of pounds were spent on security and a wide range of restrictive policies (for example, Incentives and Earned Privileges, removal of phone cards and restrictions on temporary release) were speedily implemented (particularly in the maximum security estate; see Liebling 2002; Bottoms 2003). If we compare the delayed impact of the Woolf Report on practice (see Prison Reform Trust 2001), with the speed and intensity with which the changes that followed from Woodcock and Learmont were implemented (and examined, service-wide; Liebling 2002), we have an interesting paradox to consider. If we continue with our analogy, the Woodcock and Learmont Reports appeared to act as 'raging fires' in terms of delivering change.[14] Was there any relationship between the formal (if not substantive) independence of the inquirers, the quality of the analysis in each report, the soundness of the recommendations made in each, the consensus each report generated and their impact on practice? The answer seems to be no. How can we assess or compare the independence of each of the inquirers (and their teams)?

Morgan suggests that readers should judge inquiry reports on their processes and central logic rather than what is implemented from recommendations, which has other (largely unrelated) explanations (Morgan 1991). He proposes that there is a crucial relationship between the prospects of effectiveness and an organisation's operational environment. Broad factors such as population pressures and political will or context can limit, delay or transform the nature of change, even where the outcome of the inquiry is a widely welcomed, highly regarded set of recommendations (Morgan 1992).

Inquiries that lead to instant and substantial change are not necessarily the best or the most influential in the medium–long term. The Woolf inquiry is widely regarded as having established a number of truths and a positive way forward for the Prison Service, but implementation was interrupted and to some extent reversed in the mid-1990s, because its recommendations fitted uneasily with the 'prisons work' and 'decent but austere' political credos of the time (see Sparks 1995; Liebling 2002). Two prison reports widely criticised on the grounds of their much lower quality, because they did not contribute to truth in the sense of balanced assessments set within the context of available wider knowledge, apparently led to faster and more substantial change. Other inquiries conducted since Woodcock and Learmont (such as the Laming Report into 'targeted performance management') have also had a significant impact on the way prison business gets done (see Home Office 2000).

We have, then, a set of questions to be asked of any inquiry when we are discussing its effectiveness in practice. We might want to compare methods, personnel and speed of delivery. We need to consider the context in which an inquiry begins and concludes, and the questions of independence and the quality of the analysis. Fitness for the task, integrity, mind-set, background and experience may all play a part in the methods and qualities of any inquiry. We should consider the nature, timing and extent of any change (this change can take reformist and damaging forms, which are not always easily identifiable at the time).

Truth, independence and effectiveness: an exploratory study of prison inquiries

Hancock (2002) set out to explore some of these aspects of prison inquiries, using questionnaires, appreciative interviews with inquiry stakeholders (practitioners and other interested parties), observations and an analysis of secondary data. The 'appreciative inquiry' approach was used to explore examples of inquiries perceived as 'good' or 'bad' by six groups of people: 'commissioners' of inquiries such as government ministers and senior managers; 'internal conductors' and 'external conductors' from within and outside the organisation; 'independence seekers' such as interest groups and individuals with a direct interest in the matter under inquiry; a 'legal group' with a process or representative role; and 'others' with a significant interest, such as academics, volunteers and members of other prisons or correctional systems.[15] Those who responded to the questionnaire included prison and policy personnel, academics, lawyers and coroners, a health director, two Samaritan volunteers and a railways executive.[16] Seventeen 'purposefully sampled' individuals from each of the six groups were followed up in interviews, in which questions relating to the key themes of truth, effectiveness and independence were pursued in depth.

Respondents felt that the main reason for conducting inquiries was 'to establish the relevant facts within a credible narrative'. Other commonly cited reasons were the 'prevention or reduction of a recurrence' and 'extracting learning'. Several respondents suggested that inquiries should be set up 'with protocols covering specific occurrences and initial assessments of circumstances informing judgements about whether or not fuller inquiries should follow'. The usual catalyst for action was 'when systems had failed' or 'something had gone badly wrong'. Several people felt that speedy inquiries should be tempered by a pause between initial assessment and fuller inquiry, to allow 'the dust to settle' and well-considered terms of reference to emerge. Some respondents thought there should be inquiries into well-handled incidents because much could be learned and staff could be praised when things went well.

Forty-four respondents identified 34 different inquiries which they felt were 'good'. Two prison inquiries (one external, one internal) were mentioned twelve times, across several of the groups of respondents. Twelve of 26 'good' prison inquiries were conducted by people external to HM Prison Service, two in Northern Ireland by people external to its Prison Service. Thirty-three 'bad' inquiries were identified by 40 respondents, with three inquiries (two external, one internal) identified by three or more people. Eight out of 22 'bad' prison inquiries were external. Two 'bad' Northern Ireland inquiries were identified, the internal one by one person, the external one by three people.

We shall look at the characteristics of 'good' and 'bad' inquiries below. First, let us explore the three terms we have set out to consider in the light of our explorations.

Truth

> The problem with truth is it all depends upon the perceptions of people involved. It is a question of whose account you accept. The chances are it will be a mixture of everybody's. You have to make assumptions as to what you think happened and that isn't necessarily the truth. (Interviewee)

> The best inquirers, like poets and philosophers, recognise that 'truth lies at the bottom of a well' (Heraclitus).

Bottoms reminds us in his thoughtful account of the relationship between theory and research in criminology that there are competing assumptions embedded in different accounts of the social world (Bottoms 2001: 15–16). Observations are always interpretations, and these inter-pretations are made in the light of theories, whether the observer knows this or not (ibid.: 16). The choice of what to observe is theoretically informed: thus we each construct a universe which 'fits' with our expectations about that universe. Research findings (and the reports to flow from inquiries) are largely constructions, as we suggested earlier. But some constructions can make greater claims to validity ('give a truer picture') than others (*ibid.* 17). We can judge, using certain means, 'which of two interpretations is nearer to the truth' (*ibid.* 17).

By 'truth' in this context, we mean the extent to which inquiries appear to establish accurately both the *reality of what happened* in a given set of circumstances and *knowledge-as-understanding about the organisation concerned* more generally. This can be judged, in the absence of Plato's omniscient observer, at least partially, by the extent to which a sufficient range of observers and participants seem to have reached a consensus that the facts have been approached as closely as possible. Inquirers interviewed during the course of Hancock's research emphasised the primacy of fact-finding, of creating meaningful pictures from a range of different perspectives. Blame might be apportioned for specific acts of commission or omission, but all of the inquirers felt that embarking on an inquiry with a view to establishing blame was not an approach most likely to arrive at the truth.

Establishing an account approaching truth was a central aim of any inquiry. Hancock's fieldwork suggested that internal inquiries were sometimes more likely to achieve this (for reasons we discuss below), provided that the inquirer was high quality and had a reasonably free hand. A Home Affairs interviewee argued that organisations are very good at making it difficult to get at the truth: 'How can an outsider know where all the bodies are buried?' Insider knowledge (and contacts) sometimes provided an important opening. Organisational and political factors could, and often did, impede this search for the truth.

Levels of inquiry into all public sector organisations have clearly risen since the 1980s, for a combination of reasons. Some of these are related to truth-seeking (for example, in the interests of greater and more effective managerial control) and some might be related to a more sophisticated form of institutional defensiveness, whereby the 'critique' has been incorporated into the organisation (and thereby tamed). Ryan suggests, like others, that naive trust in government has waned (Ryan 2003; see also Kramer and Tyler 1996; Braithwaite and Levi 1998):

Citizens, it is said, no longer trust governments, or politicians, or ministers, the police, or the courts, or the Prison Service. (O'Neill 2002: 8)

There is evidence of 'a culture of suspicion' (O'Neill 2002: 45) and this suspicion is widespread, rather than confined to the socially and economically excluded. The revolution in accountability seen during the 1990s is intended to rebuild such trust but it is unclear whether such information flow supports or undermines it (O'Neil 2002). O'Neill observes that constant information-seeking may bring out defensiveness in organisations. Likewise media battles with organisations can distort the truth and turn inquiries into a 'battleground' (Scraton *et al.* 1995). One interviewee (a journalist) bemoaned the 'near total collapse of defer-ence ... and lack of belief in officialdom' that Ryan addresses (in a different spirit) in his essays on 'penal policy and political culture'. Such critique of officialdom 'makes harder any consensus on what the truth about any organisation might be' (Interviewee). Ryan would no doubt welcome this 'lack of consensus' (see Ryan 2003), and we would tend to agree. O'Neill suggests that material intended for the public to inform debate might be independently assessed for its reliability and standard of reporting. In the information age, we need standards by which sources of 'truth-telling' can be evaluated.

Following the Woolf Report, and in the light of several internal inquiries we have considered, it is difficult to argue that official prison inquiries never represent the truth. With some important exceptions, we propose that the information and analyses contained in many inquiries – internally conducted and otherwise – usually contribute to knowledge. It is getting harder to predetermine the outcome of official prison inquiries.[17] There may be a significant shortfall in *implementation* of the relevant recommendations, but that part of the story of prison inquiries requires a separate and fuller analysis than we can manage here. It is salutary to consider the lack of impact of the Woolf Report in establishing a model for the conduct of future inquiries, although some of our respondents felt that if another major catastrophe occurred on the same kind of scale, then the Woolf model would be repeated.

Independence

The final thing I would say is that the issue of independence and perceived independence is more important now than ever. I think that is entirely right because people are better informed. They are less deferential and less likely to take what you say for an answer. That imposes its pressure. People are more ready to seek recourse to law in challenge of what we do and we have to respond to that. As a general principle, being open about the things that you get wrong (although in an organisation there can be quite a strong cultural bias against that) is in my view much the best way to go about it because it is more honest. (Interviewee)

Why does so much rest on the concept of independence in inquiries and what does the term mean? The argument runs as follows. The process of inquiry requires 'a fresh mind', intellectual rigour and objectivity. The 'truth' is unlikely to be reached by internal inquirers: their conclusions and recommendations will be (fatally) tainted by undue sympathy and bias towards those under investigation. No one will be found accountable, nor will effective corrective action be taken. As one interviewee said:

> A key issue is people's perception of whether the inquiry is truly independent and, of course, if it is wholly internal and comes to the conclusion that everything is perfect and nothing went wrong, even though that may indeed be the objective truth, people may then say 'Surprise surprise, an organisation investigated itself and decided that everything was fine.' That is a tension that has to be faced up to. (Interviewee)

But what is 'true independence'? The choice of 'independent inquirer' is often made with specific aims in mind. Campaigning organisations can hardly claim to be independent if their approach to 'the truth' has an agenda and a contested ideology driving it. Woolf was arguably more independent (and operated in a more acceptable operating environment) than either Woodcock or Learmont, who seemed to be driven by a Home Secretary's determination to distance himself (and the Prison Service) from the liberal penal agenda that was retrospectively held responsible for the embarrassing security lapses of the early 1990s:

> Learmont was just a general inquiry. He was toeing the political line as well and I think politicians pick people to carry out independent inquiries who they know will come up with the answer they want, and within the budget that they want. (Interviewee)

Independence can mean ineffectiveness, if it also means ignorance or incompetence. As we suggested earlier, the 'truth' may be hard to find:

> They would not know where to look, to be honest. I knew my way around. I knew some of the people involved who were still there and I knew where to dig. An outsider would never have got to the bottom of what I got to. (Interviewee)

According to Hancock's interviewees, any single independent had a 'shelf life and a sell-by date' with the 'cutting edge of independence' lost when an inquirer became a 'professional independent'.

Some events troubled the public more than others:

One of the other pressures which determine the nature of inquiry is the extent to which people are calling for independent inquiry. In truth, nobody has called for one in relation to Lincoln [there was a short-lived disturbance there in late 2002]. That is a legitimate consideration because it is about in part satisfying public expectation. If the papers for the next week had taken the line that there really must be a public inquiry there would be a different dynamic to the decision about what would be the appropriate thing to do. (Interviewee)

In practice, the evidence suggests that independence *by itself* may be less significant in practice in establishing a truthful account than fairness, impartiality and good processes. Sometimes producing soundly-based answers quickly is important and could only be accomplished by an 'insider'. Independence was one, but not the only, component of fairness (we are attracted to the term 'neutrality', as used by Tyler and Blader 2000). An independent stance was not guaranteed by outsider status. The Lord Chief Justice, in the context of a judicial review of the government's refusal to provide an 'independent investigation' into the murder of Zahid Mubarek at HM Young Offenders Institution, Feltham in 2000, said of the Prison Service's internal inquiry that:

anyone reading the Butt report will not fail to be impressed by the independent stance it takes and the comprehensive nature of the investigation ... [18]

Could an internal inquiry be widely regarded as legitimate without similar support from key stakeholders? As the head of a prominent United Kingdom penal pressure group put it:

You can do an internal inquiry with integrity but it is never independent and it is never seen to be as such. How would I ever know if an internal inquiry is better? You can tell me that but unless I see some evidence, unless there is some independent scrutiny that is published and accountable, I don't believe it. This was the problem with the Police Complaints Authority. They keep saying they are independent, that they are outside, but they are coppers, aren't they? (Interviewee)

Most respondents connected the nature of independence with factors relating to the organisation being inquired into and to the inquirers' status and quality (see Table 5.1). Commissioners of inquiries associated independence with distance from and externality to the event, and with a lack of vested interest in the organisation and its operational line. Inquirers should have 'no axes to grind' and 'no career expectations'. Independence seekers cited organisational factors above all others: independence from the organisation ('no corporate loyalty' or 'protective intent'), 'no career or financial stake' and 'credibility'.

Table 5.1. Nature of independence

	Group A	Group B	Group C	Group D	Group E	Group F	NI Group	Totals
Event	3		1		1	2		7
Truth		1		1		1		3
Remedy	1	1				3	1	6
Organisation	4	2	4	7	3	3	2	25
Inquirer – individual status	1	1	2	1	3	10	1	19
Inquirer – individual qualities	1	1	2	1	3	10	1	19
Process			1	2	1	2	3	9
Totals	10	10	14	11	11*	26**	11	93

* One respondent denied the existence of independence.
** Ditto.
See Table 5.2. for group characteristics.

Independence in inquiries consisted of two main characteristics: remoteness from external control or influence, and integrity: that is, a stance of not being influenced by obligations to or the opinions of others. There is much scope in the selection of the 'independent inquirer' for shaping the likely focus of the investigation. The selections of Woolf in 1990, Woodcock in 1994 and Learmont in 1995 constitute the beginning of the process by which inquiries are socially and politically constructed.

Effectiveness

Learmont and Woodcock were, frankly, over the top though doubtless politically necessary. But there was a will there that was very effective in terms of what happened afterwards despite the quality of the inquiry and the inquirer. (Interviewee)

Oh, god, absolutely awful [L and W]. And the results were so negative. Independent inquiries sometimes go wrong but then you ignore them. The Prison Service should have ignored both of those. (Interviewee)

Woolf was a superb analysis of what had gone wrong and pointed the way ahead. Now looking at it years later, you have to ask was some of it really realistic, was it too ambitious? It certainly got to the bottom of what caused the trouble. But then you wonder, whose was the agenda, what was the agenda? There might be an issue to investigate, but where Whitehall is involved you wonder whether there is total independence, in the sense that is someone in government pointing the way? We know how these things are done ... they are never in writing. (Interviewee)

Who is to say what 'effectiveness' is, particularly in the search to establish 'truth'? Scraton argues, in his study of the Hillsborough football stadium disaster, that the 'theatre of the law' has little to do with the discovery of 'truth' or the realisation of 'justice' (Scraton 1999). On the other hand, theatrical forms of inquiry with significant process weakness can sometimes be effective in leading to substantial change. Dennis *et al.* (2000) provide a powerful critique of the methods and conclusions of the influential Macpherson Report. The inquiry, they argue, was characterised by relaxed rules of procedure and evidence, with witnesses harassed by the inquiry team and from the public gallery. Truth and facts became distorted with a lower than balance of probability approach to truth and 'legitimate inference'.

Interviewees in this study felt that there was a significant relationship between a strong inquirer and effectiveness. But increased familiarity with an environment risked a reduction in independence and hence effectiveness. Blame cultures reduced effectiveness. One commissioner put it thus: 'We need a culture in which people can be open about things that go wrong without feeling that the whole world will fall in on them.' For another interviewee, there was a tendency to over-inquire. Inquiries had been rare events in the past, but there were now 'layers of investigations' into the same set of events, which inevitably found breaches of procedures but this sometimes made it harder to establish the facts. Processes of inquiry influenced effectiveness, often disproportionately, through the location of hearings, their logistics and organisation. The best reports were not necessarily written by those with the best manner during interviews.

Process and quality were seen by most of the questionnaire respondents as more important than the question of who conducted the inquiry or with what result (except in Northern Ireland where outcomes were stressed more often – see Table 5.2). External inquirers rated process as important more often than others. Commissioners were particularly interested in the quality of reports.

Table 5.2 Components of good inquiries

	Outcome related	Process related	Quality related	Inquirer related	Other related
A. Commissioners	3	6	8	4	0
B. Internals	3	6	3	3	0
C. Externals	4	16	6	4	0
D. Independence seekers	2	7	2	7	0
E. Legal group	3	6	6	1	0
F. Others	5	8	9	9	5
G. Northern Ireland	11	5	6	2	0
Totals	31	54	40	30	5

What made for bad inquiries? Examples of outcome related reasons included predetermined outcomes, inquiries being insufficiently fact-grounded, little learning and no outcome monitoring. Some inquiries led to too many recommendations insufficiently rooted in realism. Highly politicised contexts made successful outcomes difficult (see Table 5.3).

Table 5.3 Components of bad inquiries

	Outcome related	Process related	Quality related	Inquirer related	Other related
A. Commissioners	2	10	8	2	0
B. Internals	2	8	3	2	0
C. Externals	0	11	5	8	0
D. Independence seekers	2	7	2	8	0
E. Legal group	0	5	2	1	0
F. Others	3	11	12	10	2
G. Northern Ireland	2	4	8	5	0
Totals	11	56	40	36	2

The process weaknesses most frequently mentioned concerned imprecise terms of reference, lack of availability of relevant documentation and timelines. All groups mentioned drawn out or interrupted timescales. Commissioners stressed the importance of timescales and processes more often. Inquirers, particularly those external to the organisation being investigated, complained about imprecise terms of reference, poor record-keeping and staff preparation, and a lack of openness and consultation. For independence seekers, process weaknesses included remits that were too narrow, the exclusion of family and other 'outsiders', lack of witness compulsion and secrecy (symbolised by unpublished reports). The legal group stressed inadequate terms of reference and poor screening of complaints. Sometimes inflexibility in adjusting the terms of reference in the light of emerging evidence was a weakness. Processes were exclusive, families were not heard and inquiries were often 'process' and 'audit' driven.

Bad inquiries were superficial, assertive without justification, confusing, skewed and often voluminous. Commissioners regretted the lack of decisive conclusions and recommendations in poor quality inquiries. Inquirers considered bad reports to be narrow and defensive with little sense of history. They were insufficiently researched and had 'opaque conclusions'. Independence seekers and the legal group made few specific comments about report quality, dismissing (poor) reports in general terms (such as 'a waste of money'). For the 'others' group, poor quality was about 'sketchiness' and 'lack of focus', 'lack of curiosity and evidence-base', a 'defeatist tone', 'blindness to policy requirements and staff failings' and 'insufficient emphasis on care'.

For commissioners, bad reports could result from the inquirer becoming 'too close and subjective'. Internal inquirers pointed to 'terms of reference not being followed', external inquirers to a 'lack of independent support and back-up', 'insufficient detachment or impartial spirit', 'individual agendas' and 'prejudice'. Independence seekers referred to family exclusion (or disdain for families), lack of robustness and a bland acceptance of failure. For others, bad inquiries often had too judicial or political an approach and were often narrow, that is, they were insufficiently researched or inclusive and appeared to show little understanding of the complexities of the wider operational and political environment in which the events being examined had taken place.

Overall, process and quality were key (see Table 5.3). There was a greater tendency to refer to inquirer-related reasons for bad inquiries.

About half of the 'good inquiries' were led internally, compared to about two-thirds of the bad. Inquirers were more likely to be blamed for the bad inquiry than praised for the good. Independence was associated with inquirer status and distance from the organisation. There was much support for the concept of mixed internal and external inquiry teams with the question of who should take the lead depending on the seriousness and context of the issue. Independence mattered particularly when something went wrong and public confidence required as transparent an analysis as possible. Interested parties needed reassurance that appropriate follow-up action would be taken, with some continuing external scrutiny. It also mattered for the organisation, in the sense that those working within it had to come to terms with what had happened and feel that there was a sufficient measure of external understanding of the complexities of roles within an organisation rightly subject to the public gaze: internal legitimacy was important too.

Expectations of inquiries varied and extended well beyond establishing the facts and adding to knowledge. Although 'good' inquiries were about more than outcomes, remedies and learning scored highly in assessments of inquiry purpose. Expectations of effective follow-up action seemed less central to inquiries than might have been supposed. As with Weller's Australian study of royal commissions, inquiries are often 'stronger on investigation than cure' (Weller 1994). Effective inquiries seemed to require that a number of factors came together: clarity of purpose, scope and process, openness, inclusiveness, timescale, quality of product, quality of inquirer, teamwork and the right mix of independents and experts. When this happened the likelihood of effective change was higher, given a good financial and political wind. Effectiveness required an organisational readiness to admit mistakes and a willingness to put them right. The combination of outstanding inquirers, processes and amenable contexts for effective change was rare.

The procedural justice literature suggests that people are influenced disproportionately by their judgments about the fairness or unfairness of decision-making procedures as well as by material outcomes (that is, we distinguish between outcome fairness and outcome favourability; Tyler and Blader 2000). It matters greatly to people how they are treated and how decisions are made. People value highly, for example, the feeling of being listened to without a predetermined agenda. The fairness of a process of investigation, like the process of law enforcement and criminal justice, tends to be judged by both the quality of the decision-making and by the quality of one's treatment by the body concerned. Our judgments about fairness are, at least in part, *relational*. We make assessments about the neutrality and trustworthiness of authorities, and the degree to which we as individuals are treated with dignity:

> Interpersonal treatment is important because it communicates a message to the person about their status in relation to the group. (Tyler and Blader 2000: 90)

Tyler and Blader's four-component model of procedural justice includes the formal and informal qualities of the decision-making and the formal and informal qualities of one's treatment. We can see considerable support for this model in our study. Some of the recent prisons literature illustrates the importance of informal as well as formal procedures in relation to day-to-day life in prison (for example, Sparks *et al*. 1996; Liebling and Price 2001). These considerations of procedural fairness are clearly relevant to prison inquiries. Bereaved relatives of prisoners who died in prison custody spoke with passion about the 'importance of courtesy' and of 'receiving meaningful explanations'. They spoke of the importance of 'inclusive processes'. It did not matter, for example, if public meetings were poorly attended:

> It would be public for us. There should be *systems* that guarantee independence rather than rely on the character of an individual inquirer. (Interviewee)

This link between sound processes (including treating interested parties well) with positive perceptions of effectiveness helps explain why some internally led inquiries were more highly regarded than some external ones. If one's procedural justice needs were met then whether or not the leader of an inquiry came from within or outside the organisation being investigated became a secondary matter. The independence–effectiveness axis needs to be reconciled with what we might call a fairness–effectiveness axis:

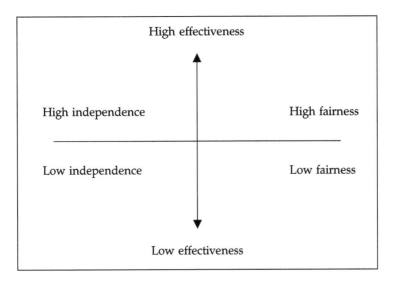

Conclusions: inquiry, legitimacy and the organisation

> A death ... should not be in vain. Something should happen as a result of it. If there are lessons to be learned, little things, then they should be applied and something should be done. (Interviewee)

> It is important that the results of an inquiry are made public. We need to be clear about the terms of reference, what the process is, who is going to be involved, what opportunity will people have to participate ... if you are the parent of the person who died, there may be questions that you want to put. There are difficult issues of representation. If we publish the results ... are those results then followed up? How can you demonstrate that you have accepted the recommendations and delivered them while recognising in some cases that the honest answer may be 'we just don't know'? (Interviewee)

Inquiries served a wide variety of purposes, for different groups of people with competing interests. Victims want the truth, the public want to know that the story has been told and that such trust as they have in organisations and governments is reasonably placed. The motivations of governments and organisations are substantially political and, increasingly, managerial. Inquiries need to meet the legitimacy needs of individual parties and observers. Organisations, like people, need to learn from the experience of what goes wrong and move on. Several interviewees suggested that there was a role for mediation and reparation (for 'restorative justice') in the inquiry process (see Braithwaite 2002).[19]

So what is a legitimate inquiry? A legitimate inquiry is established and conducted within recognised legal and moral norms, and is widely regarded as doing so. Process (including the interpersonal treatment of parties) is crucial, and is not guaranteed by independence. On the other hand, however 'good' inquiries are in terms of being rigorously conducted and establishing truth, they may still have serious 'legitimacy defects' if they are not seen by critics to be properly independent. We should think in terms of 'interior' and 'exterior' legitimacy (Sparks 1994). Inquiries have to convince the organisation and its critics that the job has been well done. Much depends on the timing and context of the inquiry. Hancock's fieldwork suggested a good case for holding independent-led inquiries supported by mixed teams for strong consultative and other processes, for caution about witness compulsion, for targeted recommendations and for a greater stress on effective report-handling and follow-up.

It might be argued that managerialism has changed the context in which modern penal institutions are investigated. In a performance-oriented and audit-saturated organisational climate, managers have new and vested interests in following their own procedures. They often feel vulnerable, as 'failure' is robustly handled internally. Prison Service senior personnel ask tougher and more frequent questions about 'what went wrong' in their own organisation than they did in the 1970s and 1980s, and this might be one of many reasons why calls for public inquiries are relatively infrequent. They also have a much better window on how business gets done, thanks to modern technology and a proliferation of performance and other management data. It is probably more difficult to get away with obfuscation in a late modern Prison Service than it was twenty years ago.[20] There are of course some complex questions to be asked about the quality and purpose of all this official information, and the processes involved in its production. We should pay greater attention to the processes of management attempts at control that underpin the self-reflexive organisation, to the relationship between management control and legitimacy, and to the relationship between official sources of knowledge about these organisations and 'alternative truths'. Truth remains contested, and power operates in new ways in late modern societies (and in their organisations). Questions about the role and nature of the prison inquiry should begin at the beginning, with the insights provided by past sociological inquiries supplying a valuable sensitising framework, but the new sociologically complex practices of knowledge production taking us in new directions.

Notes

1. The authors would like to thank Tony Bottoms and Jenny Hall for valuable assistance in the preparation of this chapter, and Brodie Clark, Rod Morgan, Mick Ryan, George Gilligan and John Pratt for helpful comments on a first draft.
2. We make no distinction here between *inquiry* – the action of seeking a combination of facts and knowledge which approximate to the truth and the process of doing so – *investigation* and *review*.
3. Mathiesen distinguished between 'positive reforms', which can help to consolidate the status quo, and 'negative reforms', which challenge current institutional arrangements (Mathiesen 1974). We tend, in this chapter, to employ the restricted meaning of securing improvements to current arrangements.
4. Wormwood Scrubs (where an internal inquiry is ongoing) provides a clear example of conflict between, in this case, the Prison Service's desire for the establishment to 'move on' while the legal processes are continuing, and others who want above all else to be satisfied about what happened.

5. The Macpherson Report examined the circumstances surrounding the racially motivated murder of black teenager Stephen Lawrence and its handling by the Metropolitan Police and looked closely at allegations of racism.

6. Currently under review. An attempt is being made to reduce its 'process and compliance' emphasis and to allow a more 'narrative', problem-solving and heuristic approach to be taken, with greater emphasis on outcomes.

7. As in England and Wales, work is ongoing in Scotland to strengthen investigation procedures and introduce further independence.

8. According to Morgan he was not the first choice, but was 'fortuitously one of the most creative of our senior judges' (Morgan 2001: 5).

9. The importance of the seminars, and some official reluctance to concede to this method, is beautifully described in Morgan (1991: 722–3).

10. Morgan contrasts the process of the Woolf Inquiry with that of the May Inquiry conducted over a decade earlier (Morgan 1991: 717; see also King and Morgan 1980).

11. The degree of consensus was unusually high. It was not universal (see Morgan 1992; Sim 1994).

12. The use of compacts, which would form the basis of 'legitimate expectations' for prisoners, has not been successful in practice (Morgan 2003: 1127–8). Prisoners are not located close to their homes; average levels of purposeful activity are low (Prison Reform Trust 2001). Remand prisoners (and local prisons) remain the 'poor relations' in the system (Morgan 2001: 9).

13. Reversals have occurred on the nature and extent of home leaves, and the form that IEP took when implemented in 1995 departed from Woolf's 'high basic threshold quality of life' maxim (see Bottoms 2003).

14. The policy response to them was more in the tradition of 'short-term exigency' than long-term strategic vision (Morgan 1991: 715).

15. We are aware that we have not asked prisoners or their families for their views about prison inquiries in this account, although clearly this would be a priority in a more developed study.

16. The questionnaire response rate was high (74%).

17. There have arguably been efforts made in the recent past to make careful (conservative) appointments to the roles of Chief Inspector of Prisons and the Prisons Ombudsman which have famously backfired.

18. Paragraph 73, Judgment 27 March 2002.

19. Braithwaite and colleagues have demonstrated that organisations respond more effectively to 'responsive' (restorative) regulation (involving praise, trust, dialogue and consensus about how to improve) than to 'prescriptive' or punitive forms of regulation (see Braithwaite 2002; Braithwaite and Makkai 1994).

20. The paradox here is that there may be new modes of 'obfuscation', whereby a stronger internal inquiry that meets external criticism more professionally may make external scrutiny of follow-up action less rigorous, keeping this 'truer test' of effectiveness weak.

References

Atkinson, J.M. (1982) *Discovering Suicide: Studies in the Social Organisation of Sudden Death*, 2nd edn. London: Macmillan Press.

Bottoms, A.E. (2001) The relationship between theory and research in criminology. In R.D. King and E. Wincup (eds) *Doing Research on Crime and Justice*. Oxford: Oxford University Press.

Bottoms, A.E. (2003) The criminological foundations of penal policy. In A. Ashworth and L. Zedner (eds) *Essays in Honour of Roger Hood*. Oxford: Oxford University Press.

Braithwaite, J. (2002) *Restorative Justice and Responsive Regulation*. Oxford: Oxford University Press.

Braithwaite, J. and Makkai, T. (1994) Trust and compliance. *Policing and Society*, 4: 1–12.

Braithwaite, V. and Levi, M. (eds) (1998) *Trust and Governance*. New York: Russell Sage Foundation.

Burton, F. and Carlen, P. (1979) *Official Discourse: On Discourse Analysis, Government Publications, Ideology and the State*. London: Routledge & Kegan Paul.

Dennis, N., Erdos, G. and Al-Shani, A. (2000) *Racist Murder and Pressure Group Politics: The Macpherson Report and the Police*. London: Institute for the Study of Civil Society.

Dixon, D. (1997) *Law in Policing: Legal Regulation and Police Practices*. Oxford: Clarendon Press.

Douglas, J. (1967) *The Social Meanings of Suicide*. London: Routledge.

Edwards, A. (2002) *No Truth, No Justice*. Winchester: Waterside Press.

Gilligan, G.P. (2002) Royal commissions of inquiry. *Australian and New Zealand Journal of Criminology*, 35(3): 289–307.

Hancock, N. (2002) What went wrong? Independence, truth and effectiveness in prison inquiries. Unpublished MSt thesis, University of Cambridge.

HMCIP (2001) *Report of an Unannounced Inspection of Wormwood Scrubs*. London: HMSO.

Home Office (1991) *Report of an Inquiry into the Prison Disturbances April 1990*, Cmnd 1456. London: HMSO.

Home Office (1994) *Report of the Enquiry into the Escape of Six Prisoners from the Special Security Unit at Whitemoor Prison*. London: HMSO.

Home Office (1995) *Review of Prison Service Security in England and Wales and the Escape from Parkhurst Prison on Tuesday 3rd January 1995*, by General Sir John Learmont KCB, CBE, Cmnd 3020. London: HMSO.

Home Office (2000) *Modernising the Management of the Prison Service: An Independent Report by the Targeted Performance Initiative Working Group*, chaired by Lord Laming of Tewin CBE. London: HMSO.

House of Commons (1998) *Report of an Inquiry into the Escape of a Prisoner from HMP Maze on 10 December 1997 and the Shooting of a Prisoner on 27 December 1997*. London: HMSO.

King, R. and Morgan, R. (1980) *The Future of the Prison System*. Aldershot: Gower.

King, R. (1995) Woodcock and after. *Prison Service Journal*, 102: 63–7.

King, R. and McDermott, K. (1995) *The State of our Prisons*. Oxford: Clarendon Press.

Kramer, R. and Tyler, T. (1996) *Trust in Organisations: Frontiers of Theory and Research*. London and Thousand Oaks, CA: Sage.

Liebling, A. (1992) *Suicides in Prison*. London: Routledge.

Liebling, A. (1994) Suicides amongst women prisoners. *Howard Journal*, 33(1): 1–9.

Liebling, A. (2000) Prison officers, policing and the use of discretion. *Theoretical Criminology*, 4(3): 333–57.

Liebling, A. (2002) A 'liberal regime within a secure perimeter'? Dispersal prisons and penal practice in the late twentieth century. In A.E. Bottoms and M. Tonry (eds) *Ideology, Crime and Criminal Justice: A Symposium in Honour of Sir Leon Radzinowicz*. Cullompton: Willan Publishing.

Liebling, A. assisted by Arnold, H. (forthcoming) *Prisons and Their Moral Performance: A Study of Values, Quality and Prison Life*. Oxford: Clarendon Press.

Liebling, A. and Price, D. (2001) *The Prison Officer*. Leyhill: Prison Service and Waterside Press.

Macpherson Report (1999) *The Stephen Lawrence Inquiry: Report of an Inquiry by Sir William Macpherson of Cluny*, Cm4262. London: HMSO.

Mathiesen, T. (1974) *The Politics of Abolition*. Oslo: Scandinavian University Books.

Morgan, R. (1991) Woolf: in retrospect and prospect. *Modern Law Review*, 54(3): 713–25.

Morgan, R. (1992) Following Woolf: the prospects for prisons policy. *Journal of Law and Society*, 19(2): 231–50.

Morgan, R. (2001) What did Strangeways really change? In *Strangeways – Ten Years On*. London: Prison Reform Trust, pp. 5–11.

Morgan, R. (2003) Imprisonment. In M. Maguire, R. Morgan and R. Reiner (eds) *The Oxford Handbook of Criminology*, 3rd edn. Oxford: Oxford University Press.

O'Neill, O. (2002) *A Question of Trust: The BBC Reith Lectures*. Cambridge: Cambridge University Press.

Power, M. (1997) *The Audit Society: Rituals of Verification*. Oxford: Clarendon Press.

Prison Reform Trust (2001) *Strangeways – Ten Years On*. London: Prison Reform Trust.

Ryan, M. (2003) *Penal Policy and Political Culture in England and Wales: Four Essays on Policy and Process*. Winchester: Waterside Press.

Scraton, P. (1999) *Hillsborough: The Truth*. London: Mainstream Publishing Projects.

Scraton, P., Jemphrey, A. and Coleman, S. (1995) *No Last Rights: The Denial of Justice and the Promotion of Myth in the Aftermath of the Hillsborough Disaster*. Oxford: Alden Press.

Sim, J. (1994) Reforming the penal landscape. In E. Player and M. Jenkins (eds) *Prisons after Woolf: Reform through Riot*. London: Routledge.

Sim, J., Scraton, P. and Gordon, P. (1987) Introduction: crime, the state and critical analysis. In P. Scraton (ed.) *Law, Order and the Authoritarian State*. Buckingham: Open University Press.

Sparks, R. (1994) Can prisons be legitimate? In R. King and M. Maguire (eds) *Prisons in Context*. Oxford: Oxford University Press.

Sparks, R. (1995) Recent social theory and the study of crime and punishment. In M. Maguire, R. Morgan and R. Reiner (eds) *The Oxford Handbook of Criminology*, 2nd edn. Oxford: Oxford University Press.

Sparks, R., Bottoms, A. and Hay, W. (1996) *Prisons and the Problem of Order*. Oxford: Clarendon Press

Stern, V. (1993) *Bricks of Shame: Britain's Prisons*, 2nd edn. London: Penguin Books.

Tyler, T.R. and Blader, S.L. (2000) *Cooperation in Groups: Procedural Justice, Social Identity, and Behavioural Engagement*. Philadelphia, PA: Taylor & Francis.

Weller, P. (ed.) (1994) *Royal Commissions and the Making of Public Policy*. South Melbourne: Macmillan.

Woolf, Lord (2001) *The Woolf Report: A Decade of Change?* London: Prison Reform Trust.

Chapter 6

Police governance and official inquiry

David Dixon

Introduction

Official discourse about policing presents in many forms and has many purposes, functions and effects. This chapter is inevitably selective, focusing on the changing role of royal commissions and similar major inquiries into policing in Britain and Australia, and the forms of official discourse which characterised the deep changes in police governance which emerged towards the end of the twentieth century.[1]

'A very fine body of men'

Official inquiries such as royal commissions present an easy target for the cynical, to whom they are 'an age-old instrument of delay and obfuscation' (Ryan 1999: 4; cf. Herbert 1961). There certainly have been royal commissions on policing which were manifestly used for these purposes. An excellent example is the Royal Commission, chaired by D.B. Jones, which was appointed in 1906 in response to concern about police corruption involving prostitution and gambling in London (Jones 1908; cf. Dixon 1991: 234–41). Rather than conducting a proactive, general inquiry, the Jones Commission invited the submission of specific complaints. One-fifth of those received were selected for investigation. Given the nature of the issues at stake, it would be generous to describe as self-delusion the Commission's claim that this procedure meant that 'every person who had ... any ground for complaining ... has had a reasonable opportunity of coming before us and being heard' (1908, vol. 1: 86–7). Critical evidence was avoided or treated warily. Bookmakers' reports of corrupt arrangements were treated as being of little value unless corroborated which, by their very nature, was unlikely. The Commission refused 'to obtain direct personal testimony' from prostitutes, discounting such evidence as 'practically worthless' (1908, vol. 1: 431).

By contrast, the Metropolitan Police Commissioner was invited to respond to allegations against his officers, and the London magistrates were asked whether police duties 'are discharged as a rule with discretion, honesty and efficiency' (1908, vol. 3: xx). This leading question elicited the desired response. Information about 32 officers disciplined for improper relations with bookmakers was treated as confidential because its publication 'would be detrimental to the interests of the administration of the Force generally, and therefore the public interest' (1908, vol. 1: 99–100).

The Jones Commission eventually reported what it had been set up to report. Policing was a difficult task in 'the complex conditions of modern life' and occasional shortcomings were inevitable (1908, vol. 1: 56). Such corruption as existed was low-level, unorganised and quickly detected. The Commissioners felt 'no hesitation in coming to the conclusion that the Metropolitan Police, as a whole, discharge their duties ... with honesty, discretion and efficiency' and reported that 'instances of positive misconduct ... are so comparatively rare as to give no cause for disquietude'. The Force was well-disciplined, performed its duties admirably and 'was entitled to the confidence of all classes of the community' (1908, vol. 1: 101, 144). *The Times* eagerly agreed, taking the opportunity to lambaste the 'gullibility or malice' of the police's critics (24 December 1908, p.7) and insisting that the police were 'a very fine body of men' (1 July 1908). This commentary was naïvely relied upon by the doyen of English police history, T.A. Critchley (1967; cf. Dixon 1991: 263). In this way, the use of a Royal Commission to blunt criticism contributed to the making of English police mythology. As will be shown below, in the shorter term, it allowed police corruption to become entrenched in London to an extent that was to be officially regarded as a matter of major concern in the 1920s.

The Jones Commission operated just as a cynic might suggest. Established as a gesture acknowledging public disquiet about policing in London, it drew the heat from the issue, rigorously defined out any criticism that could be politically damaging, provided an anodyne account in terms of 'bad apples', sat long enough for public interest and concern to wane and, finally, produced an inconsequential final report.

However, matters are rarely quite so straightforward. As a novitiate in the study of power would be aware, the powerful often believe their own rhetoric and their activities are shaped by structures of such belief. The Royal Commission on Police Powers and Procedures of 1928–29 and the Royal Commission on the Police of 1960–62 provide excellent examples of the need to set commissions in their socio-political context. The former, chaired by Lord Lee, was established at the end of a decade punctuated by scandals, complaints and rumours about police misconduct (Dixon 1991: 242–8). There was concern about lack of public confidence, police morale, press and Parliamentary criticism, the police's ability to maintain public order, and the quality of both recruits and senior officers.

While members of the Lee Commission were keen to reject claims that they set out to whitewash, their preconceptions impelled them to do so. The Chairman opened proceedings by asserting that 'our main effort must be to find means of restoring that mutual confidence ... which has been so striking and happy a feature of our national organisation'. The Commission had already reached the conclusion that it would eventually report: 'There is an instinctive and deep-rooted sympathy between the public and the police which has never really been broken, in spite of minor misunderstandings and cases of friction which occasionally ruffle the relations between them' (1929: para. 300). From this starting point of sentimentality and wishful thinking, problems were inevitably individualised and trivialised. The Commission considered it 'inevitable that ... there should be some "black sheep"'. Therefore, 'isolated instances of misconduct' did occur, but 'its extent has been greatly exaggerated' (1929: paras 262, 279).

However, the Lee Commission's own analysis exposed the poverty of this approach: it showed that corruption was an inevitable consequence of unenforceable prohibitions (notably in regard to gambling), and so treating it as individual deviance was inconsistent. The police realised this: by the time of this Royal Commission, they had begun a long campaign for reform of the criminal law in the interests of 'better police–public relations'. They convinced the Lee Commission that replacing unpopular laws (dealing with, *inter alia*, motoring, sexual offences and particularly gambling) was vital for police–public relations and, consequently, for police effectiveness. Here, the Commission's account was in terms of structural factors, not isolated 'black sheep': it was the law, not the venality of individuals, that lay at the heart of the problem (Dixon 1991: 256–61).

The Lee Commission may have identified the bases of police misconduct and corruption, but its inconsistent finding that no serious consequences were produced dissipated the urgency for action, allowing the government to shelve the relevant recommendations. More generally, the Commission was constrained by circumstances: its comments about the natural condition of police–public relations were a political necessity. To have followed the logic of their findings about the impact of unjust laws to its conclusion would have been politically dangerous. The Commissioners believed in what they needed to believe in.

The primary significance of the Lee Commission was to give authority to an account of the supposedly distinctive character of the British police officer as a 'citizen in uniform' which was to define official conceptions for the next half century. This construction was based on a historically inaccurate account of police practices. It failed to appreciate how the creation of public order offences in effect extended police powers (Dixon 1997: 54–8) and the manner in which the police had changed in the preceding fifty years from locally based patrols to coordinated units with growing pretensions to crime-fighting professionalism.

The outcome of the Lee Commission exemplified the ability of governments to sidestep uncomfortable recommendations. The Royal Commission analysed the murky history of how police had assumed power to question detained suspects. It strongly criticised police use of holding charges and recommended 'a rigid instruction to the Police that no questioning of a person in custody, about any crime or offence with which he is or may be charged, should be permitted' (1929: para. 169). However, rather than being legislated in statutory form, this instruction appeared as a Home Office circular issued with the approval of the judges. This addendum to the ambiguous and unclear Judges' Rules was supposed to guide police practice for the next three decades. In reality, the courts did not enforce the rules and routinely admitted confessions elicited by questioning during custody (Dixon 1997: 133–4). Custodial interrogation became standard practice.

The 1960–62 Royal Commission on the Police, chaired by Sir Henry Willink, provides an example of how deeply entrenched values and social constructions can lead an inquiry into misunderstanding. The royal commissioners again embraced an idealised account of police–public relations, this time as a distinctive part of the social democratic postwar 'consensus'. The Willink Commission endorsed its predecessor's account of police as 'citizens in uniform' (1962: 11). Largely written by T.A. Critchley, its secretary, the Commission's report expressed a caution which stemmed from a conservative belief in the benefit of evolutionary progress and a focus on the strengths rather than the weaknesses of institutions. This was expressed in an idiom which contrasts sharply with the auditor's staccato of more recent official reports:

... efficiency is not the sole end of a good and wise administration of the police, and ... the apparently confused police system which this country has inherited reflects not merely the British habit of adapting old institutions to meet new needs, but the interplay of conflicting principles of great constitutional importance which human minds have always found, and still find, the utmost difficulty in reconciling. (1962: 20)

The Commissioners' deliberations were permeated by an understanding of English policing which their report would do much to entrench. Their concern was the protection of the police's reputation 'in an age when certain elements of society are not as amenable to discipline as in the past'.[2]

The Willink Commission refused to examine 'the methods employed by the police in obtaining statements from suspected persons' (1962: 2) despite widespread contemporary concern and its own acknowledgment that there was 'a body of evidence, too substantial to disregard, which in effect accused the police of stooping to the use of undesirable means of obtaining statements and of occasionally giving perjured evidence in court' (1962: 11). However, serious analysis of investigative practice could find no place in the celebration of an institution. Buried in the soggy depths of the report's chapter on police–public relations, investigative malpractice was considered purely as a matter of isolated individual deviance (1962: 110–12). Despite the manifest failure of judicial super-vision, the matter was referred to the judiciary for consideration, so removing it from public debate. The outcome was a revision of the Judges' Rules which served to maintain criminal procedure in a state of gross anachronism for a further twenty years. Many police routinely either ignored or were unaware of the rules (Dixon 1997:4).

To say that these royal commissions operated within a legitimising discourse would be as insightful as the breathless discovery that the police are agents of social control. To both, the only worthwhile response is 'of course'. The challenge is to understand how specific locations and contexts influenced the course and outcomes of such inquiries.

Managerial governance and the decline of royal commissions

The distinctive feature of the twentieth-century English royal commission was that its membership comprised a selection of people from relevant professions (in the case of policing, this meant police, judges, magistracy, the legal professions) and laypeople. The professionals were intended to contribute their expertise, but not to act as sectional representatives. The vision was of a group of intelligent people who could investigate, evaluate, agree and recommend. From this perspective, the royal commission was a classic tool of social democratic politics.

In retrospect, the Royal Commission on Criminal Procedure 1978–81 (chaired by Sir Cyril Philips) marked the high point of royal commissions as a mode of police governance. It established an extensive research programme and, unlike its successor (see below), extensively used the resulting reports to inform its deliberations. Not all its recommendations were unanimous, but the Philips Report laid down a framework of basic principles and detailed recommendations which eventually produced legislative change, in the shape of the Police and Criminal Evidence Act 1984 (PACE) and the Prosecution of Offenders Act 1985.

Despite its role in this major legislation, the Philips Commission was an anachronism by the time it reported. Consensus, reliance on the great and the good, 'the quiet firm murmur of the Establishment' (Herbert 1961: 295), academic research, amateurism,[3] part-time, lengthy decision-making processes,[4] and unpredictable and potentially unpalatable recommendations were anathema to the neo-conservative government of Margaret Thatcher which had come to power in 1979. She did not need the independent collection and analysis of information, rebuking senior colleagues: 'Don't tell me what; tell me how. I know what' (Kavanagh 1987: 250). No royal commission (on any subject) would be established in the UK for a decade.

Change in governance was encouraged by Lord Rothschild (chair of a Royal Commission on Gambling which reported in 1978 and for whom Thatcher expressed 'the highest regard' – 1993: 647) who suggested that an expert departmental research unit could inquire and the Cabinet decide more efficiently than a royal commission consisting of 'a philosopher, a sports commentator, a specialist on office organization, an ex-scientist, an Olympic Medallist, a trade unionist, a journalist and two practising barristers' (1984: 88). While a royal commission might have been an appropriate tool for the minimal government administration of Victorian England (Herbert 1961: 265), external reference was less necessary when ministries had their own policy analysts, research sections and capacity to mount inquiries (Downes and Morgan 2002: 305, 306). While Rothschild's commission was under way, the Home Office research unit carried out and published a separate inquiry and a House of Commons Select Committee[5] examined a specific area within his remit. Not surprisingly, he wondered: 'Is there not something incomprehensible about such prodigality, such overkill?' (Rothschild 1984: 86).

The lack of royal commissions in the final decades of the twentieth century did not indicate a withdrawal of government from policing, but the opposite. Exempted for so long from changes sweeping through the public services, the police finally lost Conservative favour in the early 1990s. A 'profound transformation in the formal organization of police governance' began in 1993 without reference to a royal commission or other 'major public deliberations. The reforms emanated from internal Home Office inquiries with minimal outside consultation' (Reiner 2000: 197; cf. Downes and Morgan 2002: 307). The task of fundamental reconsideration that would previously have been done by a royal commission was instead divided between an Inquiry into Police Responsibilities and Rewards (Sheehy 1993), a Home Office Review of Police Core and Ancillary Tasks (Posen 1995) and a Home Office White Paper on Police Reform (Home Office 1993). In the managerialist agenda of the early 1990s, the 'entire package was premised on an official definition of the police task as "catching criminals" ... which reversed the notion of the priority of preserving public tranquility as advocated by British police tradition from Peel to Scarman. The reforms were clearly directed at imposing the disciplines of the marketplace on policing' (Reiner 2000: 209). As the familiar thumbscrews of the new public management were applied, forms of more intensive police governance were developed.

The language of performance indicators, monitoring, audit, value, efficiency and effectiveness found expression in a plethora of reports from the Audit Commission, Her Majesty's Inspectorate of Constabulary (HMIC) and the Home Office. The Audit Commission (which conducts national value-for-money police studies and is responsible for the financial audit of police authorities and auditing best-value performance plans) was 'a central component' of the government's managerialist programme and 'was used by central government to introduce a performance culture into the police service' (Savage *et al.* 2000: 37–8). Notable examples were the Audit Commission's studies of patrol and criminal investigation (1993, 1996). In turn, HMIC published 33 thematic reports between 1995 and March 2003. These were 'well publicized and powerful statements of HMIC "philosophy" in a range of areas' (Savage *et al.* 2000: 34). HMIC now publishes thematic, annual, Joint Area, Best Value Review, force inspection, and Basic Command Unit reports. In the first ten weeks of 2003 alone, 28 new reports appeared on the HMIC website. Meanwhile, streams of papers flooded from the Home Office Research, Development and Statistics Directorate. Between 1990 and March 2003, 161 Police Research Papers were published, as well as many other research studies, occasional papers, statistical bulletins and ad hoc publications on police-related topics.

A related outlet for the discourse of managerialism was the mission statement, statement of values or code of ethics (Dixon 1999a). Perhaps best known were the Metropolitan Police's Plus Programme and ACPO's Statement of Common Purpose. The language of the new managerialism spread pervasively through official documents. As Chan observes, the 'annual reports of police organizations, once devoted to routine tabulations of crime statistics and accounts of bravery and achievements among police ranks, now dazzle the readers with colourful charts of performance indicators under various management objectives, broken down by geographical or budget units' (1999: 255; cf. Davids and Hancock 1998: 47). Symptomatically, the NSW Crime Commission (a policing agency focusing on organised crime) introduced an annual 'overview' with the businesslike assurance that 'the Commission continued to increase productivity, reduce costs and expand its area of activity'. Its ability to declare a 'surplus' from the proceeds of seizures from its targets is used as a key performance indicator (Crime Commission 1997: 7).

In the 1980s and 1990s, British central government became increasingly interventionist and directive: 'The vehicle for this increased assertiveness ... was to be the Home Office circular which ... was transformed from a gentle "chief officer may consider this" type of advice to a role increasingly of a directive' (Savage et al. 2000: 32). The issuing of circular 1983/117, with its erection of the three totems of efficiency, effectiveness and economy, marked a turning point. Traditional legal and political forms of accountability were increasingly sidelined in favour of accounting via audit and evaluation. The strategy was to 'push control further into organizational structures, inscribing it with systems which can then be audited' (Power 1997: 255; cf. Chan 1999: 255). External review continues, but it is specifically tasked and directed in contrast to the broader forms of legal and political accountability which it displaces.

The most notable expression of this in the 1990s was the recasting of English police governance by the Police and Magistrates' Court Act 1994 which simultaneously strengthened the hand of central government and reconstituted the police authorities (including the creation, for the first time, of a police authority for London). The antagonism of the Thatcher administrations to local democracy was replaced by a strategy in which the local police authorities were to play key roles, not as mechanisms of democratic accountability but by setting objectives, assessing risks, monitoring and evaluating performance, carrying out audits, and drafting reports and annual policing plans reflecting the Home Office's national policing objectives (Jones and Newburn 1997). Similarly, the Crime and Disorder Act 1998 makes local authorities work in partnerships with the police and other governmental agencies to produce crime and disorder strategies based on consultation and audits (Hughes et al. 2002: part 2). Once again, the outcome must be published in a report.

A second form of governance to be reshaped was the judicial, which for much of the twentieth century had been the key mode of police accountability. This is not to say that judicial governance had been either close or effective. On the contrary, an elaborate rhetoric was developed around the concepts of constabulary independence and rule of law which served to allow substantial autonomy to the police. While phrasing their judgments in liberal terms, the courts facilitated the extension of police powers either de facto (by not exercising discretion to exclude evidence or being hostile to defence criticism) or de jure (by extending common law powers: see Dixon 1997). While not conventionally thought of as 'public inquiry', the accumulated case law on policing provides a significant source of regulation – or rather, what was generally involved, non-regulation. Issues were decontextualised and depoliticised by being treated as just individual cases, while crime control was given priority.

In the final quarter of the century, a combination of factors challenged judicial primacy and discredited laissez-faire. First, the general changes in governance discussed above undermined the concept of constabulary independence (Savage et al. 2000: 48–9; Patten 1999: 6.20). As Alderson shows, the new approach to police governance was 'authorise and regulate', with the result that extended (often merely formalised) police powers were accompanied by regulatory requirements. In Britain, the judicial and political rearguard action against acknowledging the wrongful convictions of the Birmingham Six and the Guildford Four was finally abandoned, giving a telling jolt to judicial complacency. The statutory regulation of police powers by PACE provided a refocused role for the courts in police governance. Scepticism about the courts' application of the new law has proved to be overstated (Dixon 1997: 169–77).

Finally, new institutions developed. Policing slipped out of the monopoly of the police at both high and low levels. Police forces are now 'just one agency among many' with crime-fighting capacity and responsibility (Leishman et al. 2000: 3; cf. Johnston and Shearing 2003). A key factor here has been the inability of locally-based police services to deal with organised crime, particularly drug distribution. Consequently, a series of special agencies – in the UK, the National Crime Squad, Assets Recovery Agency, National Criminal Intelligence Service, and in Australia, the NSW Crime Commission, Australian Crime Commission – emerged, and are now complemented by a range of anti-terrorist agencies following 11 September. At local level, the inability of public police to meet the demand for security has led to the proliferation of local (usually private) policing services. In policing, as elsewhere, the closing decades of the twentieth century were characterised by processes 'redefining the relationships between components of the state' (Alderson 2001: 384) and between state and civil society.

The New Labour government, elected in 1997, began another round of radical police reform in England and Wales. Its white paper, *Policing a New Century* (Home Office 2001), preceded the more general *Justice for All* (Home Office *et al.* 2002) and laid the foundation for the Police Reform Act 2002. The government acknowledged the expectation that consideration of radical change in policing required a royal commission, but 'took the view that there were important changes which should be progressed faster than a Royal Commission would allow' (Home Office 2001: 142). *Policing a New Century*, demonstrating New Labour's taste for 'evidence-based policy ... the "what works" principle in action' (Leishman *et al.* 2000: 4), is peppered with references to Home Office and HMIC reports, performance indicators, statistics and goals (but only 4 of 50 notes refer to academic research). Indeed, by early 2003 (the earliest a royal commission could have reported), substantial change was underway. This included:

- annual publication of a National Policing Plan setting priorities for the following three years;

- a legislative basis for what is (rather lamely) called 'an extended police family', allowing 'community support officers' and accredited Community Safety Organisations to relieve the regular police of some of the load of patrol and low-level order maintenance;

- establishment of the Central Police Training and Development Authority, the Persistent Offender Taskforce, the Policing Standards Unit, the National Centre for Policing Excellence (focusing on investigative techniques) and the Police Bureaucracy Taskforce; and

- implementation of a National Intelligence Model (designed to produce strategic and tactical assessments, and target and problem profiles), and a Policing Performance Assessment Framework allowing appropriate comparisons between similar forces.

The potential cost of this urgency was shown by a supposedly 'fundamental review' of the PACE. A regressive, sometimes incomprehensible, overview of 'general findings' followed by issues, options proposed, preferred action and timescale was produced in less than five months (Home Office/Cabinet Office 2002, for a critique, see Zander 2003: xv–xvii, 242–3).

New Labour's initiative marked the supremacy of the internet as the primary mode of expounding (and receiving comment upon) policing policy. A police reform page on the Home Office's site provides a 'knowledge bank' of electronically available material – reports, press releases, speeches, articles and links to official publications and parliamentary debates. Commitments to public consultation are (notionally) met by invitations to comment.[6]

Police reform is presented as part of New Labour's wider agenda of reforming public services. While managerialism remains dominant, there is a subtle drift in rhetoric away from efficiency and effectiveness towards 'raising standards' as the key objective, which is to be achieved by identifying and promulgating best practice. 'Modernisation' is summoned to sweep away 'outdated and outmoded attitudes, regulations and procedures' (Home Office 2001: i). The post-2000 reform package greatly extends central government's ability to shape and direct policing, notably by providing power to require standardisation of good practice. Its ideological context is a perceived need to improve and widen the delivery of policing services as a social justice priority. There is a shift from the individualistic moralism of Thatcherism and the civil libertarianism of Labour's years in opposition towards a social authoritarianism which retrieves an older Labour tradition of respectability and community. As in that tradition, there is a tendency to slip into an exclusionary criminology, in which 'criminals' are defined out of 'community': 'Those engaged in crime form a loosely connected society, linked by inclination, by illicit funding flows, and by the interdependence of criminal life-styles' (Home Office 2001: 40). The White Paper refers here not to 'some crime' or 'semi-organised crime', but just 'crime', i.e. the activities of 'them', not 'us'. 'They' are confidently delineated: 'There are around one million active offenders in the general population at any one time', of which 10 per cent are 'persistent offenders' upon whom policing efforts should focus. They are almost all male, two-thirds are hard drug users, half are under 21 (Home Office 2001: 52). Crime is seen not as an amorphous product of socio-economic forces, but as the activities of a group to be targeted, surveilled and controlled.

Runciman, Patten and beyond

In this new world of managerial governance, it would be anachronistic to use royal commissions and independent inquiries for the routine work of government. More focused, quicker (if less thorough) modes of governance are available in the managerial state. Nonetheless, such inquiries continue to have their uses: in time-honoured fashion, their establishment allows delay while public concern about a matter subsides and distances the government when a particularly controversial matter needs to be managed. The recurrence of scandals in policing makes the availability of this kind of institutional 'lightening conductor' (Herbert 1961: 292) all the more useful.

The suspension of Royal Commissions in England was ended by the appointment in 1991 of the Royal Commission on Criminal Justice (chaired by Lord Runciman) on the day that the convictions of the Birmingham Six were quashed. The context was

> a sense of collective shame about and responsibility for the failings of a system in which we were involved – as practitioners, as academic commentators, as politicians, as citizens. The setting up of the Royal Commission seemed to represent the only appropriately general response to the underlying problems which had led to the miscarriages of justice. (Lacey 1994: 31)

Establishing this Commission bought the government time and political distance, allowing them to insist that, while immediate action was inappropriate, their sincere commitment to putting things right was evident. There was nothing new here (Herbert 1961). However, what was novel was the extent to which the government and the Home Office used the opportunity, through setting the Commission's terms of reference and then making lengthy, authoritative submissions, to shift the nature of the inquiry decisively away from what was widely expected in 1991. From the perspective of the Home Office, there were no green fields in criminal justice policy: the imperative was to make the existing system work better, particularly to work better by increasing conviction rates. The Runciman Commission emerged from the public outrage about miscarriages of justice into something much more attractive to the government – an inquiry built around managerialist concerns for efficiency, effectiveness and economy. What had begun as a belated acknowledgment that criminal justice was prone to making gross errors which punished the innocent while letting the guilty go free ended in a series of recommendations for systemic efficiency in crime control.

A key factor in explaining why the Runciman Commission operated as it did was the change in the Home Office which has been discussed above. It now had a clear corporate, managerialist agenda which structured the Commission's agenda and which was forcefully presented to the Commission in its submissions. The Runciman Commission was instructed 'to examine the effectiveness of the criminal justice system in England and Wales in securing the conviction of those guilty of criminal offences and the acquittal of those who are innocent, having regard to the efficient use of resources' (Runciman 1993: i). Government had to respond to the public concern about the miscarriages cases in the context of a concurrent public antagonism (which it had done so much to encourage) towards 'going soft' on actual or suspected offenders:

Its solution, expressed clearly in the Royal Commission's terms of reference, was to reconstruct those cases as instances of a more general problem of the *efficient management* of the criminal process, and in particular of the process's failure in securing the conviction of the guilty. At a stroke a spectacular instance of individual injustice and the abuse of power was converted into an instance of systemic inefficiency and wastage of resources. (Lacey 1994: 40, original emphasis)

Efficient crime control does have a respectable link to concern about miscarriages of justice: people who commit offences may escape justice if innocent people are convicted in their place. Increasing police powers and resources will not produce effective crime control if the failure to provide suspects with substantial rights leads to wrongful conviction. As has been the case in the aftermath of the acknowledgment of most miscarriages of justice, the really guilty escape justice because the investigation has been misdirected for so long. The Runciman Commission's failure to appreciate fully the interdependence of due process and crime control led to a report which avoided hard questions about the fundamentals of a process which had repeatedly jailed the wrong people and had doggedly resisted acknowledgment of error. 'Efficiency' means not only convicting the guilty, but also *not* convicting the innocent. The Report avoided analysis of most police practices and procedures, and indeed had remarkably little to say about policing.

Commissions of inquiry are presented, and present themselves, as independent: it is this that gives them their kudos and authority. However, the Runciman Commission was 'part of the enterprise, not an external force delivered to put it back on the rails' (Wells 1995: 128). Recurrent techniques used by the Commission limited its responsibility and originality. First, 'there is a clear tendency to adopt the recommendations and ongoing initiatives of institutional authorities, notably the Home Office, the HM Inspectorate of Constabulary or the Association of Chief Police Officers rather than basing conclusions on the Commission's own arguments or research' (Reiner 1993: 811). Secondly, the Runciman Commission delegated responsibility on crucial matters back to the state bureaucracy: there is a 'repeated call for further inquiries, monitoring, working groups and the like rather than specific and definite measures' (*ibid.*). In effect, the Commission was deferring to the institutions of the new managerial governance.

The outcome was that the Runciman Commission unintentionally 'helped to effect a dramatic reversal in the political climate over criminal justice, from a situation of crisis engendered by miscarriages of justice to one of triumphal "law-and-orderism"' (McConville and Bridges 1994: xv). Its extent is illustrated by the fact that only three years after the Birmingham Six were released, Parliament eviscerated the suspect's right to silence during police questioning (Dixon 1997: ch. 6).

It would be wrong to make the functionalist assumption that official inquiries are doomed by the managerialist curse to be like Runciman's. A very considerable contrast is provided by the Report of the Independent Commission on Policing for Northern Ireland chaired by Chris Patten which not only set a radical plan for Northern Ireland, but implicitly provided a strong critique of contemporary developments in England and elsewhere (Patten 1999; see Walker 2000: ch. 6). While this was not a royal commission, the more important difference from Runciman concerned individual members' ability to provide original input rather than just to consider the evidence presented. The Patten Commission showed 'how it is possible to draw together key challenges and core issues of policing – including governance, integrity, culture, diversity and so on – within a comprehensive framework of analysis and policy formation' (Leishman *et al.* 2000: 6). The key figure here was Clifford Shearing, whose ability to rethink policing (e.g. Johnston and Shearing 2003) permeates a report which provides a radical reconceptualisation of policing with concrete achievable recommendations for democratic governance and accountability within a human rights framework (Walker 2000: 185–6).

Although never so radical as Patten, the long series of official inquiries into policing in Australia[7] since 1970 similarly do not fit Herbert's model of the obfuscating committee. While varying in tone, these inquiries were generally critical of police and called for substantial reform of criminal procedure. Most influential was the Australian Law Reform Commission's report on Criminal Investigation (ALRC 1975) which was on 'socially liberal/progressive/modernizing lines, with a significant civil libertarian emphasis' (Alderson 2001: 112). These reports drew antagonistic opposition from the police, notably in Victoria where police pressure forced the government away from the Beach Inquiry's recommendations (Beach 1978; Haldane 1986: 290–2). The Royal Commission into Aboriginal Deaths in Custody adopted an even more critical stance, one which brought it into direct conflict with police, as when it defined a notorious police shooting as within its terms of reference (Wootten 1991).

It is important to take account of the cumulative effect of public inquiries, especially in federal jurisdictions (Alderson 2002: 89). In isolation, an individual report might be (and often was) shelved. In the late 1970s, the reform of criminal investigation was lamented as 'a graveyard of reports' (Kirby 1979: 628). But their indirect effects should not be underestimated. Cumulatively, they amounted to a sustained, mutually reinforcing argument for change (Alderson 2002: 396). Chaired by judges, they influenced the Australian High Court which used decisions to put pressure on the states to reform police powers and practices. Most Australian jurisdictions have now done so to some extent (Dixon 1997: ch. 5).

Similarly, an inquiry may achieve totemic status, so that its influence goes beyond its specific recommendations. Indeed, its title may come to symbolise a broader programme or philosophy. The Scarman and Macpherson Reports may be seen in this way, as can anticorruption commissions – in the US, Knapp (1972) and Mollen (1994); in Australia, Fitzgerald (1989) and Wood (1997). Other official documents can have similar status: examples include Peel's original instructions to the Metropolitan Police (Critchley 1967: 52–3) and Home Office Circular 117/1983, and judicial decisions such as *Miranda* in the US, *Heron* in England, and *Williams* in Australia.[8]

Frequently, the forum for responding to crises and scandals is not a traditional royal commission but rather a judicial inquiry. A judge is appointed in response to a specific incident and is given the task of investigating it in detail (particularly by means of oral hearings conducted in a legally inquisitorial manner) and making recommendations both specific to the incident and general to the area of concern. In fact in Australia, this (rather than inquiry and consideration by committee) is the traditional form of the royal commission.

In England and Wales, two of the most significant investigations of policing have been judicial inquiries rather than royal commissions. In 1981, the Scarman Report on the Brixton disorders gave a decisive imprimatur to the development of 'community policing'. It had a pervasive influence: 'by the late 1980s his ideas had become the predominant conception of policing philosophy among chief constables' (Reiner 2000: 205–6). Scarman's crucial emphasis was that the maintenance of public order (broadly defined) is more important than the enforcement of law. Scarman stressed that the discretionary balance between law enforcement and order maintenance will only be properly achieved when another balance, that between independence and accountability, is achieved. This balance in turn depends upon the police securing the consent of the communities in which they work (1981: 4.59–60). There was nothing particularly original about this, but Scarman's report had impact because it connected vital themes in an authoritative, clearly expressed account in the context of an urgent need to respond to events which were not isolated deviance, but signs of significant fissures in social structure.

More recently, the Macpherson Report into the Stephen Lawrence case has had profound effects on policing, as well as on other aspects of criminal justice (Macpherson 1999; Marlow and Loveday 2000). It 'transformed the terms of political debate about black people and criminal justice, and is a comparable landmark to the Scarman Report' (Reiner 2000: 211). Contrary to common belief, judicial inquiries may be a higher risk than traditional royal commissions for governments to appoint. Apparently 'safe' judicial appointments may produce highly critical reports: nobody predicted that a conservative Scottish law lord such as Macpherson would condemn the criminal justice process as institutionally racist.

In Australia, the most significant inquiry into policing in recent years has been the Royal Commission into the NSW Police Service of 1994–1997, chaired by Justice James Wood. The Wood Commission was neither a governmental device of delay nor a predictable whitewash. The government opposed its establishment, which was the work of an independent MP supported by the opposition. Its outcome (a finding that a supposedly reformed police service was riddled with institutional corruption) was politically embarrassing for the government of the day.

It was widely expected that Justice Wood would conduct a judicial inquiry focusing on well-publicised allegations about police corruption, notably involving some notorious officers and their relations with criminals. For almost a year, it seemed that the Wood Commission was playing a familiar role – symbolising commitment to tackling problems but deflecting pressures for real change. Doubters were made to reassess when it became clear that the Commission was concerned with the present rather than the past, and the general as well as the specific. Wood's achievement was to combine proactive investigation into specific instances and patterns of corruption (widely defined to include 'process corruption') with an insistence that the focus of reform should not be on individual wrongdoers and their corruption, but on the institutional and cultural contexts which produced, maintained and tolerated them (Wood 1997; Dixon 1999b).

One of the strengths of such an inquiry is the relevance and urgency produced by being able to connect its investigation to identifiable, specific events. While a defining weakness of the Runciman Commission's report was its loss of contact with the miscarriages of justice which brought it about, the Wood Commission's broader analysis of cultural and institutional failings was conducted parallel to its exposure of corrupt individuals and groups. The Wood Commission made telling use of the media during its inquiry. Again and again, the media reminded the public of what the Commission was about by replaying surveillance tapes of corrupt officers taking bribes and illegal drugs. Similarly, the Macpherson Report was not just an investigation of the intangible concept of 'institutional racism'. It was an inquiry into the death of an identifiable, specific young man and the injustice caused by the failure to convict his killers, not least to his parents, who were identifiable and specific as they campaigned so effectively. There were also very identifiable wrongdoers, the five men suspected of involvement in the murder.

However, the Wood Commission illustrates the danger of overloading a commission with investigative and policy functions across wide areas. As if police corruption was not already a considerable target, Justice Wood was asked, in mid-inquiry, to widen his Commission's terms of reference to report on the criminal justice response to paedophilia. One result was that the final report was, perhaps inevitably, thin in vital areas. While it incisively investigated problems (both specific and general) and eloquently argued that reform required fundamental changes in structure and culture, it faltered when coming to the specifics of what should be achieved and how. This allowed the Police Commissioner to shift the agenda, promoting crime-fighting rather than cultural reform as the key corporate objective. In the context of highly politicised law and order panics, the reform agenda of the Royal Commission was disciplined into a much more containable and politically acceptable war on crime (Dixon 1999b; 2001).

Implementation – or not

Inquiry reports routinely insist that their recommendations should be treated as a unitary package. Typically, the Patten Report advised 'in the strongest terms against cherry-picking from this report or trying to implement some major elements of it in isolation from others' (Patten 1999: 19.2; cf. NSW LRC 1990: 53–4)). Whatever they may say when reports are delivered, governments routinely ignore this plea.

Governments feel comfortable in ignoring unwelcome recommendations, to the disappointment if not surprise of those who make them. As Lord Rothschild dryly commented: 'The purpose of a commission is to make recommendations which the Government may implement, or simply forget' (Rothschild 1984: 87). A.P. Herbert was more acerbic: 'The Home Office, like an elderly hypochondriac, is always asking for a second opinion but never accepts it' (1961: 272). Both the Philips and Runciman Commissions drew on extensive research evidence to recommend that inferences should not be drawn from a suspect's silence. (Indeed Runciman described the retention of the right to silence during police questioning as one of the fundamental principles under-lying his Commission's recommendations: 1994: 8.) However, the government, driven by ideological commitment and drawing on unreliable findings of unpublished police research, knew better: the right to silence was voided in the Criminal Justice and Public Order Act 1994 (Dixon 1997: ch. 6). Similarly, Australian governments have extended police powers without providing the safeguards which inquiries and commissions recommended as essential. Notably, legisla-tion authorising detention for questioning is not accompanied by the provision of publicly funded legal advice schemes for suspects in police custody, despite the insistence by official inquiries (e.g. NSW LRC 1990) that it is a vital corollary of the police power to detain. More recently, the British government has picked its way carefully and selectively through the Patten Report.

Only the most naïve commission member would be unaware that governments are not bound to implement recommendations and that once the report is delivered, their role is finished. As the (somewhat cynical) chair of the Royal Commission on Criminal Justice commented:

> Whatever view is taken of its recommendations by more or less disinterested observers, they will have been subjected to protracted debate before and during the passing of legislative and other measures which may bear only a tangential relationship to them. They will be chosen or rejected for other motives and on other grounds than those which influenced the members of the Commission to make them. (Runciman 1994: 8)

Australian corruption inquiries have been particularly aware that many of their predecessors' reform efforts – in New York City as well as in Australia, as the reform of the NYPD from Knapp (1972) to Mollen (1994) has been a constant point of reference – had not been sustained and that an apparently endless cycle of corruption, scandal, inquiry and reform had continued (Dixon 1999b). Consequently, they have attempted to maintain their influence by recommending the establishment of permanent oversight bodies. In Queensland, the Fitzgerald Inquiry led to the establishment of (what is now) the Crime and Misconduct Commission, while in NSW, the Wood Commission was succeeded by the Police Integrity Commission (PIC). The latter has had difficulty coping with a massive workload, with the result that some reports which should have been crucial have focused on trees in great detail, but seem to have missed the wood (e.g. PIC 2003).

In an additional innovative attempt to ensure that reform would continue in ways that would fundamentally change the institutional culture of the police service, the Wood Commission recommended that the PIC should engage an external auditor to carry out an 'external strategic audit' to report on success and failure and to advise on measures to improve the reform process (Wood 1997: 535). In three annual reports, the auditors presented a 'qualitative and strategic audit of the reform process' (QSARP). While not without weaknesses (Dixon 2001), QSARP provides a good example of what a critically informed managerialist methodology can produce (Hay Group 2000, 2002).

QSARP 3 recommended continuing to audit, but it could do nothing to avoid being consigned to a new graveyard of reports on the PIC's website (Hay Group 2002). While accepting most of the Wood Commission's specific recommendations, the government and the NSW Police side-stepped the fundamental finding that the institutional structure and culture of the service need to be fundamentally changed. Despite specific warnings by the Commission about the dangers of doing so, the Police Service promoted crime-fighting as its top priority and marginalised the reform process, including QSARP (Dixon 2001; Hay Group 2002). Closely focused on the perceived need to be tough on law and order for electoral success, the government did its best to avoid public interest in the QSARP reports, releasing them at times unlikely to attract public attention and dismissing them as 'management jargon'.[9]

So it would be wrong to assume that the new managerialism has enjoyed unchallenged success. NSW Police have displayed a consistent ability to soak up criticism, adopt whatever rhetoric is currently fashionable, and to stick to their own corporate priorities (Chan 1999; Dixon 2001). Similarly, in the UK, police organisations have fought a dogged rearguard action in some areas. For example, the conservative conclusions of the Posen Inquiry on core tasks (1995) owed much to fierce police opposition to potential loss of responsibilities (and resources). The 'old policing' has more fight left in it than some who foresee the decline of public policing would allow.

Official inquiry and police governance

Well-worn jibes about dogs burying bones and committees producing camels are no longer adequate for understanding official inquiry into policing. In the last two decades, power within the state has rapidly shifted with profound implications for police governance. The traditional royal commission and judicial (non)supervision have given way to a complex field in which official inquiry is, in myriad form, part of the everyday functioning of policing. Audit, evaluation, analysis and report have become growth industries (in the private[10] as well as the public sectors). While all too often the new managerialism speaks in bland terms (aims, objectives, targets) and (to an academic audience) is light on theory, empirical evidence and grounding in the literature, it is potentially potent and, sometimes, productive. There is space for innovative critique, even if implementation may be a different issue. Looking ahead, the current (UK) and future (Australia) impact of constitutional human rights commitments require a new direction for public inquiry and report (Loveday 2000: 229). Managerialism and human rights may just make unlikely but productive bedfellows.

Notes

1. I am grateful to Janet Chan for advice and comments.
2. Quoted with approval from the Justices' Clerks' Society (Willink 1962: 112).
3. Runciman commented that when he 'accepted the surprising invitation to chair the [Royal Commission on Criminal Justice], I knew next to nothing about the criminal justice system ... In our quaint British way, we assume that an enquiry of this nature is better headed by someone too ignorant to be prejudiced than by someone too knowledgeable to be open-minded' (1994: 1).
4. Rothschild pointed out that his Royal Commission was conducted as a part-time inquiry largely in the evenings and at weekends because members had full-time jobs (1984: 88).
5. Space limits preclude consideration of parliamentary committee reports. However, for analysis of an influential and critical (but poorly informed) committee, see Dixon (2001).
6 However, the Internet may in practice reduce local accountability. Reports may be available, but readers may be deterred by having to print their own copy. A duty to publish may be met by putting a report on www. But if its message is unwelcome, the release may not be announced, e.g. see Hay Group (2002); Dixon (2001).
7. See Wood (1997: vol. 3) for an impressive list of 22 commissions and inquiries in NSW alone.
8. *Miranda v. Arizona* [1966] 384 US 436; *R v. Heron*, unreported, Leeds Crown Court, 1 November 1993 (see Dixon 1997: 172–6); *Williams v. R* [1986] 66 ALR 385.
9. Premier Carr, quoted in the *Sydney Morning Herald*, 19 March 2001.
10. For example, Fitzgerald *et al.* (2002); Police Foundation/Policy Studies Institute (1996).

References

Alderson, K. (2001) *Powers and Responsibilities: Reforming NSW Criminal Investigation Law*. PhD thesis, University of New South Wales.

ALRC (1975) *Criminal Investigation*. Canberra: Australian Law Reform Commission.

Audit Commission (1993) *Helping with Enquiries: Tackling Crime Effectively*. London: HMSO.

Audit Commission (1996) *Streetwise: Effective Police Patrol*. London: HMSO.

Beach, B. (1978) *Report of the Board of Inquiry into Allegations against Members of the Victoria Police Force*. Melbourne: Government Printer.

Chan, J. (1999) Governing police practice: limits of the new accountability. *British Journal of Sociology*, 50: 251–70.

Crime Commission (1997) *New South Wales Crime Commission Annual Report 1996–97*. Sydney: NSWCC.

Critchley, T.A. (1967) *A History of Police in England and Wales*. London: Constable.

Davids, C. and Hancock, L. (1998) Policing, accountability and citizenship in the market state. *Australian and New Zealand Journal of Criminology*, 31: 38–68.

Dixon, D. (1991) *From Prohibition to Regulation*. Oxford: Clarendon Press.

Dixon, D. (1997) *Law in Policing: Legal Regulation and Police Practices*. Oxford: Clarendon Press.

Dixon, D. (1999a) The normative structure of policing. In D. Dixon (ed.) *A Culture of Corruption: Changing an Australian Police Service*. Sydney: Hawkins Press, pp. 69–97.

Dixon, D. (1999b) Reform, regression, and the Royal Commission into the NSW Police Service. In D. Dixon (ed.) *A Culture of Corruption: Changing an Australian Police Service*. Sydney: Hawkins Press, pp. 138–79.

Dixon, D. (2001) 'A transformed organization?' The NSW Police Service since the Royal Commission. *Current Issues in Criminal Justice*, 13: 203–18.

Downes, D. and Morgan, R. (2002) The skeletons in the cupboard: the politics of law and order at the turn of the millennium. In M. Maguire, R. Morgan and R. Reiner (eds) *The Oxford Handbook of Criminology*. Oxford: Oxford University Press, pp. 286–321.

Fitzgerald, G.E. (1989) *Report of Inquiry into Possible Illegal Activities and Associated Police Misconduct*. Brisbane: Government Printer.

Fitzgerald, M., Hough, M., Joseph, I. and Qureshi, T. (2002) *Policing for London*. Cullompton: Willan.

Haldane, R. (1986) *The People's Force: A History of the Victoria Police*. Melbourne: Melbourne University Press.

Hay Group (2000) *Qualitative and Strategic Audit of the Reform Process of the NSW Police Service: Report for Year 1*. Sydney: Police Integrity Commission.

Hay Group (2002) *Qualitative and Strategic Audit of the Reform Process of the NSW Police Service: Report for Year 3*. Sydney: Police Integrity Commission.

Herbert, A.P. (1961) Anything but action? A study of the uses and abuses of committees of inquiry. In R. Harris (ed.) *Radical Reaction*. London: Hutchinson, pp. 249–302.

HMIC (1998) *What Price Policing? A Study of Efficiency and Value for Money in the Police Service*. London: Home Office.

Home Office (1993) *Police Reform: A Police Service for the Twenty-First Century*. London: HMSO.

Home Office (2001) *Policing a New Century: A Blueprint for Reform*. London: HMSO.

Home Office/Cabinet Office (2002) *PACE Review*. London: Home Office.

Home Office, Lord Chancellor's Department and Attorney General (2002) *Justice for All*. London: HMSO.

Hughes, G., McLaughlin, E. and Muncie, J. (eds) (2002) *Crime Prevention and Community Safety*. London: Sage.

Johnston, L. and Shearing, C. (2003) *Governing Security*. London: Routledge.

Jones, D.B. (1908) *Report of the Royal Commission on the Duties of the Metropolitan Police*. London: HMSO.

Jones, T. and Newburn, T. (1997) *Policing after the Act*. London: Policy Studies Institute.

Kavanagh, D. (1987) *Thatcherism and British Politics*. Oxford: Oxford University Press

Kirby, M. (1979) Controls over investigation of offences and pre-trial treatment of suspects. *Australian Law Journal*, 53: 626–47.

Knapp, W. (1972) *Final Report of the Commission to Investigate Allegations of Police Corruption*. New York: Fund for the City of New York.

Lacey, N. (1994) Missing the wood... pragmatism versus theory in the Royal Commission. In M. McConville and L. Bridges (eds) *Criminal Justice in Crisis*. Aldershot: Edward Elgar, pp. 30–41.

Lee, L. (1929) *Report of the Royal Commission on Police Powers and Procedure*. London: HMSO.

Leishman, F., Loveday, B. and Savage, S.P. (2000) Introduction: core issues in policing revisited. In F. Leishman, B. Loveday and S.P. Savage (eds) *Core Issues in Policing*, 2nd edn. Harlow: Longman.

Loveday, B. (2000) New directions in accountability. In F. Leishman, B. Loveday and S.P. Savage (eds) *Core Issues in Policing*, 2nd edn. Harlow: Longman, pp. 213–31.

McConville, M. and Bridges, L. (1994) Foreword. In M. McConville and L. Bridges (eds) *Criminal Justice in Crisis*. Aldershot: Edward Elgar, pp. xv–xviii.

Macpherson, W. (1999) *The Stephen Lawrence Inquiry*. London: HMSO.

Marlow, A. and Loveday, B. (eds) (2000) *After Macpherson*. Lyme Regis: Russell House.

Mollen, M. (1994) *Report of the Commission to Investigate Allegations of Corruption and the Anti-corruption Procedures of the Police Department*. New York: City of New York.

NSW LRC (1990) *Police Powers of Detention and Investigation after Arrest*. Sydney: Law Reform Commission.

Patten, C. (1999) *The Report of the Independent Commission on Policing for Northern Ireland*. Belfast: HMSO.

PIC (2003) *Report on Operation Malta*. Sydney: Police Integrity Commission.

Police Foundation/Policy Studies Institute (1996) *The Role and Responsibility of the Police: Report of an Independent Inquiry*. London: Police Foundation/Policy Studies Institute.

Posen, I. (1995) *Review of Police Core and Ancillary Tasks*. London: HMSO.

Power, M. (1997) *The Audit Society*. Oxford: Clarendon Press.

Reiner, R. (1993) The Royal Commission on Criminal Justice – investigative powers and safeguards for suspects. *Criminal Law Review*, 808–16.

Reiner, R. (2000) *The Politics of the Police*, 3rd edn. Oxford: Oxford University Press.

Rothschild, V. (1984) *Random Variables*. London: Collins.

Runciman, W.G. (1993) *Report of the Royal Commission on Criminal Justice*. London: HMSO.

Runciman, W.G. (1994) An outsider's view of the criminal justice system. *Modern Law Review*, 57: 1–9.

Ryan, M. (1999) Penal policy making towards the millennium. *International Journal of the Sociology of Law*, 27: 1–22.

Savage, S.P., Charman, S. and Cope, S. (2000) The policy-making context: who shapes policing policy? In F. Leishman, B. Loveday and S.P. Savage (eds) *Core Issues in Policing*, 2nd edn. Harlow: Longman, pp. 30–51.

Scarman, L. (1981) *The Brixton Disorders*. London: HMSO.

Sheehy, P. (1993) *Inquiry into Police Responsibilities and Rewards*. London: HMSO.

Thatcher, M. (1993) *The Downing Street Years*. London: HarperCollins.

Walker, N. (2000) *Policing in a Changing Constitutional Order*. London: Sweet & Maxwell.

Wells, C. (1995) What Runciman didn't say. In E. Attwooll and D. Goldberg (eds) *Criminal Justice*. Stuttgart: Franz Steiner, pp. 127–40.

Willink, H. (1962) *Report of the Royal Commission on the Police*. London: HMSO.

Wood, J. (1997) *Final Report of the Royal Commission into the New South Wales Police Service*. Sydney: Royal Commission.

Wootten, J.H. (1991) *Report of the Inquiry into the Death of David John Gundy*. Canberra: Royal Commission into Aboriginal Deaths in Custody.

Zander, M. (2003) *The Police and Criminal Evidence Act 1984*. 4th ed. London: Sweet and Maxwell.

Chapter 7

'Politics by other means'[1]: the role of commissions of inquiry in establishing the 'truth' about 'Aboriginal justice' in Canada

Philip Stenning and Carol LaPrairie

As has been the case in many other nations with indigenous populations, the issue of the serious statistical over-representation[2] of Aboriginal people[3] in the criminal justice system is one that has persistently occupied the attention of legislators, policy-makers, judges, academics and advocacy groups during the last three decades in Canada. It is an issue that has been compounded, and thrust more prominently onto the public agenda, by a series of miscarriages of justice and other actual and perceived injustices[4] involving Aboriginal people during this same period.

Policy responses to this issue have been many and varied, especially as Canada's federal system has created uncertainty as to which level of government – federal or provincial – has the primary responsibility for addressing such issues.[5] At the federal level, the government has responded by establishing distinct Aboriginal justice and policing units within the government itself,[6] by referring the matter to parliamentary committees and the Law Reform Commission for consideration, by initiating specific legislation aimed at reducing Aboriginal over-representation, by commissioning research on it and funding various programmes to alleviate it, by funding representative Aboriginal groups which advocate on behalf of Aboriginal people, and by initiating constitutional discussions and amendments to provide special protections for Aboriginal rights. In 1991, the federal government established the Royal Commission on Aboriginal Peoples (RCAP) with a broad mandate to consider all aspects of the position of Aboriginal people within Canada, including their experiences within the criminal justice system, and to make recommendations for future reforms. The Commission submitted a report on *Aboriginal People and Criminal Justice in Canada* in 1996, and its final report later in the same year.

In this chapter, we consider three of the most influential of these various federal and provincial commissions of inquiry – the Marshall Inquiry in Nova Scotia, the Public Inquiry into the Administration of Justice and Aboriginal People in Manitoba, and the Royal Commission on Aboriginal Peoples' *Report on Aboriginal People and Criminal Justice in Canada*. We explore the ways in which these inquiries and the reports they produced have framed the issues, constituted the official and public discourses, and shaped public policy with respect to the experiences of Aboriginal people within, and their relationship with, the criminal justice system in Canada.

The Marshall Inquiry[7]

The Marshall Inquiry, which came to be so named after the Mi'kmaq Indian whose wrongful conviction for murder it was appointed to inquire into,[8] was established by the Nova Scotia government in 1986. The Order in Council establishing the Commission stated that it was to

> ... inquire into, report your findings, and make recommendations to the Governor in Council respecting the investigation of the death of Sandford William Seale on the 28th–29th day of May, A.D., 1971; the charging and prosecution of Donald Marshall, Jr. with that death; the subsequent conviction and sentencing of Donald Marshall, Jr. for the non-capital murder of Sandford William Seale for which he was subsequently found to be not guilty;[9] and such other related matters which the Commissioners consider relevant to the Inquiry...[10]

In light of the clearly predominantly 'judicial' character of the Commission's mandate, three senior judges from other provinces, none of whom was Aboriginal, were appointed as Commissioners. In considering the Commission's mandate, the Commissioners decided that an expansive approach to their task was called for. The 'hook' for such an approach, of course, was provided by the reference to 'such other related matters, which the commissioners consider relevant to the Inquiry'.

Armed with these words, the Commissioners decided to expand their inquiry in two principal directions beyond the specific circumstances of Donald Marshall, Jr's wrongful conviction – directions which would significantly increase the length, depth and expense of the inquiry.

On the one hand, the Commissioners decided that in order to fully understand how and why Marshall had been wrongly convicted, it would be necessary to conduct a broad inquiry into the social and political context in which it had occurred. The Commission decided to invite written briefs and oral submissions and to commission research on the position and experiences of Native and Black people in Nova Scotia's criminal justice system, and to expand their investigation to include two other cases involving provincial cabinet ministers in order to establish whether, and to what extent, they might provide evidence of racial discrimination or 'double standards' in the administration of criminal justice in the province.

A public inquiry which started out life as an investigation into a wrongful conviction thus quickly became a broad-ranging inquiry into the entire administration of criminal justice in the province, with particular attention to the treatment of members of Aboriginal and other visible minority groups, and to explore possible improvements to criminal justice policy and practices in the province. With respect to the three specific cases, this was accomplished by calling witnesses and examining them under oath, as well as examining pertinent contemporaneous documentation. In the case of the broader concerns of the Commission, it also received written briefs from a wide variety of interested parties and commissioned five research studies, one of which focused particularly on the experiences of native Indians and another on the experiences of African-Canadians in the criminal justice system. The Commission also convened a number of Consultative Conferences on different aspects of its mandate. One of these conferences focused on issues concerning Aboriginal people and the criminal justice system. From the written briefs submitted on the experiences of native Indians in the criminal justice system, the Commission received allegations of endemic, systemic and individual racial discrimination in the criminal justice system and calls for the establishment of separate Aboriginal justice institutions in the province as the only adequate means to ensure that such discrimination did not persist in the future. The findings and conclusions of the research study, however, were by no means so clear or emphatic. The researcher found that 'There does not exist an adequate information base in Nova Scotia regarding the needs of Native communities or the extent and nature of the involvement of Natives in the criminal justice system' (Clark 1989: 70). But despite this, the researcher concluded that:

> Aboriginal people in Nova Scotia are being adversely affected by involvement in the criminal justice system because they are aboriginal. The immediate cause of adverse effects is a series of systemic problems in the justice system that discriminate against Aboriginal people in general, including those people living in reserve communities and off-reserve. (*ibid.*: 69)

The researcher also concluded that 'The underlying cause for Micmac involvement in the criminal justice system is an historical process of social and economic development that has been thrust on them over the years and that has resulted in a "culture of poverty" and external dependence' and that this was manifested in a range of social problems, including 'comparatively high rates of incarceration, and comparatively low rates of parole' (*ibid.*). With respect to sentencing, frequently suggested as a factor contributing to Aboriginal over-representation in correctional institutions, the researcher's findings were inconclusive. 'There appears', he wrote, 'to be disparity in sentencing (both in favour of and against Natives) to the extent that many judges appear to apply different criteria to Natives than to non-Natives in their sentencing decisions' (*ibid.*: 74).[11]

Given the lack of adequate data available to determine with any certainty 'the extent and nature of the involvement of Natives in the criminal justice system', the researcher was circumspect in his recommendations for the future. These included, among others: a thorough review of the relevance and effectiveness of the criminal justice system for Micmac communities on a community-by-community basis; the establishment of a Nova Scotia Aboriginal Justice Institute; the establishment of an information base regarding the comparative involvement of Natives and non-Natives in the criminal justice system; the implementation of a Micmac Court Worker Program; and regular court sittings in each reserve community. The researcher also recommended that 'the Micmac of Nova Scotia should examine, as a long term goal, the possibility of institutionalizing an autonomous tribal justice system based on indigenous ways of justice' (*ibid.*: 72–6).

In that part of its final report dealing with 'Nova Scotia Micmac and the Criminal Justice System', the Commission commented that, 'Although some Native witnesses at the public hearings suggested the relationship between Whites and Natives in Sydney was not a particularly comfortable one, there is little evidence of overt hostility between White and Native communities, or between White and Black communities in Sydney, or between the two minority communities' (Nova Scotia, Royal Commission, 1989: 162). The Commission noted, however, that it had concluded that:

> Donald Marshall, Jr's status as a Native contributed to the miscarriage of justice that has plagued him since 1971. We believe that certain persons within the system would have been more rigorous in their duties, more careful, or more conscious of fairness if Marshall had been White.[12] (*ibid.*)

It also concluded that, 'If Marshall's treatment in this case occurred because he was a Native, then other Natives will have – and have had – similar experiences.' The Commission went on immediately to quote the following remarks which Professor Michael Jackson had made at one of its Consultative Conferences:

> ... The overrepresentation of Native peoples in our prisons is the result of a particular and distinctive historical process which has made them poor beyond poverty. And that process is the process of colonization, whereby we, as a dominant society, have come to North America and have sought to make over Native people in our image. That process has left Native people, in most parts of the country, dispossessed of all but the remnants of what was once their home lands ... it is, in my estimation, the central problem which lies at the root of horrendous figures relating to Native people in the criminal justice system.[13]

The Commission then observed that:

> Many Natives feel that the criminal justice system – including police, lawyers, judges and courts – is not relevant to their experience, not only in terms of its language and concepts but also in terms of its essential values. Natives rely on resolving disputes through mediation and conciliation, methods which emphasize reconciliation rather than laying blame.

Noting the uncertainties surrounding the content and implications of Aboriginal rights which are guaranteed protection under the Constitution, the Commission also observed that there is

> a clear trend at the Federal Government and Supreme court levels to having Native communities take increasing control over their own lands, services and futures. Our recommendations on Native issues will be set against this background.

The Commission stated that it had considered and rejected a 'piecemeal' approach in favour of recommending the establishment, on an experimental basis, of a Native Criminal Court 'that will allow Natives some measure of direct control over the administration of justice within their communities.' The Commission emphasised that it was not proposing a separate system of Native law, 'but rather a different process for administering on the reserve certain aspects of the criminal law.' Its answer to those who might question why Natives should 'get their own justice system?' was simply: 'Because they are Native.' In the Commission's view, 'the historical and cultural justifications for establishing Native justice systems must override the fear of problems which might arise.'

The Commission went on to make a further ten recommendations in this area which largely mirrored some of the more specific recommendations of its researcher, outlined above. The Commission's report thus put forward and endorsed as 'truth' the following propositions about Aboriginal people and criminal justice:

1. Aboriginal people are over-represented in the criminal justice system.

2. The 'root cause' of this situation is the historical process of European colonisation of traditional Aboriginal lands and peoples and the chronic social disadvantages, poverty and associated high crime rates which are its lasting legacy.

3. The immediate cause of Aboriginal over-representation is systemic and individual discrimination within the criminal justice system.

4. The experiences of Aboriginal people in the criminal justice system are unique.

5. The right to establish separate systems of Native justice is almost certainly embraced within the existing 'Aboriginal and treaty rights of the Aboriginal peoples' which are recognised and affirmed in the constitution. And even if it is not, it is something which is historically and culturally justified.

6. The 'predominantly White' criminal justice system has 'failed' Aboriginal people.

7. Aboriginal people have (traditional/cultural) conceptions of, and 'essential values' with respect to, justice and how to achieve it which are different from those of non-Aboriginal people (as reflected in the mainstream 'White' criminal justice system).

8.   The establishment of such Native justice systems is ultimately likely to be the only way to satisfactorily address the needs for justice of Aboriginal people and prevent further injustices of the kind that Aboriginal people experience within the 'White' criminal justice system.

9.   Reforms to the mainstream criminal justice system could not satisfactorily address and resolve these problems, and can at best be regarded as desirable interim measures pending the establishment of separate Native justice systems.

There is room for legitimate disagreement as to whether, and to what extent, these propositions and the Commission's recommendations were adequately supported and justified by the totality of the information which was put before the Commission. It is clear, however, that they were not supported or justified by the research that it commissioned, despite the similarity of many of the Commission's recommendations to those of its researcher. The researcher had candidly conceded in his report that there was not sufficient evidence available at the time to assess 'the extent and nature of the involvement of Natives in the criminal justice system' and that 'consequently, effective policy and program planning by government would be impossible, assuming that the will existed to undertake such work' (Clark 1989: 70). In addition, some of the researcher's more important 'findings' (with regard to disparity in sentencing), which were themselves inconclusive, were based on what the Commission described in its report as 'a cursory and unscientific review of files in ... prosecutors' offices' and interviews with defence lawyers and prosecutors. In making the recommendations it did, therefore, it appears that the Commission was persuaded primarily by advocates for separate justice systems (such as the Union of Nova Scotia Indians (see Wildsmith 1991) and Professor Michael Jackson), rather than by any solid evidence about the nature, extent and causes of Aboriginal over-representation in the Nova Scotia criminal justice system.

Yet the 'truth' about these matters which the Commission proclaimed and endorsed had a profound influence in shaping subsequent public discourse on this issue. Not surprisingly, its recommendations in this regard were enthusiastically welcomed by representative Aboriginal organisations in Nova Scotia and elsewhere (Wildsmith 1991).

The Public Inquiry into the Administration of Justice and Aboriginal People[14] in Manitoba

The justice system has failed Manitoba's Aboriginal people on a massive scale. It has been insensitive and inaccessible, and has arrested and imprisoned Aboriginal people in grossly dispropor-tionate numbers. Aboriginal people who are arrested are more likely than non-Aboriginal people to be denied bail, spend more time in pre-trial detention and spend less time with their lawyers, and, if convicted, are more likely to be incarcerated. (Manitoba, Public Inquiry 1991: 1)

Following a quote from the Chief of the Assembly of First Nations concerning the imposition of a 'colonial system of government and justice upon our people without due regard to our Treaty and Aboriginal rights', these are the opening words of the 1991 final report of the Manitoba Public Inquiry into the Administration of Justice and Aboriginal People (referred to hereafter as the Manitoba Inquiry).

The Inquiry was originally established in response to a tragic fatal shooting of an innocent Aboriginal man (J.J. Harper) by the police in Winnipeg, and a case involving the murder of a young Aboriginal woman (Helen Betty Osborne) in a rural Manitoba town. The Inquiry was established in 1988, so many of its hearings and deliberations were going on contemporaneously with those of the Marshall Inquiry in Nova Scotia. Unlike the Marshall Inquiry, however, the initial terms of reference of the Manitoba Inquiry were by no means limited to an inquiry into the two specific cases that had given rise to it. On the contrary, the Inquiry was given very expansive terms of reference to 'inquire into, and make findings about, the state of conditions with respect to Aboriginal people in the justice system in Manitoba and produce a final report for the Minister of Justice with conclusions, options and recommendations.' The Inquiry was also to 'consider whether and to what extent Aboriginal and non-Aboriginal persons are treated differ-ently by the justice system and whether there are specific adverse effects, including possible systemic discrimination against Aboriginal people, in the justice system' (Manitoba, Public Inquiry 1991: 763).

The establishment of the Inquiry and its terms of reference were confirmed through an Act of the Manitoba Legislature. The preamble referred to 'the unique problems with and concerns about the administration of justice in Manitoba' which 'Aboriginal peoples'[15] had and the possible reasons for these problems and concerns. It also referred to the fact that 'leaders of the Aboriginal peoples of Manitoba have been increasingly concerned about the relationship between the administration of justice in Manitoba and the legitimate aspirations of Aboriginal peoples for greater self-government.' Section 3 of the Act provided that the Commissioners should be 'guided by but not limited to the terms of reference set out in the Schedule.'

The Inquiry was thus given great latitude to determine the scope and manner of its inquiries, while at the same time it was given clear signals as to what were some of the key issues and considerations which should frame them. In particular, some of the key elements of the 'problems and concerns' which were objects of investigation by the Marshall Inquiry in Nova Scotia seemed to be almost taken as givens in the preamble to the Act and the Inquiry's terms of reference, which also clearly signalled a 'relationship between the administration of justice and the legitimate aspirations of Aboriginal peoples for greater self-government.'

Two Commissioners, both from within Manitoba, were appointed to head up the Inquiry – one the non-Aboriginal Associate Chief Justice of the province, the other the Aboriginal Associate Chief Judge. It seems likely that, as with the Marshall Inquiry, judges were chosen for this role particularly because of that part of the Inquiry's mandate which required it to investigate the circumstances of the Harper and Osborne cases.

Armed with a mandate which it was authorised to consider merely as a 'guide' to its inquiries, the Inquiry immediately took a decision which was to greatly influence public perceptions of what it would be all about and which would likely pave the way for public acceptance of radical recommendations. Specifically, it styled itself, in all its communications, letterhead, public logo, etc., as the 'Aboriginal Justice Inquiry', set in a logo with an Aboriginal motif. This self-presentation was adhered to faithfully in all its public hearings right through to the cover of its final report, which was mastheaded as the 'Report of the Aboriginal Justice Inquiry of Manitoba'. The official name of the Inquiry ('Public Inquiry into the Administration of Justice and Aboriginal People') was relegated to a much less conspicuous font at the bottom of the page.

All of this gives rise to a reasonable suspicion that the Inquiry's account of 'the truth' about Aboriginal people and the criminal justice system in Manitoba, which was presented and endorsed in the findings and recommendations of its final report, was, to a large extent, pre-figured even before it started its work. Predictably, the report's recommendations included not only a raft of reforms to the mainstream criminal justice system, similar to those recommended earlier by the Marshall Inquiry, but also that 'Federal, provincial and Aboriginal First Nations governments [should] commit themselves to the establishment of tribal courts in the near future as a first step to the establishment of a fully functioning, Aboriginally controlled justice system'.[16]

In its final report, the Commission said little about the research it commissioned in support of its inquiry process, and the influence of this research on its conclusions:

In addition to the hearings, we conducted research projects covering a wide range of subjects. Some of the research was done by our own research staff, including a survey of inmates at seven correctional institutions, a survey of crown and defence lawyers, and a survey of members of the judiciary. We also commissioned experts in various areas to prepare background papers for us. We combined this information with our own experience and the presentations made to us during committee hearings to come to the conclusions we reached. (Manitoba, Public Inquiry 1991: 5)

No details as to terms of reference, sampling, methodologies or analyses for any of this research were provided by the Commission, making it difficult to assess the quality of the research or the validity of conclusions drawn from it.[17] Noteworthy, however, was the fact that neither the Director of Research nor the Senior Research Officer for the Commission had any significant social science research experience.[18] Only certain findings of some of the studies were cited in the report.

Royal Commission on Aboriginal Peoples[19] criminal justice reference

For the past several decades there has been considerable activity at the political level in Canada devoted to redefining the relationship between Aboriginal and non-Aboriginal people, including systems of governance. Control over education, economic development, health, social services, language and culture have all been part of the self-government agenda and the preceding public inquiries into Aboriginal people and justice moved the issue of justice into the self-government discourse. The Royal Commission on Aboriginal Peoples (RCAP) was established in August 1991, immediately after the Manitoba Inquiry submitted its report,[20] to address some of the outstanding political, social, economic and cultural issues, and to provide direction for the future relationship between Aboriginal and non-Aboriginal Canada. There were several components to the work of the Commission including a reference on criminal justice.

Given its broad, Canada-wide mandate and the enormous resources at its disposal,[21] the Commission was well placed to explore some important aspects of the national situation with respect to Aboriginal people and criminal justice that the earlier provincial inquiries, because of their more limited mandates, were not in a position to do. As was made clear in the following excerpt from the preface to its 1996 report, *Bridging the Cultural Divide: A Report on Aboriginal People*[22] *and Criminal Justice in Canada* (referred to hereafter as the report), however, the Commission made a conscious choice, right at the outset of its work, not to pursue this opportunity:

> In this report we review the historical and contemporary record of Aboriginal people's experience in the criminal justice system to secure a better understanding of what lies behind their over-representation there. Our mandate requires us to do more, of course, than provide a framework for understanding. It also charges us with providing a framework for change. That framework has two distinctive yet interrelated dimensions. The first dimension is the reform of the existing criminal justice system to make it more respectful of and responsive to the experience of Aboriginal people; the second dimension is the establishment of Aboriginal justice systems as an exercise of the Aboriginal right of self-government.
>
> The first dimension is one that has been the subject of literally hundreds of recommendations by task forces and commissions of inquiry that have preceded ours.
>
> *At an early stage we determined that it would make little sense for this Commission to replicate the work of these inquiries or recite all their recommendations.*[23] *Instead we have sought to provide a framework for implementing these recommendations with a view to reforming the existing criminal justice system.*
>
> Our primary focus in this report, however, is the second dimension of reform, the recognition and establishment of Aboriginal justice systems. This recognition is an integral part of the right of self-government. The development of such systems, based upon Aboriginal concepts and processes of justice, will, in the long term, enable Aboriginal peoples to address crime and the social disintegration associated with it in ways that promote responsibility and healing for victims, offenders and communities. (Canada, Royal Commission 1996: xi–xii) (our italics)

This passage makes it quite clear that at the outset of its work the Commission had accepted *in toto*, and as unquestionable, 'the truth' about Aboriginal people and criminal justice as presented and endorsed by earlier inquiries such as the Marshall Inquiry and the Manitoba Inquiry[24] and previously identified in this chapter. The task which the Commission saw for itself was simply to develop a framework for the implementation of the recommendations which had flowed from it, especially those for the establishment of a separate Aboriginal justice system – and a framework which, preferably, would be politically 'saleable' in the mid-1990s and beyond.

This approach is clearly manifested in the structure of the report. Only half of one of the six chapters (26 out of a total of 315 pages) is devoted to information about 'current realities' or the aetiology of over-representation, and no new research findings emerge, only a careful selection of existing research that fits the primary 'framework for change' approach. This treatment presents no new information on the subject, simply reviewing some earlier literature and the findings and conclusions of the earlier provincial inquiries. The five chapters devoted to the framework for change include discussions of the right of self-government and the constitutional authority for the establishment of Aboriginal justice systems, current Aboriginal justice initiatives, creating conceptual and constitutional space for Aboriginal justice systems, and reforming the existing justice system. The report concludes with a discussion of the way in which the criminal justice system has 'failed' Aboriginal people and recommendations for developing and implementing an Aboriginal controlled system.

The research framework for the crime and justice reference of the RCAP did little to promote new empirical research that might have advanced an understanding of the aetiology of Aboriginal over-representation.[25] Much of what is presented in the report in the form of selective historical writings, submissions of Aboriginal politicians, findings of previous inquiries (based on similar methodologies) or out of context and out of date research findings appears to be designed to reinforce and support the broader political and self-government objectives of the Commission, rather than to identify, and support with compelling empirical evidence, real justice solutions to real justice problems.

The self-government agenda which underlies the report is most apparent in Chapter 4, 'Creating Conceptual and Constitutional Space for Aboriginal Justice Systems'. In this chapter, the Commission supports the establishment of separate Aboriginal justice systems, not on the basis that there is evidence of their likely superior effectiveness[26] in addressing and reducing the myriad of problems faced by Aboriginal people in the mainstream criminal justice system, which the report had highlighted, but simply on the basis that 'the Aboriginal right of self-government encompasses the right of Aboriginal nations to establish and administer their own systems of justice'[27] (Canada, Royal Commission 1996: 177).

Unlike the Marshall and Manitoba Inquiries, which were specific to particular provinces, the RCAP's report purported to review the situation with respect to Aboriginal people and criminal justice across the country. In simply accepting 'the truth' on these matters presented by these earlier inquiries without question, the Commission added to this 'truth' the idea that Aboriginal people everywhere in the country have the same experiences in the criminal justice system regardless of where they live, the nature of their life circumstances and their socio-economic differences, and that the kinds of recommendations for change promoted by the earlier inquiries are equally necessary and appropriate for all Aboriginal communities.

The inquiries' 'truth' becomes the official truth

We have shown how 'the truth' about Aboriginal people and criminal justice which was presented and endorsed by the Marshall Inquiry in its 1989 report was constantly repeated and elaborated upon by the various provincial inquiries, and eventually by the Royal Commission on Aboriginal Peoples which followed it during the first half of the 1990s, without much serious challenge or significant new research commissioned by them. In the latter half of the 1990s, this 'truth' was enthusiastically adopted and endorsed as the official truth on the matter by the Federal government and the Supreme Court of Canada.

In 1994, the federal government introduced a Bill in Parliament which provided for extensive reform of sentencing. This Bill, which became law two years later, included a provision which required sentencing judges to take into account a set of principles including the principle that

(e) all available sanctions other than imprisonment that are reasonable in the circumstances should be considered for all offenders, *with particular attention to the circumstances of Aboriginal offenders...* (our italics)[28]

In introducing the Bill in 1994, the Minister of Justice stated that 'The reason we referred specifically there to Aboriginal persons is that they are sadly over-represented in the prison populations of Canada' and went on to cite the findings of the Manitoba Inquiry in support of this explanation for the provision.[29]

By 1999, a case involving the application of paragraph 718.2(e) of the Criminal Code to an Aboriginal woman convicted of manslaughter reached the Supreme Court of Canada, in which the Court concluded that the reference to Aboriginal offenders in this paragraph constituted a 'direction to sentencing judges to undertake the process of sentencing

Aboriginal offenders differently [than in cases involving non-Aboriginal offenders], in order to endeavour to achieve a truly fit and proper sentence in the particular case' (*R. v. Gladue* [1999] 1 SCR 688, at para. 33).[30] During the course of its lengthy judgment in the case, the Court referred repeatedly to the findings and conclusions of the various provincial inquiries (especially the Manitoba Inquiry), as well as the RCAP report on Aboriginal people and criminal justice largely to the exclusion of any dissenting or competing explanations (Stenning and Roberts, 2001). It paid similar deference to the 'truth' about this issue presented by these various public inquiries in a further consideration of paragraph 718.2(e) in the subsequent case of *R. v. Wells* [2000] 1 SCR 207.[31]

Possibilities for alternative versions of 'the truth' about Aboriginal people and criminal justice

Four possible explanations for Aboriginal over-representation that warranted serious research attention by these inquiries were: (a) differential processing in the criminal justice system as a result of culture conflict and racial discrimination (most importantly, do police over-charge and crowns over-prosecute?); (b) higher Aboriginal offending levels; (c) disproportionate commission of the kinds of offences that are likely to result in carceral sentences; and (d) the differential impact of criminal justice policies and practices.

Few of the inquiries into Aboriginal people and criminal justice in Canada have conducted the kinds of comprehensive and systematic research required to determine which of these possible explanations can best be supported empirically. Although it had the mandate and the resources to undertake such research, the Royal Commission on Aboriginal Peoples chose not to do so. Instead, the work of the various public inquiries has generally institutionalised the public inquiry process in place of standard social science research as the leading methodology. Research findings inconsistent with what has, over the past two decades, become the conventional wisdom about Aboriginal criminal justice in Canada are often ignored. In the most recent commission reports these omissions have included existing findings on the sentencing of Aboriginal and non-Aboriginal offenders (Hann and Harman, 1993; Clark and Associates 1989); social stratification in reserve communities, the migration of 'have-nots' to urban areas and the role of certain cities in contributing to the over-representation problem (LaPrairie 1994); regional variations in over-representation (LaPrairie, 1992); and critical analyses of popular justice and customary law (Depew 1994; McDonnell 1992). These reports and research findings were generally not included or presented in a way that would expand the discussion and understanding of the issues.[32] The analyses in the RCAP and other commission reports relied heavily on research that presented a particular view of the 'problem'.[33]

Research to explain the variation in Aboriginal involvement in the criminal justice system in different regions of Canada should have been conducted in select geographic locations and explored population characteristics, migratory patterns, employment, education, age distributions, income, etc. This kind of analysis could have significantly furthered knowledge about the aetiology of Aboriginal involvement in the criminal justice and correctional systems.

The frequent calls for a separate Aboriginal justice system in Canada would suggest that the inquiries should also have explored all aspects of a separate system, particularly whether the mainstream criminal justice system is incapable of meeting the needs of Aboriginal offenders and communities, in light of recent law reform and restorative justice initiatives.

The inquiries refer to universal Aboriginal conceptions and 'world-views' of justice without any acknowledgment that the Aboriginal experience in Canada is very diverse. For example, more Aboriginal people in Canada live in urban areas than on reserves, generally regarded as the bastions of Aboriginal culture. On many reserves mainstream and evangelical religions and diversity of lifestyles and beliefs (as reflected in values about individual rights, wage labour and private property ownership) are flourishing and have generated 'world-views' which diverge substantially and in important respects from the more traditional Aboriginal outlooks of earlier times (see, for example, McDonnell 1992).

Some of the critical questions not answered by the Commission are as follows: Would an Aboriginal justice system reduce Aboriginal over-representation in whatever control institutions were established, and if so, how? Does the mainstream justice system reflect only non-Aboriginal cultural values and does a consensus exist among Aboriginal people themselves about cultural values which would/could be adequately reflected in a separate justice system?

There are also some notable omissions in the various reports, including the lack of recognition or explanation for the variation in Aboriginal over-representation across the country. The RCAP report notes that 'Aboriginal people are at the bottom of almost every available index of socio-economic well-being' (p. 42) but also fails to discuss social stratification in Aboriginal communities (LaPrairie 1994). For example, the 1991 Aboriginal People's Survey (1991) data that showed that the university education rates for some Aboriginal groups in the three Maritime provinces are higher than for the non-Aboriginal populations would have been available to the Commission. The implementation and effectiveness of Aboriginal community-based justice projects should also have been carefully evaluated and a comprehensive community justice project evaluation strategy developed by the Royal Commission. The end result would have been information about specific projects and about the feasibility of approaches such as restorative justice.

Several of the fundamental premises upon which the various reports are based minimise both the complexities of the issues, and the social, political and economic changes that had occurred prior to the Commissions as the result of explicit government policies. Many of these changes are in the justice area.[34] Other policies that relate to health, education, affirmative action and employment equity are in the social policy area but will have important implications for Aboriginal offending, and these policies continue to have a profound impact on the well-being and prosperity of Aboriginal people in Canada.[35] However, the RCAP report does not reflect the past, present or likely future impact of any of these policies on reducing the problem of Aboriginal over-involvement in the criminal justice system.

Conclusions

Widely accepted objectives of commissions of inquiry, as stated previously, are 'the education of the public, the shaping of public discourse, and the development of public policy'. In addition, as suggested by Mr Justice Cory, they are about 'fact-finding' and uncovering 'the truth'. In other words, through the public inquiry process public monies are expended and human and other resources are mobilised to advance the state of knowledge, to address or redress a problem of national import and to influence public policy. However, we argue here that when Aboriginal justice was identified as the 'problem' in the late 1980s and early to mid-1990s, in the form of the mandates given to the three commissions of inquiry considered in this paper, these objectives were compromised by politics, political agendas and advocacy. The end result was that although considerable amounts of money were expended to 'study' the problem of Aboriginal people in the Canadian criminal justice system, we know little more today about the aetiology of over-representation than we did when the first inquiry was commissioned. The underlying assertion in the reports of the various commissions has been that over-representation was evidence that the mainstream criminal justice system had 'failed' Aboriginal people, and that their processing by the system is discriminatory and biased. The only solution to these problems that is proposed is the establishment of Aboriginal-controlled systems of criminal justice, which are said to be necessary because the problems faced by Aboriginal people, when involved with the criminal justice system, are unique to them.

There is strong reason, however, to question the claims made by these inquiries that the criminal justice experiences of Aboriginal people are unique. Many of the reports make much of the argument that Aboriginal people are uniquely disadvantaged by race, class and culture in their dealings with the criminal justice system and that laws, structures and processes of the system do not represent their interests or values. There is plenty of evidence, however, that other groups in Canadian society are equally and similarly disadvantaged. As LaPrairie recently concluded:

> As a group, Aboriginal people may be more vulnerable to the commission of crime and criminal justice processing because of their more generally disadvantaged position in Canadian society but disadvantaged non-Aboriginal people are equally vulnerable and are also over-represented in the criminal justice and correctional systems in Canada. The difference is that a much larger proportion of the Aboriginal population is disadvantaged and severely disadvantaged so their over-representation, when compared to the non-Aboriginal population, is more obvious and more understandable (if not acceptable). (2003: 23)

There have been no submissions in Canada from non-Aboriginal groups or from government that juries, for instance, should be comprised of poor white males, or that appearing in front of a well-educated, middle-class judge may be as foreign and intimidating to the majority of non-Aboriginal offenders as it is to the majority of Aboriginal offenders. Nor have these disadvantaged non-Aboriginal groups (who are also seriously over-represented in correctional institutions), or the areas of towns and cities in which many of them live, been the subject of discussions about over-policing, the need to be policed by members of their own group and/or to have their own justice system. The possibility that proposals for separate Aboriginal justice systems, combined with inattention to the plight of such other disadvantaged groups, could generate feelings of injustice and inequity,[36] has not been seriously addressed in the reports of any of these inquiries.

If we are truly serious about redressing injustices and 'doing justice' differently, what genuine justice issues separate Aboriginal and non-Aboriginal offenders and communities? This question should have been the starting point for understanding and contextualising the current situation with respect to Aboriginal people and criminal justice.[37] Identifying the fact that criminal justice often presents similar problems for certain Aboriginal and non-Aboriginal groups would have allowed the various inquiries to occupy a position of authority from which to argue the need for more fundamental change and reform to the entire criminal justice system, and to re-examine social policies which affect the most disadvantaged segments of the population, regardless of race.

Notes

1. 'Law is simply politics by other means' (Kairys 1982: 17).
2. For a discussion of some of the complexities of this seemingly straightforward concept, see Roberts and Stenning (2002), at pp. 79–80.
3. Canada has three distinct Aboriginal groups (nowadays often referred to as 'First Nations') – Indians (or Dene), Metis (who are the progeny of intermarriage between Indians and (mostly French) European Canadians) and Inuit (formerly referred to as Eskimos). Of these three groups, which together account for about 3% of Canada's population, Indians are the most numerous and, unlike the other two, have been the subject of treaties and special federal legislation (the Indian Act).
4. These have included wrongful convictions, excessive use of force (including lethal force) by police, and allegations of racial discrimination throughout the criminal justice system.
5. Under Canada's constitution, the federal Parliament and government have responsibility for enacting criminal law and procedure as well as for laws with respect to Canada's Aboriginal peoples, while the provincial legislatures and governments have responsibility for the administration of justice (including criminal justice) in their respective provinces.
6. These are in the Department of Justice and the Ministry of the Solicitor General respectively, and are in addition to the substantial bureaucracy of the Department of Indian and Northern Development (DIAND) which has primary responsibility for administering the Indian Act.
7. For other accounts of the Marshall Inquiry, see Kaiser (1990), Wildsmith (1991), Roach (1995) and Stenning (2000).
8. Its formal name was the Royal Commission on the Donald Marshall, Jr, Prosecution.
9. Donald Marshall, Jr spent eleven years in the penitentiary following his original conviction for this offence.
10. Nova Scotia, Royal Commission (1989: 301).

11. In its final report, the Commission referred to this research in the following terms: 'Our researcher did a cursory and unscientific review of files in the Truro and Sydney Crown prosecutors' offices, and interviewed various players in the system. This review did not indicate a significant variation in sentencing between Natives and non-Natives, or between courts. However, the researcher indicated a clear consensus among those interviewed that certain judges are more – or less – lenient in sentencing Native people' (Nova Scotia, Royal Commission 1989: 181).

12. This conclusion was based not only on evidence the Commission heard concerning the Marshall case itself, but also on its comparison between the handling of the Marshall case and the handling of the other two criminal investigations (involving provincial cabinet ministers) which it investigated. From this comparison it concluded that 'there is a two-tier system of justice – that system does respond differently, depending on the status of the person investigated' and that 'officials in the Department of Attorney General ... require substantially more likelihood of conviction before charging a politician than an Indian' (Nova Scotia, Royal Commission 1989: 220–221).

13. This argument had been developed more fully in the Canadian Bar Association's 1988 report, *Locking Up Natives in Canada*, which Professor Jackson had authored (Jackson 1988 and 1989), and was subsequently endorsed in the report of the Osnaburgh/Windigo Tribal Council Justice Review Committee in Ontario (Ontario, Osnaburg/Windigo 1990), the Manitoba Inquiry (see below) and the Royal Commission on Aboriginal Peoples (see below).

14. The terminology used to refer to the subjects of these inquiries has varied interestingly over the years. Thus, in the three inquiries considered in this chapter, we find the terms 'Natives', 'Native people', 'Native peoples', 'Aboriginal people', 'Aboriginal peoples' and 'Aboriginal persons' used more or less interchangeably even though one might think that such terms have rather different connotations ('peoples' referring to distinct collectivities). The choice of terms, however, does not, as one might expect that it might, appear to be related to how committed the authors are to the promotion of the need and justifiability of separate Aboriginal justice systems.

15. See note 14, above. The title of Volume 1 of the Manitoba Inquiry's report ('The Justice System and Aboriginal People') reflected the official name of the Inquiry ('The Public Inquiry into the Administration of Justice and Aboriginal People').

16. This was to include '(but need not necessarily be limited to)': a policing service; a prosecution branch; a legal aid system; youth, family, criminal, civil and appellate court systems; a probation service; a mediation/counselling service; a fine collection and maintenance enforcement system; a community-based correctional system; and a parole system (see p. 266 of the Commission's report).

17. The Provincial Court Study, which was the most frequently cited study in the Commission's report, contained no description of its methodology or analysis, or its terms of reference.

18. The Director of Research for the Marshall Inquiry was also a lawyer with no formal social science research qualifications.

19. See footnote 14, above.

20. The Manitoba Inquiry report was presented on 12 August 1991.

21. At a cost of $58 million, the Commission was the most expensive public inquiry of its kind in Canadian history.
22. See footnote 14, above.
23. This decision was apparently reached on the basis of recommendations of the Commission's own research staff. A report written by the Commission's Research Directorate, entitled 'Aboriginal Justice Inquiries, Task Forces and Commissions: An Update', noted that the reports of only two of the previous inquiries (the Manitoba Inquiry and the Law Reform Commission of Canada) had advocated establishment of separate Aboriginal justice systems, and that only easy recommendations from previous inquiries had been implemented. It concluded that: 'It is evident that the problem does not need further study. Solutions have been identified and are within reach; it is now time for these solutions to be put into place' (Canada, Royal Commission 1993: 15–41, at p. 38).
24. At the beginning of the 'Introduction' to its report the Commission cites the report of the Manitoba Inquiry as authority for this 'truth' (Canada, Royal Commission 1996: 1–2).
25. What was included in the final justice report, *Bridging the Cultural Divide*, was selective, existing research. This research was often taken from other inquiry reports or from sources that identified the problem in a particular way and/or supported the underlying need for Aboriginal justice systems. Where other research findings were included, these were presented in such a way as to make the case for Aboriginal controlled systems. Original empirical research and/or comprehensive secondary analyses are notably absent from the report. This absence may result from the fact that basic research questions about the aetiology of and/or geographic variation in over-representation or other relevant justice issues were never clearly identified.
26. In the preceding chapter of the report, in which the Commission reviews a number of existing Aboriginal justice initiatives, it cites no systematic evidence of their effectiveness. The evaluation of one of these initiatives, from which the Commission quotes in its report (pp. 154–6), was a process ('implementation') evaluation, not an outcome evaluation (see Moyer and Axon 1993). This was also the case with the Hollow Water evaluation (cited in footnotes 257 and 274 of the RCAP report). Its authors noted that it was not possible to get the data required for an outcome evaluation (Lajeunesse and Associates 1996).
27. Providing a familiar echo of the Marshall Inquiry's insistence that 'Natives' are entitled to 'their own justice system' simply 'Because they are Natives' (Nova Scotia, Royal Commission 1989: 168).
28. Now paragraph 718.2(e) of the Criminal Code.
29. Canada, House of Commons, Standing Committee on Justice and Legal Affairs, Minutes of Proceedings and Evidence, 17 November, 1994, at p. 62:15.
30. In a further consideration of the provision in the subsequent case of *R. v. Wells* [2000] 1 SCR 207, the Supreme Court held that although the provision required 'a different methodology for assessing a fit sentence for an Aboriginal offender', it did not 'mandate, necessarily, a different result' (at para. 44).
31. For an extensive discussion of the Aboriginal provision in para. 718.2(e) and the interpretations and application of it by the Supreme Court of Canada in the Gladue and Wells cases, see Stenning and Roberts (2001), and the 'Colloquy' on

that article which was published in the *Saskatchewan Law Review*, 65(1) (2002), at pp. 1–105.

32. All three inquiries ignored research findings that have been available for over twenty years, which reveal that Aboriginal offenders consistently receive shorter sentences, particularly in federal institutions (e.g. Canfield and Drinnan 1981; Muirhead 1981; LaPrairie 1990; Hann and Harman 1993). More recently, research has established that Aboriginal offenders are more likely than non-Aboriginal offenders to receive conditional sentence orders despite being at higher risk to reoffend (Roberts 2002).

33. In the RCAP report *Bridging the Cultural Divide*, Chapter 2, 'Current Realities', makes some attempt to deal with the aetiology of over-representation, but does so in a way that leads directly and quite overtly to making the case for Aboriginal control of justice (see p. 57).

34. These include the creation of Aboriginal justices of the peace, Aboriginal police forces, Aboriginal justice departments with special Aboriginal justice funds and various initiatives at all levels of government including Aboriginal programmes and policies in courts, corrections, policing, after-care, Aboriginal and restorative community justice.

35. A notable example of this is the huge increase in the past twenty years in the number of Aboriginal university graduates resulting from government policies to provide funding for Aboriginal students.

36. See, for example, Seeman (2001). Interestingly, the Grand Chief of the Assembly of First Nations openly acknowledged the legitimacy of such concerns in his testimony to the House of Commons Standing Committee on Justice and Legal Affairs, in its consideration of the sentencing reform Bill in 1995: see Minutes of Proceedings and Evidence (2 March 1995) at p. 88:7.

37. The Marshall Inquiry, for instance, chose to compare the way Aboriginal people were treated in the Nova Scotia criminal justice system with the way prominent provincial cabinet ministers and Black people were treated, rather than with the way underprivileged and disadvantaged members of the White majority population were treated.

References

Canada, House of Commons, Standing Committee on Justice and Legal Affairs (1994) *Minutes of Proceedings and Evidence*, 17 November.

Canada, Royal Commission on Aboriginal Peoples (1993) *Aboriginal Peoples and the Justice System: A Report of the National Roundtable on Aboriginal Justice Issues*. Ottawa: Minister of Supply and Services.

Canada, Royal Commission on Aboriginal Peoples (1996) *Bridging the Cultural Divide: A Report on Aboriginal People and Criminal Justice in Canada*. Ottawa: Minister of Supply and Services Canada.

Canada, Statistics Canada (1993) *1991 Aboriginal People's Survey*. Ottawa: Statistics Canada, Vols 1–6.

Canfield, C. and Drinnan, L. (1981) *Comparative Statistics: Native and Non-Native Federal Inmates – A Five-Year History*. Ottawa: Ministry of the Solicitor General.

Clark, S. (1989) *The Mi'kmaq and Criminal Justice in Nova Scotia*. A research study prepared for the Royal Commission on the Donald Marshall, Jr, Prosecution, and published as Vol. 3 of the Commission's Final Report. Halifax: Government Printer.

Clark, G.S. and Associates (1989) *Sentencing Patterns and Sentencing Options Relating to Aboriginal Offenders*. Ottawa: Department of Justice, Policy, Programs and Research Sector.

Depew, R.C. (1994) *Popular Justice and Aboriginal Communities: Some Preliminary Considerations*. Department of Justice: Aboriginal Justice Directorate.

Hann, R. and Harman, W. (1993) *Predicting Release Risk for Aboriginal Penitentiary Inmates*. Corrections Branch, Ottawa: Ministry of the Solicitor General, User Report 1993–21.

Jackson, M. (1988) *Locking Up Natives in Canada: A Report of the Canadian Bar Association Committee on Imprisonment and Release*. Vancouver University of British Columbia.

Kairys, D. (1982) Legal reasoning, traditional jurisprudence and legal education. In D. Kairys (ed.) *The Politics of Law: A Progressive Critique*. New York: Pantheon Books, pp. 9–17.

Kaiser, H. (1990) The aftermath of the Marshall Commission: a preliminary opinion. *Dalhousie Law Journal*, 13: 364–75.

Lajeunesse and Associates (1996) *Evaluation of the Hollow Water Community Holistic Circle Healing Project*. Ottawa: Solicitor General Canada.

LaPrairie, C. (1990) The role of sentencing in the over-representation of Aboriginal people in correctional institutions. *Canadian Journal of Criminology*, 32: 429–40.

LaPrairie, C. (1993) *Dimensions of Aboriginal Over-representation in Correctional Institutions and Implications for Crime Prevention*. Ottawa: Corrections Branch, Ministry of the Solicitor General, Supply and Services.

LaPrairie, C. (1994) *Seen But Not Heard: Native People in the Inner City*. Ottawa: Justice Canada.

LaPrairie, C. (2003) *Aboriginal Governance and Criminal Justice: No Single Problem, No Simple Solution*. Paper prepared for the State of the Federation Conference, 'Reconfiguring the Geometry of Aboriginal Self-Determination', Queen's University, Institute of Intergovernmental Relations, 1–2 November 2003.

McDonnell, R. (1992) *Justice for the Cree: Customary Beliefs and Practices*. Nemaska: Cree Regional Authority/Grand Council of the Crees.

Manitoba, Public Inquiry into the Administration of Justice and Aboriginal People (1991) *Report: Vol. I: The Justice System and Aboriginal People*. Winnipeg: Queen's Printer.

Moyer, S. and Axon, L. (1993) *An Implementation Evaluation of the Native Community Council Project of the Aboriginal Legal Services of Toronto*. Ontario: Ministry of the Attorney General.

Muirhead, G. (1981) *Analysis of Native Over-representation in Correctional Institutions in B.C.* Vancouver: Ministry of the Attorney General.

Nova Scotia, Royal Commission on the Donald Marshall, Jr, Prosecution (1989) *Commissioners' Report: Findings and Recommendations Vol. 1*. Halifax: Government Printer.

Osnaburgh/Windigo Tribal Council Justice Review Committee (1990) *Report of the Osnaburgh/Windigo Tribal Council Justice Review Committee*. Prepared for the Attorney General (Ontario) and Minister Responsible for Native Affairs and the

Solicitor General (Ontario).

Roach, K. (1995) Canadian public inquiries and accountability. In P. Stenning (ed.) *Accountability for Criminal Justice: Selected Essays*. Toronto: University of Toronto Press, pp. 268–93.

Roberts, J. (2002) *Responding to Over-representation of Aboriginal Offenders: Policy Implications of Correctional Trends in Canada*. Draft Paper.

Roberts, J. and Stenning, P. (2002) The sentencing of Aboriginal offenders in Canada: a rejoinder. *Saskatchewan Law Review*, 65(1): 75–95.

Seeman, N. (2001) Two kinds of justice is no justice at all. *Globe and Mail*, 6 December, p. A23.

Stenning, P. (2000) Independence and the Director of Public Prosecutions: the Marshall Inquiry and beyond. *Dalhousie Law Journal*, 23(2): 385–405.

Stenning, P. and Roberts, J. (2001) Empty promises: Parliament, the Supreme Court, and the sentencing of Aboriginal offenders. *Saskatchewan Law Review*, 64(1): 137–68.

Wildsmith, B. (1991) Getting at racism: the Marshall Inquiry. *Saskatchewan Law Review*, 55: 97–126.

Chapter 8

Penal truth comes to Europe: think tanks and the 'Washington consensus' on crime and punishment[1]

Loïc Wacquant

Over the past dozen years, a moral panic has been sweeping across Europe that is capable, by its scope and virulence, of redirecting state policies and durably remaking the character of the societies it affects. Its *apparent objective* – too apparent indeed since it has hogged public debate: 'youth' delinquency, 'urban violence', the disorders of which 'sensitive' or 'problem neighbourhoods' are taken to be the crucible, and the 'incivilities' of which their residents are believed to be both the prime victims and the foremost perpetrators. So many terms that one is well-advised to keep them in quotation marks, since their meaning is as vague as the phenomena they allegedly define – phenomena which nothing proves to be in any way specific to 'youths', to certain 'neighbourhoods' and still 'urban'. Yet one finds them characterised thus everywhere, and because of this very fact they appear to be self-evident. They swell the speeches of politicians, saturate the daily papers, invade and dominate television, and there is no shortage of media-savvy politologists and sociologists adept at surfing the wave of 'current issues' to deliver on-the-spot those 'minute-maid books' that, under the cover of 'debunking received ideas', grant them the dignity of *faits de société* or even categories of analysis.

Now, these notions did not spring spontaneously, ready-made, out of reality. They make use of a vast discursive constellation of terms and theses that come from America, on crime, violence, justice, inequality, and responsibility – of the individual, the 'community', the national collectivity – that have gradually insinuated themselves into European public debate to the point of serving as its framework and focus. These terms and theses owe the force of their power of persuasion to their sheer omnipresence and to the restored prestige of their originators.[2] The banalisation of these *topoi* conceals *a stake* that has little to do with the problems to which they ostensibly refer: namely, the redefinition of the perimeter and mission of the state, which is everywhere withdrawing from the economic arena and asserting the need to reduce its social role and to enlarge as well as harden its penal intervention. In the manner of a parent who for too long has been overly tender and lax, the European welfare state would henceforth be duty-bound to get 'lean and mean', to 'downsize', and then deal severely with its unruly flock by elevating 'security', narrowly defined in physical terms and not in terms of life risks (occupational, social, medical, educational, etc.), to the rank of paramount priority of public action.

This chapter traces how this emerging 'penal common sense' – a new configuration of self-evident 'truths' about crime and punishment aiming to criminalise poverty and thereby normalise precarious wage labour – has been incubated in America and is being internationalised alongside the neo-liberal economic ideology that it translates and complements in the realm of 'justice'. Three operations are distinguished in the transatlantic diffusion of these US-made *doxa* on 'security': (a) the gestation and dissemination, by American think tanks and their allies in the bureaucratic and journalistic fields, of terms, theses and measures that converge to penalise social insecurity and its consequences – a new kind of official discourse originating outside of government but assuming the tone of official authority and setting the agenda for renewed public action on crime; (b) their borrowing, through a work of adaptation to the national cultural idiom and state tradition, by the officials of the different receiving countries; (c) the 'academicisation' of the categories of neo-liberal understanding by pseudo-scientific research that serves to ratify the abdication of the social and economic state and to legitimise the bolstering of the penal state.

Withering away of the economic state, diminution and denigration of the social state, expansion and glorification of the penal state: civic 'courage', political 'modernity', even progressive boldness (under the marketing name of 'the third way' or 'social liberalism'), would now demand that one embrace the most worn-out law-and-order clichés and measures. 'Republicans, let us not be afraid!' is the gallant exhortation of the French proponents of a new state repression that bills itself 'of the left' – among them are two former ministers and an advisor of Mitterrand, an editorialist for the centre-left cultural weekly *Le Nouvel Observateur* and two directors of the catholic-left magazine *Esprit* – in an opinion piece published with much ado by *Le Monde* in September 1998 that openly expresses the new official thought on the subject: in the name of the people, in their well-understood (by us) interest, let us re-establish law and order so that we may snatch victory in 'the sprinting race that has now been entered into between reactionary restoration and republican radical reform'.[3]

One would need to reconstitute, link by link, the long chain of institutions, agents and discursive supports (advisers' memoranda, commission reports, official missions, parliamentary exchanges, expert panels, scholarly books and popular pamphlets, press conferences, newspaper articles and television reports, etc.) by which *the new penal common sense fashioned in America and aiming to criminalise poverty is being internationalised,* under forms more or less modified and unrecognisable (including sometimes by those who propagate them), in the wake of the new dominant economic and social ideology founded on radical individualism and unfettered commodification. Here, I shall content myself with selective indications bearing on the most visible channels, which nonetheless suffice to give an idea of the transcontinental scale and impact of this operation of worldwide ideological marketing. I shall also limit myself to the relations between the United States and Western Europe, noting that Washington's influence, on both the economic and penal planes, is even stronger in Latin America and – by a supreme irony of history – in many of the countries born of the break-up of the former Soviet empire.[4]

I shall likewise limit myself to retracing the impact of only one 'think tank' or policy institute each in the United States and in England even though it would be necessary, to give my analysis its full force, to reconstitute the complete network of multiplex relations that tie these manifold organisations to each other, on the one hand, and to a varied range of agents and institutions that occupy positions of power within the political, economic, journalistic and academic fields on the other. For the success of this or that protagonist (person or organisation) in the vast transcontinental traffic in ideas and public policies within which the internationalisation of the criminalisation of poverty takes place is not due to the 'influence' that it enjoys in its individual capacity – to suppose so would amount to taking the effect for the cause. It is due, rather, to the position that it occupies within the structure of relations of competition and collusion, subordination and dependence, that ties it to the whole set of the other protagonists, and which is at the principle of the effects it is capable of wielding. This much to stress, against the charismatic conception of the intellectual as lone knight mounted on his writings and armed with his sole ideas, and its collective complement, conspiracy theory, that the authors and organisations whose proposals and activities are analysed in this chapter are, from the angle that interests us here, nothing other than the personal and institutional materialisation of systems of material and symbolic forces that run through and beyond them.[5]

Manhattan, crucible of the new penal reason

The wide-ranging network of diffusion of the new penal common sense originates in Washington and New York City and crosses the Atlantic to lash itself down in London. From there, it stretches its channels and capillaries throughout the Continent and beyond. It is anchored by the complex formed by the organs of the American state officially entrusted with implementing and showcasing 'penal rigour', among them the Department of Justice (which periodically leads veritable *dis*information campaigns on crime and incarceration) and the State Department (which, through the agency of its embassies, actively proselytises, in each host country, in favour of ultra-repressive criminal justice policies, particularly regarding drugs), the semi-public and professional associations tied to the administration of police and corrections (the Fraternal Order of Police, the American Correctional Association, the American Jail Association, etc.), as well as the media and the commercial enterprises that partake of the punishment economy (private firms in the areas of detention, carceral health care, construction, identification and surveillance technologies, but also insurance and financing; see the overview by Donziger 1996: 63–8).

But, in this domain as in a good many others since the denunciation of the Fordist-Keynesian social compact, the private sector makes a decisive contribution to the conception and implementation of 'public policy'. In point of fact, the pre-eminent role assumed by neo-conservative 'think tanks' in the constitution and subsequent internationalisation of the new punitive *doxa* spotlights the organic bonds, ideological as well as practical, between the decline of the social wing of the state and the deployment of its penal arm. For the very foundations and institutes that paved the way for the advent of 'real (neo)liberalism' under Ronald Reagan and Margaret Thatcher by painstakingly undermining Keynesian notions and policies on the economic and social front between 1975 and 1985 (see especially Smith 1991) have operated, a decade later, as a pipeline feeding the political and media elites with concepts, principles and measures designed to both justify and speed up the establishment of a penal apparatus at once prolix and protean. The same parties, politicians, pundits and professors who yesterday mobilised, with readily observable success, in support of '*less* government' as concerns the prerogatives of capital and the utilisation of labour, are now demanding, with every bit as much fervour, '*more* government' to conceal and contain the deleterious social consequences, in the lower regions of social space, of the deregulation of wage labour and the deterioration of social protection.

On the American side, more so than the American Enterprise Institute, the Cato Institute or the Heritage Foundation, it is the Manhattan Institute that has popularised the discourses and policies aimed at repressing the 'disorders' fostered by those whom Alexis de Tocqueville already called 'the lowest rabble of our big cities'. In 1984, this organisation founded by Anthony Fischer (Margaret Thatcher's mentor) and William Casey (who would become CIA director during Reagan's first term as president) to apply market principles to social problems, launched *Losing Ground*, the book by Charles Murray (1984) that served as the 'bible' of Reagan's crusade against the welfare state. This tome massages and misinterprets data to 'demonstrate' that the persistence of poverty in America is due to the excessive generosity of policies intended to support the poor: such support, we are warned, rewards sloth and causes moral degeneracy among the lower classes, and it is directly responsible for this 'illegitimacy' that allegedly breeds all the ills of modern societies.

Having been consecrated the premier 'idea factory' of the New American Right federated around the trinity of the free market, individual responsibility and patriarchal values, and armed with a budget in excess of $5 million, the Manhattan Institute organised in the early 1990s a conference on the 'quality of life' that led to a special issue of its journal *City*. (This magazine sets as its goal to 'civilize the city' and invests heavily in this project: ten thousand copies of every issue are distributed free of charge to politicians, senior public officials, business-men and influential journalists, so that it has quickly become one of the main common references of the state decision-makers in the Northeast of the USA.) The key idea of the conference was that the 'sanctity of public space' is indispensable to urban life and, *a contrario*, that the 'disorder' in which the poorer classes revel is the natural breeding ground for crime. Among the participants in this 'debate' was the star federal prosecutor of New York City, Rudolph Giuliani, who had just lost the mayoral elections to the black Democrat David Dinkins, and who would draw from it the themes of his victorious campaign of 1993.[6] In particular, Giuliani took from this debate the guiding principles of the police and justice policy that would turn New York into the world showcase for the doctrine of 'zero tolerance' which gives the forces of order *carte blanche* to hunt out petty crime and to drive the homeless and the derelict back into dispossessed neighbourhoods.

It is yet again the Manhattan Institute that popularised the 'broken window theory' formulated in 1982 by George Kelling and James Q. Wilson (the leading light of conservative criminology in the United States) in an article published by the *Atlantic Monthly* magazine. A derivation of the popular saying 'he who steals an egg, steals an ox', this so-called theory (based on experiments by a Stanford psychologist on people's propensity to pilfer an abandoned car whose windows had been smashed) maintains that it is by fighting inch by inch the small disorders of everyday that one can vanquish the large pathologies of urban crime. The Institute's Center for Civic Initiative, whose objective is 'to research and promulgate creative, free-market solutions to urban problems', and which counts among its fellows Richard Schwartz, the architect of the Giuliani administration's 'workfare' programmes and CEO of Opportunity of America (a private 'job placement' firm for welfare recipients), financed and promoted the book by George Kelling and Catherine Coles (1996), *Fixing Broken Windows: Restoring Order and Reducing Crime in Our Communities.*[7]

The 'broken windows' theory, which has never been validated empirically, served as a criminological alibi for the reorganisation of police work instigated by William Bratton, the head of security for the New York City subway promoted to chief of the city's police. The primary objective of this reorganisation was to soothe the fear of the middle and upper classes – those that vote – by means of the continual harassment of the poor engaging in untoward behaviour in public spaces (streets, parks, transit stations, buses and subways, etc.). Towards this goal three means were deployed: large increases in the personnel and equipment of the police squads, the 're-engineering' of bureaucracy via the devolution of operational responsibilities to precinct captains with mandatory quantified target goals, and a computerised monitoring system that (together with its centralised database of criminal and cartographic information that can be consulted via portable computers on board patrol cars) makes possible the ongoing redeployment and almost instantaneous intervention of police forces, resulting in an inflexible enforcement of the law, particularly the sanction of such minor nuisances as drunkenness, public urination, disturbing the peace, panhandling, solicitation and 'other antisocial behaviors associated with the homeless', according to Kelling's own terminology.

It is this new policy that city leaders, but also the national and international media (followed by certain European researchers whose principal source of data on the American city is their dutiful reading, from Paris, London or Stockholm, of the *International Herald-Tribune*), are quick to credit for the decline in the crime rate posted by New York City in recent years – conveniently ignoring the fact that this decline *preceded* by several years the introduction of these police tactics, and the fact that crime has also dropped in cities that do not apply them. Among the 'lecturers' invited in 1998 by the Manhattan Institute at its prestigious 'luncheon forum' to enlighten the upper crust of politics, journalism and philanthropic and research foundations on the Eastern seaboard: William Bratton, billed as an 'international consultant' in urban policing, who cashed in on the glory of having 'reversed the crime epidemic' in New York City (and on the agony of having been fired by Giuliani for being more popular than the Mayor) with his pseudo-autobiography with which he preaches the new credo of 'zero tolerance' to the four corners of the globe (Knobler and Bratton 1998) – beginning with England, the land of welcome and acclimation chamber for these policies on their way to the conquest of Europe.

London: trading post and acclimation chamber

On the British side, the Adam Smith Institute, the Centre for Policy Studies and the Institute of Economic Affairs (IEA) have worked in concert to disseminate neo-liberal ideas in matters economic and social as well as the punitive theses elaborated in America and introduced under John Major before being carried forth and amplified by Tony Blair.[8] For example, in late 1989, the IEA (founded, like the Manhattan Institute, by Anthony Fischer, this time under the high intellectual patronage of Friedrich von Hayek) orchestrated at Rupert Murdoch's initiative and with much fanfare a series of meetings and publications around the 'thought' of Charles Murray. Murray used this platform to implore the British to hasten to roll back their profligate welfare state – absent the possibility of eliminating it – so as to check the emergence in the United Kingdom of a so-called 'underclass' of alienated, dissolute and dangerous poor, close cousins to the hordes said to be 'devastating' the cities of America in the wake of the 'lax' social measures implemented as part of the 'War Against Poverty' of the 1960s.[9]

This intervention, trumpeted by *The Sunday Times* and followed by a veritable blizzard of generally laudatory articles in the British press (in *The Times*, *The Independent*, *The Financial Times*, *The Guardian*, etc.), led to the publication of an edited volume in which one can read, alongside Murray's ruminations on the need to bring the weight of the 'civilizing force of marriage' to bear on 'young males [who] are essentially barbarians' and on their partners who are so prone to get pregnant since, for them, 'sex is fun and [having] babies endearing' (Murray 1990: 41–5), a chapter in which Frank Field (1990: 58–9), then charged with welfare in the Labour Party and Blair's future Minister of Welfare Reform, advocates punitive measures designed to prevent single mothers from having children and to force 'absentee fathers' to assume financial responsibility for their illegitimate offspring as well as an 'availability-to-work' test to push people into whatever employment slots are available. One discerns a solid consensus taking shape, between the most reactionary segment of the American right and the self-proclaimed avant-garde of the European 'New Left', around the idea that the 'undeserving poor' ought to be brought back under control by the (iron) hand of the state, and their errant behaviours corrected by public reprobation and by tightening the noose of administrative constraint and penal sanction.

By the time Murray returned to the attack in 1994, on the occasion of a London sojourn sponsored by *The Sunday Times* during which he again received generous and complacent press coverage, the notion of an antisocial 'underclass' was well established in the language of UK policy as well as in the social sciences – under the impulse of research bureaucracies anxious to demonstrate their usefulness by sticking close to the political-journalistic themes of the moment – so that he had little difficulty convincing his audience that his dismal predictions of 1989 had come true: 'illegitimacy', 'dependency' and crime, the three leading indicators of the growth of the loathsome 'underclass', had increased in unison among Albion's new poor and, together, they threatened the sudden death of Western civilisation (Lister 1996).[10] And so in 1995, it was the turn of his ideological comrade-in-arms, Lawrence Mead, the neo-conservative political scientist from New York University, to come and explain to the British at yet another IAE colloquium that, if the state must imperatively refrain from helping the poor materially, it behoves it to support them *morally* by imposing upon them the requirement of (substandard, low-pay) work. This is the theme, since made canonical by Tony Blair, of the 'obligations of citizenship' that purports to justify the mutation of welfare into workfare and the institution of forced wage labour under conditions that exempt persons 'dependent' on public aid from social and labour law – in 1996 in the United States and three years later in the United Kingdom (see Deacon 1997).

The paternalist state wished and called for by Lawrence Mead must also be a punitive state: in 1997, the IAE brought Charles Murray yet again, in order, this time, to promote before an audience of prominent policy-makers and hand-picked journalists the idea, much in vogue in American neo-conservative circles, that 'prison works', and that correctional expenditures are a reasoned and profitable investment for society.[11] (This thesis, supported by America's highest judicial authorities since the 1980s, is so glaringly untenable as soon as one ventures outside the borders of the United States, in view of the fact that there exists *no correlation whatsoever between crime rates and incarceration rates* on the international level, that the IEA had to resign itself to formulating it in the interrogative in its conference volume). Murray relies on a cooked-up statistical study by the US Department of Justice which concludes that, by the mere virtue of its 'neutralising' effect, the tripling of the incarcerated population of the United States between 1975 and 1989 prevented 390,000 murders, rapes and robberies in 1989 alone, to assert that 'short of the death penalty', prison is 'by far the most effective' means of 'restrain[ing] known, convicted criminals from murdering, raping, assaulting, burglarizing, and thieving'. And he articulates in these forthright terms the penal policy that should go hand in hand with the retrenchment of the social state: 'A lawful system has only a minor interest in the reasons why someone commits the crime. The criminal justice system is there to punish the guilty, exonerate the innocent, and serve the interests of the law-abiding' (Murray 1997: 19, 26). To put it plainly, the state need not concern itself with the causes of crime among the poorer classes, other than their 'moral poverty' (the new explanatory 'concept' in fashion), only with its consequences, which it should punish with zeal and efficacy.

A few months after Murray's visit, the IAE invited the former police chief of New York City, William Bratton, for purposes of advertising 'zero tolerance' at a press conference dressed up as a research colloquium, in which the police officials of Hartlepool, Strathclyde and Thames Valley took part (the first two having taken the initiative of introducing 'proactive policing' in their districts). This was only logical, since 'zero tolerance' is the indispensable police complement to the mass incarceration produced by the criminalisation of poverty in Great Britain no less than in America. At this meeting, which was again well covered by docile media, one learned that 'the forces of law and order in England and the United States agree more and more that criminal and subcriminal [*sic*] behaviors such as littering, verbal abuse, tagging, and vandalism should be firmly checked to prevent more serious criminal behaviors from developing' and that there is an urgent need to 'restore the morale of police officers who for years have been undermined by sociologists and criminologists who insist that crime is caused by factors, such as poverty, over which the police has no control'.

This pseudo-conference was prolonged, as is customary, by the publication of a collective book, *Zero Tolerance: Policing a Free Society* (Dennis *et al.* 1997), whose title summarises well its political philosophy: 'free', that is (neo)liberal and non-interventionist 'above', in matters of taxation and employment; intrusive and intolerant 'below', for everything to do with the public behaviours of the members of the working class caught in a pincer movement by the generalisation of underemployment and precarious labour, on the one hand, and the retrenchment of social protection schemes and the indigence of public services, on the other hand. Widely diffused among the experts and members of Tony Blair's government, these notions directly informed the law on Crime and Disorder voted by New Labour in 1998, widely recognised as the most repressive penal legislation of the postwar period. And to avoid any ambiguity as to the target of these measures, the British Prime Minister justified support for 'zero tolerance' in terms that could hardly be clearer: 'It is important that you say we don't tolerate the small crimes. The basic principle here is to say, yes it is right to be intolerant of people homeless on the streets.'[12]

From the United Kingdom, where they constitute the yardstick by which all authorities are henceforth enjoined to measure their police and judicial practices, the notions and measures promoted by the neoconservative 'think tanks' of the United States and their British trading posts have spread throughout Western Europe, in Sweden, Holland, Belgium, Spain, Italy, Germany, and France. So much so that it is difficult nowadays for an official of a European government to express him or herself on 'security' without some 'Made in USA' slogan coming out of his or her mouth, be it dressed up, as national honour no doubt demands, with the adjective 'republican' or qualified by '*à la*' (French, Spanish, German, etc.). Vitriolic denunciations of 'rampant crime' and increased surveillance of 'problem neighbourhoods', curfews for 'youth' in immigrant areas and the diligent targeting of petty drug violators, the erosion of the juridical boundary between minors and adults, increased imprisonment of repeat offenders, deregulation and privatisation of criminal justice services, 'zero tolerance', 'prison works': all these mottos, notions and policies forged by neo-conservative think tanks in the United States and their British trading posts have spread throughout Western Europe where they foster the transition from a social-welfare to a penal management of rising marginality in the dualising metropolis. The crown of the hypocrisy or ignorance of politicians on the Continent is that their proponents present them as national innovations necessitated by the unprecedented evolution of 'urban violence' and crime in their localities.

Importers and collaborators

Indeed, it is plain that the export of these law-and-order themes and theses hatched in America for the purpose of reaffirming society's moral ascendancy over its 'undeserving' poor and bending the (sub)proletariat to the discipline of the new labour market is thriving only because it is meeting with *the interest and approval of the authorities of the importing countries*. This approval assumes a variety of forms, ranging from the jingoistic enthusiasm of Tony Blair to the shameful and awkwardly denegated acceptance of Lionel Jospin, with a whole range of positions in between (as testified by Schröder's oscillations between these two poles). This implies that that one must include among the agents of this transnational enterprise of symbolic conversion – an enterprise aimed at making the new *punitive ethos*, necessary to justify the rise of the penal state, accepted as self-evident by universalising its self-proclaimed truths (within the narrow circle of the capitalist countries that think of themselves as the universe, that is) – the leaders and officials of the European states who, one after the other, are converting to the imperative of the 'restoration' of (republican) order after having converted to the benefits of the ('free') market and the necessity of a smaller (social) state. In those fallow areas where the state has given up on bringing in firms and jobs, it will put up in their stead police stations and patrols, perhaps in anticipation of building prisons later. The expansion of the policing and penal apparatus can even make a significant contribution to the creation of jobs in the surveillance of those who have been expelled from the world of work by capitalist restructuring: the 20,000 'adjunct security officers' and 15,000 'local mediation agents', who are expected to be massed in 'sensitive neighbourhoods' before the end of 1999 in France, represent a good tenth of the 'youth jobs' promised by the Socialist government.

The countries that import the American instruments of a resolutely offensive penality, fit for the enlarged missions incumbent upon the police, courts and penitentiary in advanced neo-liberal society, do not content themselves with passively receiving these tools. They often borrow them on their own initiative and they always adapt them to their needs as well as to their national traditions (political and intellectual). Such is the purpose of those 'study missions' that have multiplied in recent years across the Atlantic. Following in the steps of Gustave de Beaumont and Alexis de Tocqueville, who set out in the spring of 1831 on a carceral excursion on the 'classical soil of the penitentiary system', elected officials, high-ranking civil servants and penologists of the European Union's member countries regularly make the pilgrimage to

New York, Los Angeles and Houston, with the aim of 'penetrating the mysteries of American discipline' and the hope of activating the 'hidden springs' of its inner workings back in their own homeland.[13] Thus, it was in the wake of such a mission, graciously financed by Corrections Corporation of America, the leading private incarceration firm in the United States (and the world) – as measured by sales (over $400 million), inmates (almost 50,000) and the yield of its stock on the NASDAQ market (its value multiplied forty-fold between 1988 and 1998) – that Sir Edward Gardiner, head of the Commission on Interior Affairs in the House of Lords, was able to discover the virtues of prison privatisation and to steer the United Kingdom onto the road to for-profit imprisonment. He later demonstrated that his personal endorsement of privatisation was sincere by taking up a position on the board of directors of one of the main firms that compete for the booming and lucrative punishment market: the number of inmates in British private prisons exploded from 200 in 1993 to nearly 4,000 in 1999.

Another medium for the diffusion of the new penal common sense in Europe is official reports, those *pre-thought* writings by means of which politicians cloak the decisions they intend to make for purely political (and often narrowly electoral) reasons[14] in the garb of the pseudo-science that those researchers most attuned to the state-media problematic of the moment are particularly adept at producing on command. These reports are based on the following (sucker) contract: in return for a fleeting media notoriety – which the hired researcher will apply him or herself to cashing into academic prebends and privileges in the most hetero-nomous sectors of the university field – he or she agrees to abjure intellectual autonomy, which would require *ex definitione* a break with the official definition of the 'social problem' assigned and to analyse its political, administrative and journalistic *pre*-construction. To take a recent French example: this would mean tracing the invention and political usages of the recently proliferating category of *'violences urbaines'*, which is a pure *bureaucratic artefact* devoid of statistical coherence and sociological consistency, rather than docilely embarking on a quest for its presumed causes and possible remedies (as done by Body-Gendrot, 1998, Le Guennec and Herrou 1998).

These reports typically rely on the support provided by reports produced under analogous circumstances and according to similar canons in the societies taken as 'models' or singled out for a 'comparison' that typically boils down to fantasised projection, such that the governmental common sense of a given country finds a warrant in the state common sense of its neighbours through a process of circular reinforcement and mutual misrecognition. One example among others:

one is dumbfounded to discover as an appendix to the official report of the mission given by French Prime Minister Jospin to two socialist house representatives, Christine Lazerges and Jean-Pierre Balduyck, on *Responses to Juvenile Delinquency*, a note by Hubert Martin, Adviser for Social Affairs at the French Embassy in the United States, which delivers a veritable panegyric on the curfews imposed on teenagers in major American cities (Lazerges and Balduyck 1998). This zealous civil servant parrots, without voicing the slightest doubt or the most timid criticism, the results of a dubious survey in the form of a plea carried out and published by the National Association of Mayors of the big cities of the United States with the express aim of defending this police gimmick that occupies a choice place in their media 'showcase' on crime and safety. According to the accounts of their promoters, which, conveniently, no serious study comes to qualify or correct (although there exists a good number of such studies, and they are not difficult to find), the institution of such curfews is supposed to be 'a useful tool for the maintenance of public order' because it stimulates the sense of responsibility of parents and prevents acts of violence through a 'good use of the time and services of the police', thanks to 'serious preparation of the field aimed at obtaining a local consensus'.

This official of the French government thus makes himself the mouthpiece of the American mayors who 'have the feeling' that curfews 'have contributed to the current decline in juvenile delinquency'. In reality, these programmes have no measurable impact on delinquency, which they merely displace in time and space. They are very onerous in personnel and resources, as they make it necessary to arrest, process, transport and eventually detain tens of thousands of youths every year who have not contravened any law (more than 100,000 in 1993, or twice the number of minors arrested for theft, excluding car theft). And, far from being the object of a 'local consensus', as Hubert claims, they are vigorously fought in the courts on account of their discriminatory enforcement and their repressive purpose, which contributes to criminalising youths of colour in segregated neighbourhoods (see, for example, among several quantitative studies, Ruefle and Reynolds 1995). One sees in passing how a police measure devoid of effects – other than criminogenic and liberticidal – and shorn of justifications – other than as a media ploy – manages to generalise itself, each country invoking the 'success' of the others as a pretext for adopting a technique of surveillance and harassment, which, although it fails everywhere, finds itself validated by the very fact of its wide diffusion.

The academic pidgin of neo-liberal penal thought

First there is the gestation and dissemination, national and then international, by the American think tanks and their allies in the bureaucratic and journalistic fields, of terms, theories and measures that, articulated together, converge to penalise social insecurity and its consequences. Second comes their borrowing, partial or wholesale, conscious or unconscious, necessitating a more or less elaborate work of adaptation to the cultural idiom and state traditions peculiar to the different receiving countries by the officials who then implement them, each in his domain of competence. A third operation redoubles this work and accelerates the traffic in the categories of neo-liberal understanding, which circulate now in rush production mode from New York City to London, and then on to Paris, Brussels, Munich, Milan and Madrid: their 'academicisation', that is dressing them up in scholarly garb.

It is through the agency of exchanges, interventions and publications of an academic kind, real or simulated, that intellectual 'smugglers' (*passeurs*) reformulate these categories in a sort of *politological pidgin*, sufficiently concrete to 'hook' political decision-makers and journalists anxious to 'stick close to reality' (as projected by the authorised vision of the social world), but sufficiently abstract to strip those categories of any overly flagrant idiosyncrasy that would tie them back to their originating national context. And so these notions become semantic commonplaces where all those meet up who, across the boundaries of occupation, organisation, nationality and even political affiliation, spontaneously think advanced neo-liberal society as it wishes to be thought.

We find a striking illustration of this in that exemplary specimen of false research on a false object entirely *pre-constructed* by the political-journalistic common sense of the day, and subsequently 'verified' by data gleaned from news magazine articles, opinion polls and official publications, but duly 'authenticated', in the eyes of the novice reader at least, by a few quick visits to the neighbourhoods incriminated (in the literal sense of the term), in the book by Sophie Body-Gendrot (1998), *Cities Confront Insecurity: From the American Ghettos to the French Banlieues*.[15] The title is by itself a sort of prescriptive précis of the new state *doxa* on the question: it suggests that it is now *de rigueur* to think about the new police and penal rigour, which it proclaims to be at once inescapable, urgent and beneficial. One short citation, drawn from the book's opening lines, will suffice here:

> The inexorable growth of phenomena of urban violence plunges all the specialists into perplexity. Must we opt for 'all-out repression',

concentrate our means on prevention, or seek a middle road? Must we fight the symptoms or attack the deep causes of violence and delinquency? According to a public opinion poll...

One has here, conveniently gathered in one place, all the ingredients of the pseudo political science that is gobbled up by the technocrats of ministerial staffs and the 'Debate' pages of major dailies: as the point of departure, a fact that is anything but established ('inexorable growth') but which, one maintains, disconcerts even 'specialists' (it is not said which ones, and for good reason); a category of bureaucratic understanding ('urban violence') under which each can put whatever suits him or her, since it corresponds to just about nothing; a public opinion poll that measures little more than the activity of the institute that produced it (and the coverage of the newspapers which commission such polls); and a series of false alternatives answering to a logic of bureaucratic intervention (repression or prevention) which the researcher sets out to resolve even though they have already been implicitly settled in the way the question is formulated. Everything that follows, a kind of catalogue of American clichés about France and French clichés about America, will allow the writer to present *in fine* as a 'middle way', in conformity with reason (of state), the penal drift advocated by the socialist government currently in place if the country is to avert disaster – the back-cover of the book hails the citizen-reader thus: 'It is a matter of great urgency: by 'reinvesting' entire neighborhoods, one seeks to prevent the middle classes from sliding towards extreme political solutions' (read: the National Front).[16] An added precision: by reinvesting them with police officers, not with jobs.

By means of a twofold, crossed projection onto each other of the national pre-notions of the two countries considered, this American-ologist in favour with the French Interior Ministry[17] manages at the same time to tack onto French neighbourhoods with high concentrations of public housing the American mythology of the ghetto as a territory of dereliction (rather than as instrument of *racial domination*, which is hardly the same thing – see Wacquant 1998), and to force the ghettoised areas of New York City and Chicago into the French administrative fiction of the 'sensitive neighbourhood' (*quartier sensible*), a bureaucratic term designed to efface the responsibility of the state in creating areas of urban dispossession. Hence a series of pendulum swings passing themselves off as an analysis, in which the United States is utilised, not as one element in a methodical comparison – which would reveal at once that the alleged 'inexorable rise' in 'urban violence' is above all a political and media thematic designed to facilitate the redefinition of social problems in terms of security (and thence 'law and order' – see, on this subject, the incisive study by Beckett 1997) – but rather by turns as bogeyman to be shunned and as model to be emulated, albeit with precaution. By raising, in a first moment, the spectre of 'convergence', the United States serves to elicit horror – the ghetto, never that in our society! – and to dramatise discourse so as better to justify taking 'entire neighbourhoods' into police hands. It then remains only to sing the Tocquevillian refrain of grassroots citizen initiative, this time expanded on a world scale (since, thanks to globalisation, 'inhabitants of the entire planet have discovered a common identity for themselves, that of Resistance fighters for democracy' [sic]), to justify the importation into France of American techniques for the local enforcement of public order.

At the end of a meandering essay fit for Poli-Sci undergraduates on the hackneyed theme of 'the city as social laboratory', the 'stakes of the post-city' and (to put on a truly scientific air) 'operational criminality in a fractal world', about which the author asserts – no joke – that its 'script is borrowed from Mandelbaum's mathematical theories on fractalization', Body-Gendrot puts forth this forceful conclusion, which seems to have come right out of a Manhattan Institute 'luncheon forum': notwithstanding the 'French regal might' which regrettably 'slows the transformation of mentalities', *governments are gradually surrendering to the evident facts:* community-based management of problems must be developed, juvenile crime police squads bolstered, the training of officers intensified, parents held criminally responsible' and 'every delinquent act by a minor punished in a systematic, swift, and visible manner' (Body-Gendrot 1998: 346, 332, 320–1, my italics).[18] These self-evident facts are henceforth shared in New York, London, and Paris, and they impose themselves a little more each day in the other European capitals by an effect of imitation – even Sweden is wondering whether it should inflict 'zero tolerance' on itself in order to get in line with its continental neighbours to the south.

In short, *Les Villes face à l'insécurité* comes at just the right moment to ratify the abdication of the social (and economic) state and to legitimise the bolstering of the penal state in formerly working-class neighbour-hoods sacrificed on the altar of the 'modernisation' of French capitalism. Like most works which have recently sprouted forth on the 'feeling of insecurity', 'incivilities' and 'urban violence', this book is part and parcel of the very phenomenon it purports to explain: far from supplying an analysis of it, it contributes to the political construction of a strengthened and proactive penality entrusted with containing the disorders caused by the generalisation of unemployment, underemployment and precarious wage work.

The expression 'Washington consensus' is commonly used to designate the panoply of measures of 'structural adjustment' imposed by the rulers of global finance on debtor nations as a condition for international aid (with the disastrous results that were in glaring evidence in Russia and Asia in the late 1990s), and, by extension, the neo-liberal economic policies that have triumphed in all Western capitalist countries over the past two decades: budgetary austerity and fiscal regression, cutbacks in public expenditures and the strengthening of the rights of capital, the unbridled opening of financial markets and foreign exchanges, privatisation, the flexibilisation of wage work and the reduction of social protection.[19] It is now necessary to extend this notion to encompass the punitive treatment of the social insecurity and urban marginality that are the socio-logical consequences of such economic policies.

Notes

1. This is a revised and abridged version of a paper that first appeared as 'How penal common sense comes to Europeans: notes on the transatlantic diffusion of neoliberal doxa,' *European Societies*, vol. 1 n. 3 (Fall 1999), pp. 319–52.
2. On the social conditions and mechanisms of cultural diffusion of this new planetary accepted reading, whose fetish-terms, seemingly shot up out of nowhere, are nowadays everywhere – 'globalisation' and 'flexibility', 'multi-culturalism' and 'communitarianism', 'ghetto' or 'underclass', and their 'postmodern' cousins: identity, minority, ethnicity, fragmentation, etc. (see Bourdieu and Wacquant 1999).
3. Régis Debray, Max Gallo, Jacques Juillard, Blandine Kriegel, Olivier Mongin, Mona Ozouf, Anicet LePors, and Paul Thibaud, 'Républicains, n'ayons pas peur', *Le Monde*, 4 September 1998 (the number and supposed dispersal across the political spectrum of the signatories aim to give the appearance of neutrality and thus of reason to the position being advocated).
4. These regions, however, have the (convenient) excuse of rates of homicidal violence comparable to that of the United States, and some of them are also directly subordinated, economically and diplomatically, to the United States. Such is the case with Mexico, which has to writhe before the U.S. Congress each winter to prove that it is waging the 'War on Drugs' ordered by its 'Big Brother to the North' with the requisite fortitude and zest.
5. On this crucial distinction between 'empirical' individual (or institution) and 'epistemic' individual (or institution), see Bourdieu (1988: 21–35).
6. All the accounts of the Manhattan Institute's rise on the public scene describe Giuliani furiously filling up his notepad at these conferences and report the regular presence of his advisors at key meetings held there.
7. The original article which is extended and illustrated by the book is James Q. Wilson and George Kelling (1982), 'Broken windows: the police and neighborhood safety'. If this 'common sense theory' is true, one wonders why it took

more than fifteen years to realise it.

8. They were later joined by Demos, the officially accredited 'think tank' of Tony Blair's team, which plays a similar role from 'across' the political divide.

9. 'I arrived in Great Britain earlier this year, a visitor from a plague area come to see whether the disease is spreading' (Murray 1990: 25). On the origins and social usages of the pseudo-concept of 'underclass', which is now in circulation in several European countries, see Wacquant (1996).

10. Murray's rhetoric relies on a dichotomous opposition between 'the new Victorians' (a term designating the middle and upper classes who are allegedly rediscovering the virtues of work, abstinence and the patriarchal family) and 'the New Rabble' of the dregs of society, mired in promiscuity, the rejection of (underpaid) work and predatory crime.

11. As in 1989 and 1994, The *Sunday Times* kindly accorded full pages to a two-part article by Charles Murray that gave it an instant national visibility that no lifelong British student of crime and prison has ever enjoyed, even though (or perhaps because) Murray's sophomoric statements are a mere rehash of well-worn works by America's leading conservative criminologists and crime ideologues such as James Q. Wilson and John DiIulio.

12. Tony Blair's statement was reprinted by *The Guardian* on 10 April 1997. I am grateful to Richard Sparks, Professor of Criminology at Keele University, for the precise information he supplied on these developments.

13. The expressions in quotation marks are those of Gustave de Beaumont and Alexis de Tocqueville (in Tocqueville 1984: 11).

14. That is to say, in the present conjuncture in France (spring 1999), to attract the voters of the *Front National*, particularly those left disoriented by the party's abrupt split in December 1998. This is the banal explanation for the sudden speeding up of the measures announced by the Jospin government to 're-establish' (republican) order and to 'reconquer' the *banlieues* (declining housing estates) – another term borrowed from the military language of the American state and its 'War on Crime', which would have us believe that these *banlieues* have been 'invaded' by an enemy (immigrants). This also explains the sudden about-turn of the same Prime Minister in favour of increased criminalisation of juvenile delinquency, as the latter was propelled to the rank of priority for state action, even though a close-up examination of the existing statistics published in the official report submitted to the government on the question (which apparently neither its authors nor its sponsors took the trouble to read attentively) demonstrates that the physiognomy of juvenile delinquency has hardly changed in recent years, contrary to media and political hype (cf. the appendix by criminologist Bruno Aubusson de Cavarlay (1998a), 'Statistiques'; see also Aubusson de Cavarlay (1998b).

15. According to the law of the genre, the book mixes scientific works (to give authority to its pronouncements) and journalistic reporting (to be accessible to decision-makers and the media), as attested by the motley mix of its references, which have Jean Baudrillard rubbing shoulders with William Julius Wilson, articles from *Science* with pieces from the *International Herald-Tribune*, interviews with judges, editorials from the fadish news magazine *Le Nouvel Observateur* and pamphlets by former members of the Reagan Administration.

16. The promotional flyer sent by the publisher for the book's launch asks the question more abruptly still: 'Between the French *banlieues* and the American ghettos, *convergences exist*: a rise in youth delinquency, drugs, fighting among gangs, etc. For all that, can the policies of massive incarceration that have been *successfully* adopted in the United States apply in France?' (my italics).

17. Jean-Pierre Chevênement, the minister in charge of police, had previously commissioned her to write a 'Report on Urban Violence' and the Interministerial Agency for City Policy financed the 'mission' of a few weeks which permitted her to 'live some experiences in the sensitive neighbourhoods of the United States' (*sic*).

18. The work closes on the following moving flight of moralising lyricism, which easily rivals magazine politology, and which no Minister for Urban Affairs would repudiate, even one belonging to the Socialist Party: 'Let the police be placed at the service of the inhabitants, let the school be a neighbourhood's locus of life, let elected officials deploy citizen innovations, let the struggle against crime become also the business of the residents, and you will see another horizon dawn on the City.' In other words, when city life is good, it will be jolly good.

19. On the construction of this notion at the intersection of the academic and bureaucratic fields, see the provocative article by Dezalay and Garth (1998).

References

Aubusson de Cavarlay, B. (1998a) Statistiques. In C. Lazerges and J.-P. Balduyck, *Réponses à la délinquance des mineurs; Mission interministerielle sur la prévention et le traitement de la délinquance des mineurs*. Paris: La Documentation française, pp. 263–91.

Aubusson de Cavarlay, B. (1998b) *La mesure de la délinquance juvénile*. Paris: Cesdip.

Beckett, K. (1997) *Making Crime Pay: Law and Order in Contemporary American Politics*. Oxford: Oxford University Press.

Body-Gendrot, S. (1998) *Les Villes face à l'insécurité: Des ghettos américains aux banlieues françaises*. Paris: Bayard éditions,

Body-Gendrot, S., Le Guennec, N. and Herrou, N. (1998) *Mission sur les violences urbaines; Rapport au Ministère de l'intérieur*. Paris: Bayard Éditions.

Bourdieu, P. ([1984] 1988) *Homo Academicus*. Cambridge: Polity Press.

Bourdieu, P. and Wacquant, L. ([1998] 1999) On the cunning of imperialist reason. *Theory, Culture and Society*, 16: 41–57.

Deacon, A. (ed.) (1997) *From Welfare to Work: Lessons from America*. London: Institute of Economic Affairs.

Dennis, N. *et al.* (1997) *Zero Tolerance: Policing a Free Society*. London: Institute of Economic Affairs.

Dezalay, Y. and Garth, B. (1998) Le 'Washington consensus': contribution à une sociologie de l'hégémonie du néolibéralisme. *Actes de la recherche en sciences sociales*, 121–122: 2–22.

Donziger, S. (1996) *The Real War on Crime*. New York: Basic Books.

Field, F. (1990) Britain's underclass: countering the growth. In C. Murray (ed.) *The*

Emerging British Underclass. London: Institute of Economic Affairs.

Kelling, G. and Coles, C. (1996) *Fixing Broken Windows: Restoring Order and Reducing Crime in Our Communities*. New York: Free Press.

Knobler, P. and Bratton, W. (1998) *Turnaround: How America's Top Cop Reversed the Crime Epidemic*. New York: Random House.

Lazerges, C. and Balduyck, J.-P. (1998) *Réponses à la délinquance des mineurs; Mission interministérielle sur la prévention et le traitement de la délinquance des mineurs*. Paris: La Documentation française.

Lister, R. (ed.) (1996) *Charles Murray and the Underclass. The Developing Debate*. London: Institute of Economic Affairs.

Murray, C. (1984) *Losing Ground. American Social Policy 1950–1980*. New York: Basic Books.

Murray, C. (ed.) (1990) *The Emerging British Underclass*. London: Institute of Economic Affairs.

Murray, C. (ed.) (1997) *Does Prison Work?* London: Institute of Economic Affairs.

Ruefle, W. and Reynolds, K. (1995) Curfews and delinquency in major American cities. *Crime and Delinquency*, 41: 347–63.

Smith, J. (1991) *The Idea Brokers. Think Tanks and the Rise of the New Policy Elite*. New York: Free Press.

Tocqueville, A. de (1984) Le Système pénitentiaire aux États-Unis et son application en France. In *Oeuvres complètes. Vol. IV: Écrits sur le système pénitentiaire en France et à l'étranger*. Paris: Gallimard.

Wacquant, L. (1996) L'underclass urbaine dans l'imaginaire social et scientifique américain. In S. Paugam (ed.) *L'Exclusion: l'état des savoirs*. Paris: Éditions La Découverte,

Wacquant, L. (1998) ' "A Black city within the White": revisiting America's dark ghetto'. *Black Renaissance – Renaissance Noire*, 2: 141–51.

Wilson, J.Q. and Kelling, G. (1982) Broken windows: the police and neighborhood safety. *Atlantic Monthly*, March: 29–38.

Part 3
Official discourse as closure, healing or crisis management

Chapter 9

From Brixton to Bradford: official discourse on race and urban violence in the United Kingdom

John Lea

Recourse to riot by those dispossessed of any other means of representing their interests or simply defending themselves from attack and harassment has a long history (Hobsbawm 1959). What is perhaps more remarkable is its survival into the mature liberal democracies of advanced capitalism. In the United States since the Second World War the riots in Los Angeles (1965), Detroit and many other cities (1967), in Los Angeles following the police beating of Rodney King together with numerous lesser disturbances have all been theatres in which the grievances of the poor and socially excluded have been played out. In the United Kingdom, which is the focus of this chapter, during the same period numerous disturbances, though small by comparison with the American examples, have concentrated the minds of political and policy-making elites. 1958 saw the first postwar disturbances in the Notting Hill area of London. During the 1980s there were significant disturbances in Bristol (1980), London, Bradford and Liverpool (1981), and in Birmingham and other Midland towns (1985). The 1990s saw outbreaks in the North East, Oxford and Bristol (1991–2), and Bradford (1995). The beginning of the present century was greeted with further outbreaks of rioting in Bradford, Burnley and Oldham (2001)

A notable feature of all the incidents mentioned here, on both sides of the Atlantic, has been their connection with race and ethnicity. While by no means all participants in the riots have been ethnic minorities, racism and the various injustices of discrimination, blocked opportunity and police harassment which continue to be visited upon non-white communities in the advanced capitalist democracies have been major components. Whatever else they indicate about social fractures and the state of the poor, riots have almost always been read as barometers of the state of ethnic relations.

Most of these events have called forth official or semi-official inquiries chaired variously by judges, politicians and bureaucrats (rarely, if at all, by social scientists). Over time these come to serve as museums of official discourse through which the practical working out, and metamorphosis, of dominant political ideologies about the relationship between ethnicity and social stability are revealed. This chapter will trace these ideological shifts in the context of major official inquiries into ethnic-related urban violence in the United Kingdom from the Scarman Report of 1982 to the recent official investigations of events in the North of England in 2001

Colour and citizenship

The disturbances of 1958 in which gangs of white youth attacked members of the small and recently arrived West Indian community in West London focused the mind of the political elite on the need for a 'race relations' strategy. Immigrants from the Commonwealth were being drawn in to meet shortages of low wage labour during the postwar economic boom. As Commonwealth citizens they had permanent residence rights and would eventually aspire to full social citizenship. If their aspirations, particularly those of the second and subsequent generations, to upward social mobility were blocked by racial discrimination then further social tensions could be envisaged. But if full integration took place then of course they would less readily accept their role as a low-wage labour force. The resolution of this dilemma involved two components. First, the focus of recruitment of low-wage labour would be switched from Commonwealth immigrants with permanent settlement rights to migrant labourers with short-term work permits drawn from non-Commonwealth countries. As numbers of the former were progressively restricted the latter expanded (Lea 1980).

Second, positive steps would be taken to speed the integration of existing ethnic minorities of Commonwealth origin by means of legal outlawing of discrimination combined with the establishment of new institutions to promote an ethnic integration which, in the words of the then Home Secretary Roy Jenkins speaking in 1966, would be seen '... not as a flattening process of assimilation but as equal opportunity accompanied by cultural diversity in an atmosphere of mutual tolerance' (Rose and Deakin 1969: 25). Of major importance was the fact that the new institutions tended to circumnavigate rather than confront the major structures of power and ethnic segregation. Rather than affirmative action or a frontal assault on labour market discrimination the National Committee for Commonwealth Immigrants (later the Commission for Racial Equality) and its local committees and funded projects emphasised ethnic identity and cultural issues. Thus the 'multiculturalist settlement' (Kundnani 2002) which became the foundation stone of British race relations policy for over three decades established structures which

> did not integrate the Third World immigrants into the politics of institutionalised class conflict that characterise the liberal collectivist age, but rather set up alternative political structures to deflect the politics of race from Westminster to the National Committee for Commonwealth Immigrants, and from local political arenas to the voluntary liaison committees. (Katznelson 1973)

Official discourse thus incorporated the multiculturalist settlement: initially as the basis for an understanding of the dynamics of 'good race relations' and then, as we shall see, as an explanation of their collapse.

The first problem was that integration failed to get off the ground. During the late 1960s and the 1970s numerous commentators pointed to a lack of social mobility of blacks into the mainstream (Rex and Tomlinson 1979). Entrenched white racism, manifested in the temporary growth of support for Enoch Powell and the extreme right National Front during the mid-1970s, combined with a rate of economic growth insufficient to overcome discrimination in labour and housing markets for existing ethnic minorities of Commonwealth origin. A black middle class emerged but it remained small and weak, certainly not an effective stabilising leadership. Established black working-class communities remained concentrated in the same labour market positions as they had entered on initial immigration. By the end of the 1970s they were suffering high unemployment rates, particularly concentrated among second-generation youth.

Rescuing multiculturalism: Scarman and the riots of 1981

Black unemployed youth spent a high proportion of time on the streets and bore the brunt of an aggressive policing style which, by intensive use of blanket 'stop and search' tactics, maximised the alienation of police from the black community (Lea and Young 1993). These tensions came to a head towards the end of the 1970s and during the next decade. They generally involved street confrontations between black youth and police. The main disturbances took place in 1976 in Bradford, 1980 in Bristol (St Pauls), 1981 in London (Brixton) and Liverpool (Toxteth) and 1985 in Birmingham (Handsworth) and other Midland towns.

Brixton was the most important. The disturbances of 10–12 April 1981 were provoked by *Swamp 81*, a police operation involving aggressive stop and search directed at black youth. The response saw several hundred young people involved in building barricades, overturning cars and using petrol bombs for the first time on mainland UK. Twenty-eight buildings were destroyed or damaged by fire and 279 police officers were recorded as injured. While the immediate government response was to characterise the events as an outburst of criminality, the rapid initiation of an inquiry by a senior High Court Judge, Lord Scarman, brought forth a report which is a classic of its type (Scarman 1981).

Scarman showed a sensitivity to the problems of young blacks whose 'lives are led largely in the poorer and more deprived areas of our great cities. Unemployment and poor housing bear on them very heavily: and the educational system has not adjusted itself satisfactorily to their needs. Their difficulties are intensified by the sense they have of a concealed discrimination against them' (Scarman 1981: para. 2.35). It is hardly surprising then that many of them '... live their lives on the street, having often nothing better to do: they make their protest there ... The recipe for a clash with the police is therefore ready-mixed: and it takes little, or nothing, to persuade them that the police, representing an establishment which they see as insensitive to their plight, are their enemies' (*ibid.* para. 2.37). Scarman went as far as it is possible to go within his liberal paternalist framework to understand the viewpoint of the rioters. Many young blacks 'believe with justification, that violence, though wrong, is a very effective means of protest: for, by attracting the attention of the mass media of communication they get their message across to the people as a whole (*ibid.* para. 2.38).

Brixton was thus read, by Scarman at least, as a demand for inclusion in social citizenship rights by those who had become marginalised through a combination of racial discrimination and economic decay. His proposed reforms were directed to this end. He criticised the tactics of 'hard policing' such as mass stop and search operations like operation 'Swamp 81'. He did not for a moment doubt that such operations were 'necessary to combat street crime' (*ibid.*: para. 7.2). Rather he recommended that such stops be made more rule governed through a process of written recording of the reasons for such stops and searches. This was made statutory for some categories of stops under the Police and Criminal Evidence Act of 1984 (PACE). Such police actions against street crime would, moreover, be more acceptable to local communities if the latter were consulted about such operations and their interests taken into account by police managers. 'Community relations are central, not peripheral, to the police function. I question whether this truth was as fully understood by all concerned before the riots as it is now' (*ibid.*: para 4.80). He called for local police–community liaison committees. These were made statutory under PACE.

Finally, Scarman saw the existence of 'ill-considered, immature and racially prejudiced actions of some officers in their dealings on the streets with young black people' (*ibid.*: para. 4.63) as a factor in the breakdown in relations with the black community. Besides the direct individual racism of 'bad apples' in the police force there was the fact that public bodies, including the police, may adopt practices which are 'unwittingly discriminatory against black people' (*ibid.*: para. 2.22). He failed, however, to elaborate this observation into a more developed theory of what later came to be called 'institutional racism'.[1] He did make explicit, however, that 'police attitudes and methods have not yet sufficiently responded to the problem of policing our multi-racial society' (*ibid.*: para. 4.70).

The orientation of the Scarman Report was that of the relationship between the community and the state, crystallised as the relationship between black youth and the police. Scarman's aim was to secure the effective citizenship of the black community by eliminating discriminatory attitudes and practices on the part of the police and ensuring effective representation, through consultation, of local interests in police policy-making.[2] Scarman's liberalism was reinforced by the methodology of the *judicial inquiry* over which he presided. This contrasted with that of the bureaucratic *investigation into pathology* chaired by a civil servant or other bureaucrat. If the latter reinforces the silence and subordination of the *problem population* under examination, the former gave a voice to the poor – even if for a fleeting moment – as *party to a dispute* on equal terms to other parties, notably the police.

The implications of Scarman and of the riots more generally were thus understood by the political elite as urging a speeding up and reinforcement of the existing strategies designed to integrate black communities: an intensification of the multiculturalist settlement. Consequently, as well as the particular reforms affecting policing noted already, there was a further intensification, during the 1980s, of the strategies outlined already. The Commission for Racial Equality acquired progressively greater legal powers to act against discrimination in widening areas of public life.[3] Police–community liaison committees in black communities became part of a spectrum of consultation commit-tees, race awareness training and equal opportunities policies. But, alongside, this developed mechanisms of local funding for community projects allocated along ethnic lines. These latter were particularly emphasised in Labour local authorities and the London-wide local authority, the Greater London Council.[4]

The positive role of such activities was obvious. They were able to short-circuit entrenched discrimination by giving ethnic minorities direct access to funding and resources for the development of their own community life. Many black people were able to move into influential positions, particularly in local government and politics. The mid-1980s also saw a flourishing of a more general 'identity politics' involving gender and sexual orientation which helped to raise the profile of equal opportunities and diversity. At the same time older more traditional class politics, expressed through local institutions such as trades councils, were in decline under the impact both of the collapse of traditional manufacturing employment and restrictions of trade union rights by the Conservative governments of Margaret Thatcher.

But the negative side of the celebration of cultural identity and difference was a displacement of energies away from confrontation with the core structures of discrimination. This shift enhanced the power of conservative leaders within the ethnic minority communities (Kundnani 2001, 2002; Malik 2001). At the same time it has proved notoriously difficult to make much advance on some of the main goals set by the Scarman Report, particularly in relation to ethnic minority recruitment to police and a reduction of heavy policing involving stop and search.[5] To the extent that black and ethnic minorities remain, despite some social mobility, concentrated in relatively powerless poor communities then it is inevitable that they bear the brunt of such policing and have minimal power to enforce *de facto* changes in police policy (Lea 2000).

This illustrates the downside of the judicial inquiry. The equality of the parties is precisely fleeting, achieved only in the context of the inquiry itself rather than in any shift in the structures of social power. Recommendations are made and then the inquiry packs its bags and moves on. The power of the judge is by its nature episodic and momentary: the sentence of the court. Where there is no sentence but rather a series of recommendations to be enacted by others over a substantial period of time, the weakness of the judge as social engineer is made manifest. Once Scarman had packed his bags, what then was to stop policing returning to its grim normality?

The white riots of the early 1990s

While the consequences of these developments were working themselves out, public attention shifted from London and the Midlands northwards to the decimated industries and dismal housing estates of Tyneside and other places where white youth appeared to be erupting. During 1991 and 1992 there were 13 major disturbances, mainly in the North East of England (but also in Oxford, Coventry and Bristol). They generally occurred in large deprived, low-income housing estates with very high rates of unemployment and high concentrations of young people. They took the form of street battles among youth gangs and between youth and police, the joyriding of stolen cars, and the wrecking and burning of buildings, including community centres (Power and Tunstall 1997). These riots actually passed off without inquiry: as if these non-policed, socially redundant areas were no longer of interest to anyone except those who had to live in them.

These riots were quite different to those to which Scarman had directed his attention. They lacked the focused attention of the Brixton rioters on the specific issue of police harassment. As Beatrix Campbell commented, 'The prelude to the 1981 riots saw "flooding" saturation policing which overwhelmed and criminalised communities; but the 1991 riots were preceded by the absence of police from the neighbourhoods that erupted' (Campbell 1993: 97). The riots seemed less oriented to a confrontation between a community and state agencies perceived as oppressive and denying equal treatment, and more symptomatic of socially excluded communities turning in on themselves.

> All the areas where riots broke out had a previous history of disorder and 'rumbling riots'. The police and community had tolerated, or were forced to put up with, unusual levels of violence and law-breaking by young men prior to the riots. Disorder had gradually mounted and there was weak social control, serious intimidation, an unwillingness by residents to act as witnesses and irregular policing. (Power and Tunstall 1997: 2)

Yet it would be a mistake to deny elements of inchoate protest. The joyriding (racing) of stolen cars could be seen as 'a particularly apt expression of the combination of marginality and relative deprivation, kids who are denied access to the labour market taking the status symbols of the consumer society and testing them to destruction!' (Lea and Young 1993: xxi). Also much of the rage directed against local community centres could have been associated with the fact that the construction of these buildings, funded by government grants to deprived areas, had mainly benefited outside contractors rather than brought jobs to local people.

Riot by the unpoliced rather than the overpoliced, as an exaggeration of criminality preying on the community itself rather than directed against the state, speaks of fundamental changes taking place in the social structure and governance of advanced capitalist democracies. Continuous aggressive patrolling of populations perceived as recalcitrant gives way to a more episodic regime. Incursions into deprived areas in the form of stop and search, or 'zero tolerance' régimes, occur as and when particular incidents or conditions require. Poor communities may be left to their own devices and then encounter a sudden massive police presence in response to joyriding, arson or gang fights.

Such communities came to be seen less as facing obstacles to the exercise of effective citizenship and more as 'self-excluded' by welfare dependency and other pathologies. There is a return to older notions of the 'culture of poverty' except that such communities are enjoined to take a significant degree of responsibility for their own social reintegration. These perspectives gathered pace during the 1990s under the Thatcher government and its neo-liberal inspiration. They would come to have a decisive influence on the official discourse concerning the nature and courses of urban violence.

Behind them lay changes in the dynamics of globalised capitalism, changes which both neutralised any pressure to undermine race discrimination and to draw ethnic minority communities into the mainstream semi-skilled working class, while at the same time expelling semi-skilled white workers, particularly the young and old, from traditional manufacturing industries. Whereas black youth in Brixton in 1981 could focus their attention on the police as the immediate vehicle of their oppression, white youth in the decaying industrial communities in 1991 faced the unmediated irresponsibility of global capital as it turned on its heels and went elsewhere in search of cheap labour. To this they could only react with a theatre of destruction.

Globalisation and the new racism

By the early 1990s it was clear not simply that the British economy had slipped behind its competitors but that the impact of fundamental changes both in the world economy and the political systems of nation states were working themselves through. Such developments can only be schematically indicated here.[6]

Manufacturing capital, increasingly able to move globally in search of cheap labour and low taxation, has become consequently reluctant to fund welfare state expenditure and tolerate high wage labour régimes in the advanced capitalist countries. State action to fund welfare programmes and stabilise social tensions is continually fiscally constrained by the fear of provoking capital flight. There has been, therefore, a tendency to progressively shift responsibilities in these areas to private funding and community initiatives. But at the same time as communities are asked to take more responsibility for their own cohesion, economic stagnation and capital flight exacerbates community fragmentation and social tensions. Private citizens, communities and the state all of necessity shift their preoccupations in the direction of security, protection, and the neutralisation of populations defined as recalcitrant.

These trends are repeated on an international scale. Growing inequality of wealth and income between states and regions, particularly in the global south and the former USSR and its satellites, and the weakening of economic infrastructures in these areas, is accompanied by deficits in effective governance by states, ethnic fragmentation and localised warfare. One result is increased population movement to escape economic disruption, war and political instability through asylum in more stable regions where opportunities in informal and low-wage sectors of the economy are available. Another is the development of new forms of global identity politics, as exemplified by a resurgent militant Islam, aiming to overthrow, by all available means including terrorism, corrupt political régimes sustained by western capital.

In Western Europe increased immigration and asylum seeking in conditions of economic instability, community fragmentation and preoccupations with security has provided a base for a new defensive racist nationalism exemplified in the growth of the extreme right. Such groupings have made considerable headway by weaving together an ideological fantasy linking an imaginary economic threat from immigration with Islam and terrorism. This new constellation of economic, political and cultural forces set the backdrop to the official response to riots in the Asian dominated communities of the North of England at beginning of the new millennium.

Bradford, Burnley and Oldham 2001

The riots in Bradford, Burnley and Oldham in the spring and summer of 2001 were the worst for twenty years. They involved mainly young men from both white and Asian communities. Attacks on Asians by whites were partly inspired by the high-profile activity of certain extreme right organisations, in particular the National Front and the British National Party, that had been active in local election campaigns and which were able to play on fears and resentments in the poor white communities. Asians defended themselves and attacked property such as pubs which were perceived to be strongholds of white racists.

These towns, at the core of the old and decaying textile and steel manufacturing industries of Lancashire and Yorkshire, are among the 20% most deprived areas in the UK. The unemployment rate for young Asian males is estimated at around 40%. These areas are a graphic illustration of the way economic forces have sabotaged ethnic integration. The Asian community, mainly Pakistani and Bangladeshi, grew during the 1960s and 1970s as migrants were drawn in to work the night shifts in the textile mills and steel foundries. But with the decay of these industries they have been the first to lose their jobs. Most employment which still exists is low-paid service sector work. But alongside the poorest areas in Britain are some of the most wealthy. In Oldham, Bradford and Burnley, affluence and multiple deprivation live cheek by jowl. So the sense of relative deprivation among unemployed youth is high (Webster 2003a, 2003b).

There were several reports into the events of 2001. The most important were Sir Herman Ousely's report on the disturbances in Bradford (Ousely 2001), the report into the Oldham disturbances by David Ritchie (Ritchie 2001), the more general reports on the lessons of the disturbances by Ted Cantle (Cantle 2001) and the report of the Ministerial Group on Public Order and Community Cohesion (Denham 2002). These reports function as sources of information about the events but, far more importantly, as markers for a new official discourse about race and the problems of social disorder. In this discussion the focus will be on the Ousely and Cantle reports as exemplars of the key themes.

The events of 2001 reproduce many of the characteristics of the riots by white youth at the beginning of the 1990s: firstly, that these were communities 'falling apart from within' (Kundnani 2001: 105) under the impact of years of decay and discrimination; secondly, that the state of police–community relations, however bad, is no longer seen as the main precipitating factor. Indeed, the police are seen as having tolerated crime and disorder in the Asian communities. Earlier disturbances in Bradford in 1995 were widely seen as anti-police but even then a major source of resentment was based on 'a perception of the police as unable or unwilling to maintain order or civility on the street or address their concerns about crime' (Webster 2003b: 3). Police were seen as tolerating drugs and prostitution in Asian areas. The Ousely report noted that in

Bradford 'policing is inconsistent and law enforcement is driven by containment policies and "keeping the peace"' (Ousely 2001: para. 2.5.10). This was echoed by Cantle who claimed that in Oldham there were 'now some virtual "no-go" areas in respect of tackling drugs' (Cantle 2001: para. 5.11.1). To the extent that police are criticised it is therefore for failure to act against crime. Absent is any sustained discourse about police racism. There is, in fact, plenty of evidence of aggressive policing of Asians in these areas (Kundnani 2001; Kalra 2001) while inactivity can be as much an indication of racism as overtly aggressive policing. Moreover, the complaint is not in itself new. Scarman, visiting the Asian area of Southall in London during his 1981 inquiry, noted that whereas the complaints of the black community focused on police harassment, 'the chief complaint of Asian leaders appears to be that the police do not do sufficient to protect their community from alleged attacks by racist members of the white community' (Scarman 1981: para. 2.26).

The subtle change between 1981, 1991 and 2001 is rather this: in 1981 irrespective of whether the police were overly aggressive or inactive the main issue was the relationship between the ethnic minority communities and the state: were the ethnic minorities being treated as citizens? In 1991, the absence of official inquiry was indicative of the way in which predominantly poor whites had effectively slipped into a status as non-citizens. When we come to read Ousely, Cantle *et al.* the issue is different: how have the socially excluded communities – poor whites and Asians – got into this mess, and what can be done – in particular what can *they* do – to restore their 'community cohesion'?

From multiculturalism to community cohesion

Ousely is quite direct in a criticism of 'community leaders [who] tend to retain their power base by maintaining the segregated status quo, even when unrepresentative' (Ousely 2001: para. 2.5.2). This situation had reinforced a division between poor whites and Asians in which different communities seek to protect their identities and cultures, discouraging and avoiding contact with other communities and institutions' (Ousely 2001: para. 2.5.4). Multiculturalism, once part of the solution, is, by virtue of having led to 'ethnic fiefdoms' (Kundnani 2002), now recognised as part of the problem. Different ethnic communities compete for local development funding and hence turn against one another. Whites mistakenly believe that Asian areas are disproportionately funded and vice versa (see Ousely 2001: paras 2.5.8 and 3.2; Cantle 2001: para. 2.7).

It is hardly surprising then that there has been a tendency to community segregation. It is, however, seen as 'self-segregation'. Partly this is recognised by Ousely as a 'self-segregation...driven by fear of others, the need for safety from harassment and violent crime and the belief that it is the only way to promote, retain and protect faith and cultural identity and affiliation' (Ousely 2001: para. 2.5.5). But this drive to segregation can become self-induced. Thus the White community feels

> resentment about a perceived dominant presence of visible minorities with strong religious affiliation [while the Muslim community] is, to an extent, resentful of perceived as well as actual unfair and unequal treatment [and] therefore tends to draw on the comfort and security derived from staying together, retaining its strong culture, religious affiliation and identity, to live in self-contained communities and maintain strong links with Pakistan. (Ousely 2001: para. 3.5)

These themes are reproduced in the other reports. It is this alleged self-induced segregation which is stressed. There is little more than a passing nod in the direction of the history of racial and economic discrimination in the labour and housing markets which produced the segregation in the first place, or the contribution of 'white flight' out of inner-city areas to Asian segregation. This emphasis then leads to remedies which are, again, focused on neither economic development, nor the need to combat institutional racism but on 'community cohesion'.

Ousely sees community divisions as the main barrier to local economic development and so the body of his recommendations consists of worthy proposals based around the ideas of citizenship education in schools, the creation of a Centre for Diversity, behavioural competency (the ability to work across cultures), and equality and diversity contracts (no funded project should work with only one community). Denham puts the same theme succinctly. Commenting on the high levels of unemployment, he identifies a need 'to understand the obstacles that prevent some ethnic minority communities from being more successful in local labour markets' (Denham 2002: para. 2.36). Presumably he means not being prepared to work for starvation wages.

Scarman, only twenty years before, never had these qualms about the lack of cohesion even of the marginalised and rioting black youth of the inner city. He regarded the inner cities as 'not human deserts: they possess a wealth of voluntary effort and goodwill' (Scarman 1981: para. 6.7). He warned, however, that 'in order to secure social stability there will be a long term need to provide useful, gainful employment and suitable educational, recreational and leisure opportunities for young people, especially in the inner city' (Scarman 1981: para. 6.29). We now see the consequences of the failure to heed his warnings and we have turned to blaming the victims for their lack of community cohesion and lack of an ability to be 'successful' in local labour markets.

The theme of community cohesion is more starkly emphasised in the Cantle report which produced an elaborate schema of five domains of community cohesion:

- common values and a civic culture (common moral principles and codes of behaviour);

- social order and social control (absence of general conflict and incivility, effective informal social control, tolerance and respect for differences);

- social solidarity and reductions in wealth disparities (equal access to services and welfare benefits, redistribution of public finances and opportunities, and ready acknowledgment of social obligations);

- social networks and social capital (high degree of social interaction within communities and families, voluntary and associational activity and civic engagement);

- place attachment (an intertwining of personal and place identity).

All these are seen as having weakened and led to community divisions and antagonisms which both produced the riots and which explain the lack of economic resources in the area (Cantle 2001: para. 3.2).

Community cohesion has certainly declined under the impact of economic decay but its reconstruction is hardly feasible. In the twenty-first century world of 'lightly engaged strangers' community 'is constantly reinvented and the boundaries redrawn and redrafted' (Young 2001: 38). Cohabitation and sharing of space by different groups is more plausibly represented as a process of 'prosaic negotiation' involving 'a vocabulary of rights of presence, bridging difference, getting along. These are not achievements of community or consensus, but openings for contact and dialogue with others as equals, so that mutual fear and misunderstanding may be overcome and so that new attitudes and identities can arise from engagement' (Amin 2002: 972). These don't necessarily arise from or imply common values or an intertwining of personal and place identity.

The absence of any significant empirical indicators which would enable the achievement of such cohesion to be demonstrated is therefore hardly surprising. The most politically high-profile proclamation to date has been the suggestion that ethnic minorities should prioritise the use of the English language, as if the young Asian rioters in Oldham or Bradford did not have a grasp of the language every bit as authentic as the police officers and white youth with whom they were engaged in conflict.

In such a context the agenda of Cantle *et al.* acquires repressive connotations. This becomes clearer when the discourse of cohesion is linked to that of citizenship. While all sections of the community, including whites, are encouraged to 'improve their knowledge and understanding of other sections and thereby reduce their ignorance and fear' the non-white communities are enjoined 'to develop a greater acceptance of, and engagement with, the principal national institutions' (Cantle 2001: para. 5.1.10). This is translated into a call for greater participation in national mainstream political parties 'without the burden of "back home" politics' which get in the way of community cohesion (Cantle 2001: para. 5.1.12). This theme concludes with a proposal, echoed as we shall see in other government documents, that 'the rights – and in particular – the responsibilities of citizenship need to be more clearly established and ... should then be formalised into a form of statement of allegiance' (Cantle 2001: para. 6.1).

To say the very least, a concept of cohesion recalling the vanished world of the classic industrial city combined with a notion of citizenship implying disengagement from politics elsewhere in the world is, under today's conditions of globalisation, perverse. The political functions of such discourse will be examined presently. In the meantime it is important to stress, with Kundnani, that the appearance of these discourses marks the end of the multiculturalist settlement.

> The 1980s solution to riots – a higher dose of 'culture' – now appears to make the problem worse. Whereas before, black youths were assumed to be rioting because of a lack of culture (what was referred to as 'ethnic disadvantage'), now youths were rioting because of an excess of culture – they were too Muslim, too traditional. For the state, the laissez-faire allowances of earlier had to be ended and cultural difference held on a tighter rein. The 'parallel cultural bloc' was now seen as part of the problem, not the solution. (Kundnani 2002)

As if to make the point, the judiciary handed out remarkably stiff sentences to the rioters – four years and nine months for throwing stones, much tougher than are habitually imposed on petrol bomb throwing youth in Belfast (Bodi 2002). Citizenship has to be learned the hard way it seems.

It is worth concluding this part of the discussion with a little 'thought experiment'. Imagine Cantle transported to the ethnic hothouse of, say, Chicago in the 1920s with its corrupt ethnic-based 'machine politics' and destructive activities of the Mafia. Imagine the call going out for community cohesion as a solution to this precarious state of affairs. What broke the power of the Mafia and weakened the corrupt political machines was, as Robert Merton pointed out long ago, the coming of the welfare state (in the form of Roosevelt's New Deal) which reduced the importance of local ethnic nepotism in favour of impartially administered social security and Federal job creation programmes (Merton 1957: 194). Ethnic groups, meanwhile, learned not 'community cohesion' but shifting alliances, political wheeler-dealing and the processes of prosaic negotiation. But of course it is precisely the national welfare state with its combination of social citizenship rights and channels of political negotiation – exemplified by the trade union movement – which are today progressively enfeebled. It is hardly surprising therefore that what once functioned as a multicultural route to some form of social citizenship now ends up as local 'machine politics'.

Citizenship and community

Though prompted by the riots of 2001 the various reports considered above echo wider themes related to the position of Britain in the current global political and economic context. These themes and discourses crop up in other key documents. Of particular importance are two recent White Papers produced under the auspices of the Home Secretary at the time of writing, David Blunkett. The first, *Secure Borders, Safe Haven: Integration with Diversity in Modern Britain* (Blunkett 2002), starts from the question of immigration and asylum seekers but, as its title implies, connects with the themes of community cohesion and citizenship discussed above.

The starting point is the perceived need to update policy on nationality, immigration and asylum in response to the pressures of globalisation which have resulted in accelerated migration flows (Blunkett 2002: 26) As regards immigrants and asylum seekers it is proposed to prioritise skilled workers through a 'Highly Skilled Migrant' programme and a more 'managed system' of dealing with asylum applications and measures to tackle immigrant smuggling. The other concern is that acquisition of citizenship is not linked strongly enough to competence in English language and that 'some applicants for naturalisation do not have much practical knowledge about British life or language, possibly leaving them vulnerable and ill-equipped to take an active role in society. This can lead to social exclusion and may contribute to problems of polarisation between communities' (Blunkett 2002: 32). To remedy this requires the promotion of language training, and a new 'citizenship pledge' which 'will make clear the fundamental tenets of British citizenship: that we respect human rights and freedoms, uphold democratic values, observe laws faithfully and fulfil our duties and obligations' (Blunkett 2002: 34).

However, the focus of these concerns is wider than that of new immigrants and asylum seekers. Early on in the discussion our attention is drawn to the previous summer's disturbances in Bradford, Oldham and Burnley which 'signalled the need for us to foster and renew the social fabric of our communities, and rebuild a sense of common citizenship. In this context, citizenship is not just for those entering the country – it is for all British citizens' (Blunkett 2002: 10). Global migration and asylum seeking is linked to community cohesion:

> If we are to maintain and develop social cohesion and harmony within the United Kingdom it is crucial that we make sense of these global flows. Our domestic and social policies in relation to nationality, immigration and asylum applications must therefore respond both to the reality beyond our borders and the danger posed by well meaning but indecisive drift at home. (Blunkett 2002: 27)

One does not have to be too paranoid to see the implied connection: we have people in our midst who are not really acting as citizens, who are far too preoccupied with 'back home' politics – or even support for Islamic terrorism – and this is an ingredient of the lack of community cohesion. These people are not just asylum seekers and new immigrants but include large sections of the settled Asian communities with their global connections and their religion. The black community, increasingly smeared by the media with international organised criminal associations and gun culture, has since the onset of the 'war on terrorism' following the events of 11 September 2001, been partly displaced by an equally distorted image of politicised Islam as the archetypal threat to state security. The new racism based on insecurity and threat, fuelling the advance of the extreme right in continental Europe and which played a significant role in the disturbances of 2001 in Britain, is now read as indicating the need for a new type of citizenship which functions as a guarantee of passivity.

But, finally, the white working class are also there. Lack of 'community cohesion and commonality of citizenship' 'is true of those in white working-class communities whose alienation from the political process, along with their physical living conditions and standards of living, leaves them feeling excluded from the increased wealth and improved quality of life which they see around them' (Blunkett 2002: 10). This commonality of citizenship is to be achieved in a similar way. Gone are the older notions of social citizenship we have referred to previously. Citizenship now means simply security: not posing a threat. This is the minimalist citizenship of the state which, having abandoned all pretence at social democracy, makes itself useful to global capital through adopting 'the role of little else than oversized police precincts' (Bauman 1998: 120) to guarantee the security, and of course the high returns to, hoped-for inward investment.

The second recent White Paper is concerned with the local rather than the global. *Respect and Responsibility – Taking a Stand Against Anti-Social Behaviour* (Blunkett 2003) aims to enable communities to develop a sense of responsibility for anti-social behaviour. The latter is defined to include: children out of parental control, noise from neighbours or places of public entertainment, selling drugs, dumping of waste, rowdy behaviour and intimidation by gangs of youth, graffiti and street begging. The assumption is that dealing with low-level anti-social behaviour or incivility of this type will prevent the development of more serious crime in a neighbourhood. The control of such activity can therefore be considered an important aspect of community cohesion. The White Paper proposes a number of measures whereby the state will assist communities to regulate such behaviour in their midst. The emphasis is on the criminalisation of low-level incivilities through fixed penalty fines administered by police, local authority or private security officers, court enforced 'anti-social behaviour' orders, making repeated street begging a criminal offence, etc.

This is not the place to enter the debate over the coherence or efficacy of such measures. It is, however, important to understand how such thinking coheres with the community cohesion discourse discussed above. The important common framework is that the community is the key level at which renewal will take place. The criminal justice role of the state, the guaranteeing of security, is more important than either welfare or economic development. The idea that secure and worthwhile employment at decent wages will get young people off the streets and give them lives and thereby reduce anti-social behaviour is now reversed. While there is some funding available under various programmes, the key assumption is that if communities can check the advance of crime through nipping it in the bud at the level of anti-social behaviour, they will thereby present themselves as attractive for investment and jobs. Criticism and blame are directed away from the state and the economic system towards the community itself as responsible for its own development.

In this way the White Paper parallels and reinforces the perspectives of Ousely, Cantle *et al.* They all agree that there is no way out of inner city decay by means of a Keynesian New Deal. That is gone forever in the world of footloose global capital which is progressively emancipating itself from the burdens associated with social responsibility. They all agree that communities have to sort themselves out, develop cohesion and thereby reduce crime, become active and develop the conditions to become more 'successful in the labour market'. The role of the state is rather to provide security back-up: at a national level with new citizenship requirements and oaths of allegiance, and at a local level with new police powers and 'zero tolerance' of low-level incivilities. Community cohesion and community responsibility are the hallmarks of the post welfare state in globalised capitalism

Conclusion

We have moved a long way from Scarman. He did not doubt, even though he produced his report when a Conservative government was already established and determined to begin the process of rolling back the state, the social nature of citizenship. It meant inclusion in the economy, in welfare rights and in legal and civil rights. The focus was on the relationship between the community and the state, how to break down discrimination and extend equal rights to ethnic minorities. The multicultural settlement was a particular way of doing this which served the interests of pacification by establishing separate institutions which would facilitate the development of a middle class in the black community which would have a pacifying 'leadership' effect steering black workers away from working-class militancy. Nevertheless many black and Asian people moved into influential positions in local government.

Much of the Scarman agenda, such as the reform of police stop and search operations (while not questioning their actual purpose), repeated almost twenty years later by Macpherson, failed. The disproportionate stopping of blacks is as high as ever (Dodd 2003). However, the time-bomb ticking away was that under conditions of economic decay and the decline of social citizenship and structures of political compromise, the colonial structures of the race relations industry would continually function less as subaltern structures of ethnic integration but would develop a tendency to become variants of 'machine politics' and ethnic fiefdoms in which competition between blacks, Asians and poor whites would channel what power and resources were left at a local level into the hands of conservative ethnic leaderships on the one hand and the extreme right on the other. The losers would be the working class: black, white or Asian. In 1991, the dominant Thatcherite orthodoxy, allied to the sheer helplessness of the poor white communities who simply had no one at all of any standing to speak on their behalf (although the National Front did see this opportunity), ensured that there was no need for any official inquiry.

Ousely and Cantle, it has been suggested, epitomise a new era. The contrast with Scarman could not be greater. Integration into the channels of political compromise and stable employment is no longer a route to community cohesion. There is little room for the old politics of the 'social contract' when economic integration is a myth, social exclusion is widespread among whites as well as blacks and there is a growing danger of conflict between the two sections of the socially excluded, spurred on by the extreme right. Integration, it is more politically convenient to imagine, is now a matter of oaths of allegiance and 'behavioural competency', of getting communities to take responsibility for the reversal of their own social decay. If perhaps, the reasoning goes, we can get the blacks, Asians and the poor whites to become paragons of passivity and offer their services to global capital as the cheapest labour in the world, then and only then is there a chance of renovating the inner cities and preventing further riots. Hardly a placid scenario.

Notes

1. For a fuller discussion of the dynamics of police racism see Lea (1986). The concept of institutional racism was taken up in the Macpherson Report of 1999 following the failed police investigation into the murder of a black teenager, Steven Lawrence, by white racists. The report is not discussed here as it was concerned not with riot and police harassment but the role of racism in the alleged failure of police detectives to conduct an effective murder inquiry. Macpherson did, however, include a more general discussion of continuing experience by black and Asian communities of police harassment in the form of stop and search operations. For a discussion see Lea (2000) and Bridges (2001).
2. Scarman baulked at any suggestion that policing policy be made formally accountable to democratically elected local authority bodies as was being advocated by radicals in local government at the time (Lea and Young 1993; Kinsey, Lea and Young 1986).
3. The Race Relations (Amendment) Act 2000 increases the powers of the CRE to initiate investigations and places a statutory duty on public bodies to promote

good race relations in all their activities.

4. Abolished in 1986 by the Conservative Thatcher government and reinstated, in a much weakened form, by the Blair Labour government in 1998.

5. Scarman called for an increased recruitment of ethnic minority officers having noted that in 1981 black officers constituted 0.5% of the Metropolitan Police (Scarman 1981: para. 5.6). The proportion of minority officers is currently 3.3%, a figure still dwarfed in comparison to the 20% of London residents who are members of ethnic minority communities. Similarly, various forms of race awareness training have been on the agenda of police forces throughout the United Kingdom for many years. Scarman called for training aimed at 'an understanding of the cultural background of ethnic minority groups...' and indeed was 'satisfied that improvements in police training are in hand' (Scarman 1981: paras 5.16, 5.17). Macpherson found, however, 18 years later (Macpherson 1999: para. 6.45) 'that not a single officer questioned before us in 1998 had received any training of significance in racism awareness and race relations throughout the course of his or her career' (see Lea 2000).

6. For a fuller discussion of various aspects of these changes see Lea (2002), Young (1999) and Bauman (1998).

References

Amin, A. (2002) Ethnicity and the multicultural city: living with diversity. *Environment and planning*, 34(6): 959–80.

Bauman, Z. (1998) *Globalization: The Human Consequences*. Cambridge: Polity Press.

Blunkett, D. (2002) *Secure Borders, Safe Haven: Integration With Diversity in Modern Britain*, Cmnd 5387. London: Home Office.

Blunkett, D. (2003) *Respect and Responsibility – Taking a Stand Against Anti-social Behaviour*, Cmnd 5778. London: Home Office.

Bodi, F. (2002) Muslims got Cantle. What they needed was Scarman. *The Guardian*, 1 July.

Bridges, L. (2001) Race, law and the state. *Race and Class*, 42(2): 61–76.

Campbell, B. (1993) *Goliath: Britain's Dangerous Places*. London: Methuen.

Cantle, T. (2001) *Community Cohesion: A Report of the Independent Review Team*. London: Home Office.

Denham, J. (2002) *Building Cohesive Communities: A Report of the Ministerial Group on Public Order and Community Cohesion*. London: HMSO.

Dodd, V. (2003) Black people 27 times more likely to be stopped. *The Guardian* 21 April.

Hobsbawm, E. (1959) *Primitive Rebels: Studies in Archaic Forms of Social Movement during the Nineteenth and Twentieth Centuries*. Manchester: Manchester University Press.

Kalra, V. (2001) *'We want to make this a no-go area for Whites': Multiculturalism and Minority Rights (and Wrongs) in England*. Paper presented to conference on 'Rights of Groups and Differentiated Citizenship', Department of Political Science, University of Stockholm, 21–22 September.

Katznelson, I. (1973) *Black Men, White Cities: Race, Politics and Migration in the United States, 1900–30, and Britain, 1948–68*. Oxford: Oxford University Press.

Kenan, M. (2001) *The Trouble with Multiculturalism*. Spiked Central (http://www.spiked-online.com/Articles/00000002D35E.htm).

Kinsey, R., Lea, J. and Young, J. (1986) *Losing the Fight Against Crime*. Oxford: Blackwell.

Kundnani, A. (2001) From Oldham to Bradford: the violence of the violated. *Race and Class*, 43(2): 105–31.

Kundnani, A. (2002) The death of multiculturalism. *Institute of Race Relations*. (http://www.irr.org.uk/2002/april/ak000001.html).

Lea, J. (1980) The contradictions of the sixties race relations legislation. In National Deviancy Conference (ed.) *Permissiveness and Control: The Fate of the Sixties Legislation*. London: Macmillan, pp. 122–48.

Lea, J. (1986) Police racism: some theories and their policy implication. In R. Matthews and J. Young (eds) *Confronting Crime*. London: Sage Publications, pp. 145–65.

Lea, J. (2000) The Macpherson Report and the question of institutional racism. *Howard Journal of Criminal Justice*, 39(3): 219–33.

Lea, J. (2002) *Crime and Modernity: continuities in the left realist criminology*. London: Sage Publications.

Lea, J., and Young, J. (1993) *What Is To Be Done About Law and Order?* London: Pluto Press.

Macpherson, Lord (1999) *The Stephen Lawrence Inquiry*, Cmnd 4262-I. London: HMSO.

Merton, R. (1957) *Social Theory and Social Structure*. New York: Free Press.

Ousely, H. (2001) *The Bradford District Race Review*. Bradford: Bradford Vision.

Power, A. and Tunstall, R. (1997) *Riots and Violent Disturbances in Thirteen Areas of Britain*, Joseph Rowntree Trust: Social Policy Research Findings No. 116. London: Joseph Rowntree Trust.

Rex, J. and Tomlinson, S. (1979) *Colonial Immigrants in a British City: A Class Analysis*. London: Routledge & Kegan Paul.

Ritchie, D. (2001) *The Oldham Independent Review*. Oldham: Oldham Independent Review Panel.

Rose, J. and Deakin, N. (1969) *Colour and Citizenship*. Oxford: Oxford University Press.

Scarman, Lord Justice (1981) *The Brixton Disorders 10–12 April 1981*, Cmnd 8427. London: Home Office.

Webster, C. (2003a) Race, space and fear: imagined geographies of racist violence. *Capital and Class*, 80: 26–35.

Webster, C. (2003b) Policing British Asian communities. In R. Hopkins Burke (ed.) *'Hard Cop/Soft Cop': Dilemmas and Debates in Contemporary Policing*. Cullompton: Willan Publishing.

Young, J. (1999) *The Exclusive Society: Social Exclusion, Crime and Difference in Late Modernity*. London: Sage.

Young, J. (2001) Identity, community and social exclusion. In R. Matthews and J. Pitts (eds) *Crime, Disorder and Community Safety: A New Agenda?* London: Routledge, pp. 26–53.

Chapter 10

Exhausting whiteness: the 1996–98 Belgian parliamentary inquiry into the handling of a paedophilia affair

Ronnie Lippens

Introduction

At the time of writing (September 2002), with the trial of Marc Dutroux and his accomplices scheduled to take place in 2003, the Dutroux case which broke out during the summer of 1996, and the events surrounding the unique and massive *White March* that followed in its wake (people taking part in that silent March were dressed in white or carried something white; hence the *whiteness* in the title), are still conspicuously present in much of Belgium's press and media coverage. This chapter will focus on what arguably has turned out to be one of the most crucially important political documents in Belgian postwar history, a document that had a significant impact on the country's constitution, i.e. the *Parliamentary Inquiry Report into the Handling by the Police and the Judiciary of the Dutroux and Consorts Case* (henceforth the *Report*). A few introductory notes with regard to this *Report*'s immediate antecedents are appropriate.

When, in August 1996, in the south of the country, two girls were freed by the police from what later became known as Dutroux's 'dungeons', where they had been locked-up and sexually abused, this *'fait divers'* [literally, an item in the 'various news' section of a newspaper, RL] (to echo a phrase used by a Paris based weekly that, in 1999, considered the Dutroux affair as one of the three most important *'fait divers'* of the twentieth century) did not initially stir any significant interest among journalists. The latter had not been very interested in the disappearance of the girls, months previously, either. Only when a few days later the lifeless bodies of two girls, also victims of Dutroux and his accomplices, were exhumed (two more bodies were to be exhumed a few weeks later), did micro-dynamics among journalists seem to have been able to gather critical momentum (De Mulder and Morren 1997: 189–209). When, the day after, the local procurator organised his second press conference (at the time this was a highly unusual thing for a procurator to do), the Dutroux affair was destined to dominate the press and other media in Belgium for the next two and a half years. With hindsight, one could point to two recurrent themes in this coverage that, from fairly early on, managed to mobilise public sentiments to an almost extreme degree. The first theme was that of the alleged 'incompetence' of the Belgian police and judiciary. This theme had already emerged by the end of August 1996, when it gradually became clear that the deaths of the four girls might have been prevented if only the three main police forces as well as the judiciary had co-operated (e.g. by exchanging information efficiently) instead of waging a *'guerre des polices'* among themselves. At about the same time, a second theme emerged. This latter theme, i.e. the 'corruption' of the police and judiciary, and of 'politics' as such, was later to overshadow the former 'incompetence' theme. This theme, a mantra in the Belgian media as well as everyday discourse since the early 1980s, was able to tap into a large reservoir of discontent and served as a focal point for both press coverage and everyday talk from September 1996 onwards. We will show below how this focus was never completely dissipated, the Parliamentary Inquiry and the *Report* notwithstanding.

In September 1996, the *juge d'instruction* (examining judge) who was assigned to the case, made an error of judgment. The judge, who had already become a folk hero, attended a party that was organised by one of the legal parties in the Dutroux case, on which occasion he accepted a free pasta dish. This prompted Dutroux's legal counsel to object to the judge before the *Cour de Cassation* for reason of his being apparently partial to some of the legal parties. The *Cour*, although being urged by all political parties to be 'creative', could do nothing but replace the judge. This so-called 'Spaghetti decree' (see on this, for example, Tanghe 1997) immediately caused riots and spontaneous strikes throughout the country. Neither authorities nor trade unions tried to prevent this from happening. Press coverage reported on a 'pre-revolutionary climate'. Most of the popular reproach at this stage was violently directed against the alleged 'arrogance' and 'unworldliness' of the judiciary. A week later, on 20 October, a massive though silent White March slid through

Brussels' streets in protest (Lippens, 1998). The then government coalition (Christian Democrats and Social Democrats) quickly accepted the neo-liberals' proposal for a cross-party Parliamentary Inquiry into the handling by the police and the judiciary of the Dutroux affair.

Belgian parliamentary inquiries

In Belgium, the majority of parliamentary inquiries have taken place since 1980 (Dupont 1990; Fijnaut *et al.* 1998). Between 1830 and 1980, there were only nine. They dealt with the state of the country's industry and commerce (1840), with election results (1859 and 1864), educational policy (1882), the military draft (1908), monetary policy (1935), one case of fraud in a particular government department (1951), the 1959 riots leading to the independence of the Congo, a former Belgian colony (1959), and advertising and public broadcasting (1972). Between 1980 and 2000, however, 16 inquiries took place. This is not just a massive quantitative increase. A closer look also shows that most of the inquiries conducted after 1980 differed qualitatively from those before 1980, in that many tended to deal with crime and criminal justice matters, while most followed significant popular unrest or were accompanied by popular emotional distress. Inquiries were held with regards to (in chronological order): private policing and private militias (1980–81), public order enforcement during the disastrous Liverpool-Juventus soccer match at the Heysel stadium (1985), arms trade (1987–89), fraud in the nuclear industry (1988), the fight against 'banditry' and terrorism (1988–90), army purchases (1990), clandestine intelligence organisations (1990–91), human trafficking (1992–94), organised crime (1996), religious and Satanic sects (1996–97), then another inquiry into (the inquiry into!) the fight against banditry and terrorism (1996–97), police reform (1997), the handling by the police and the judiciary of the Dutroux affair (1996–98), the killing in 1994 of Belgian UN troops in Rwanda (1997), the 1999 dioxins food poisoning crisis (1999), and, after 2000, the possible involvement of Belgian officials in the murder of Patrice Lumumba at the time of the Congo's early independence (2001–2).

At the time when, in October 1996, the Dutroux inquiry was installed, there had already been a decade and a half of inquiries into, and reports on, the deficiencies of the Belgian criminal justice system. Indeed, most of the findings and recommendations in the Dutroux *Report* were already known to many as they had already been extensively covered following previous inquiries, or by media coverage of particular cases of fraud and corruption. Although criminal policy did start to gear towards improving the quality of policing and jurisprudence from about 1988 onwards (Huyse and Verdoodt 1999), effective improvements on the ground were few and far between, as the Dutroux case seemed to have illustrated. In the popular imagination and discourse, these alleged deficiencies ('incompetence' and 'corruption'), over the years, mixed with journalistic and popular rumour and conspiracy theories (about 'states within the state' trying to 'destabilise' the country) that were prominent during the best part of the 1980s. In addition, there had been extensive press coverage of a number of scandals and cases of corruption that were never the object of parliamentary inquiries. Academics and commentators who critically examined and undermined rumour and conspiracy theories often found themselves to be targeted in the press by proponents of a kind of investigative journalism that, throughout the 1980s and early 1990s, was flourishing and very successful in speculating and publishing about (alleged) corruption and conspiracies (Fijnaut, in Fijnaut *et al.* 1998: 126–35). The Dutroux case, however, pushed to the surface this very tenacious blend of rumour and conspiracy theories that had been accumulating for years. One little line spoken, in the early days of the outbreak of the Dutroux case, by the procurator assigned to the case, conjured up this blend. Asked whether he thought he would be able to get to the bottom of the case, the procurator enigmatically replied: 'si on me laisse faire' ['provided they let me', RL], thereby instantly connecting onto this dormant reservoir of distrust. The procurator never explained what he meant by these words (indeed, he may just have been referring to the trouble journalists were causing him at the time when they published information that might have endangered police investigations) but this single little phrase did manage to unleash massive social energy and did structure, as we will see, to a large extent, much of the motivation, logic and effort of the inquiry.

The Inquiry Commission was installed by the end of October and was therefore in a position to make use of the provisions of the 30 June 1996 Parliamentary Inquiry Act that, just before the outbreak of the Dutroux affair, supplemented the much older 1880 Act. After more than a decade of negative experiences in parliamentary inquiry commissions, this 1996 Act, although respecting the older principle of non interference with current judicial investigations (which would forbid inquiry commissions to hear individuals who have been indicted in ongoing trial proceedings), did extend the powers of investigation for parliamentary inquiry commissions, and granted inquiry commissions, for example, the right to see any judicial document pertaining to ongoing cases. The Dutroux parliamentary commission, despite having to counter severe resistance from senior magistrates, made ample use of these provisions. Let us have a closer look at this inquiry commission's activities and its *Report*. But first a theoretical note.

The Dutroux Inquiry as a gift

Parliamentary inquiries produce a form of 'official discourse' (Burton and Carlen 1979). Much of the literature on official discourse, particularly the literature written during the 1970s and 1980s, was largely inspired by Gramscian notions such as 'hegemony'. This notion tends to read official discourse as the result of largely rational and strategically planned options. Hegemony, in other words, is that which is aspired to by coherent, rationally and strategically planning 'centres of calculation' (to use a phrase of Latour's, 1990) where 'facts' and discourses are generated that aim at the universalisation, or at least at the *hegemonisation*, of particular truths and practices. Apart from assuming coherence and rationality in such centres of strategic calculation, such Gramscian writings in a way were often implicitly haunted by some Marxian notion of 'false consciousness', i.e. as that which is being spread in and through the strategic practice of hegemony (for critical notes on this, see Gilligan 2002), in order, for example, for 'the state' (a centre of calculation *par excellence* in many of those writings) to be able to 'maintain, repair, renew or reformulate ... objective political conditions' and 'survive continuous crises of hegemony' (Burton and Carlen 1979: 132). This chapter looks at 'official discourse' in a somewhat different vein and takes its clues from Marcel Mauss's anthropological writings on the gift.

In his seminal *Essai sur le Don* (originally published in 1925) Mauss, in a passage on the economic dimensions of the gift, is at pains to stress that the latter is 'a notion neither of purely free and gratuitous prestations, nor of purely interested and utilitarian production and exchange; it is a kind of hybrid' (1980 translation: 70). A gift, any gift, Mauss implies, is essentially, ontologically, a multiplicity, and is therefore able to hold and generate a multitude of discourses about it. Reading a gift as that which happens in rationally and strategically planned hegemonic practice may surely have a ring of 'truth' about it. But a gift is much more than the enactment of some rationally calculated strategic ploy. Gifts also play out or express something of gratuitous expenditure, of emotional sociality, sometimes even of what Michel Maffesoli (1996) would later identify as excessive, 'Dionysian sociality'. Any object that changes hands as a gift in a way is always an item for consumption, as the receiver is always supposed to do something with the gift (even doing nothing with it constitutes consumption). But any gift is always and simultaneously also a piece of technology. One is supposed to be doing something with the gift, that is to produce something with this object of the gift. The gift, in so far as it aims at something beyond itself (and it always does), constitutes technology: gifts, as technology, for instance, produce selves, identities and communities. Furthermore, a gift simultaneously embodies power and submission. The receiver is at the same time powerful (he or she is in a position where gifts are given to him or her) and in submission (for exactly the same reason), while the reverse (and yet the same) also holds true for the giver. Gifts, moreover, are as much technologies towards the production of an often uneasy mix of both conflict and consensus as they are items through which consumption of this very mix is made possible. The practice of giving, and therefore also the object of the gift, in a Maussian reading, appear as multiplicities that are very hard to grasp by singular discourses such as the Gramscian discourse on 'hegemony' or any Marxist discourse on, for example, the 'reproduction of relations of production' or 'social formations'.

Below we shall read the Dutroux Inquiry Commission's activities, but their *Report* in particular, as a gift. However, here is probably the place to introduce one more idea before taking up a close reading of said *Report*. With Bruno Latour (1990) we could consider this *Report* as an example of what he, writing about the production of scientific 'facts', once called 'immutable mobiles', that is, more or less coherent objects (photographs, mathematic equations, scientific articles, ...) that can easily be reproduced and transferred and exchanged in order to produce scientific truth. Actor-network theorists like Bruno Latour or John Law (e.g. Law 1994 and 2001) often illustrate how objects and events (such as immutable mobiles) have origins, both in what they call 'Euclidean' (physical, geographical, linear) and 'non-Euclidean' space, that are too complex, diverse, tangled and heterogeneous for sociologists to hope to be able to chart them in any detail. We can therefore never hope to adequately chart the Euclidean and non-Euclidean forces that are 'drawn together' into the immutable mobile object or event (the *Report* for example), nor those that will drag (parts of) this object or event into innumerable contexts, where they will be dealt with – adopted possibly, although adapted, or 'betrayed', is more likely – in ever so many diverging ways. However, what we would like to achieve below is a close reading of the *Report*, this hybrid gift, as an immutable mobile, and hopefully to frame its discursive elements within what we think are crucial developments in Belgium's social and political life, i.e. the gradual erosion of welfare (state) provisions since about 1980; the gradual 'de-pillarisation' of Belgian social and political life since about the end of the 1980s ('pillars' are ideologically bound networks of service-providing organisations who, as executive subcontractors of state-funded policies, were able to structure social and political life and everyday experience towards the predictabilities within largely separated communities, and to simultaneously facilitate the 'pre-packaged' or streamlined solution of social unrest and/or political conflict); and the emergence of a consumer culture and a consumer 'logic' that formed in the wake of both former developments. The gift of the *Report*, we will argue, was a gift *of* (the *Report* as a consumer item to be consumed, passively), as well as a gift *towards* (the *Report* as a piece of technology, to be used actively) what could be called a victim democracy.

The gift of whiteness

Any gift, we could argue in a somewhat Maussian vein, is always already a countergift. This should also be the case with the *Report*, which could be read as a countergift following an original gift of whiteness during the so-called White March. There were no slogans during the White March in October 1996. Nobody spoke. People were dressed in white, and marched, silently. There have been attempts to read a particular meaning in this gift of whiteness (see, for example, Licata, 2000: 273ff.), a gift that did not have a precedent in Belgium. Some commentators thought that the whiteness of the White March somehow expressed 'innocence', the innocence of the murdered children for example. Others labelled the White March as a 'march for Truth'. Whiteness here symbolises the Truth that is aspired to, the Truth that, in a place like Belgium, was allegedly constantly falling prey to 'cover-ups' by incompetent/corrupt criminals/officials/politicians. Or the Whiteness, according to yet others, symbolised political 'neutrality', seemingly much desired in a de-pillarising country that, almost out of necessity, previously always cherished a culture of party-political patronage. But whiteness could also simply have been speechlessness, as it often accompanies 'shock' or 'anger', as when, for example, people come to realise that the police and the judiciary, in an uncertain, de-welfarising, de-pillarising society where opportunities and dangers seem to be popping up and disappearing everywhere, and unpredictably so, have very little on offer that might be able to replace yesteryear's steady comforts. Or it may have been the result of tactics pure and simple, of a carefully crafted decision not to speak at all in order to be able to keep a very fragile momentum of sociality, of emotional solidarity, going. A hybrid multiplicity of unspoken contradictions, this whiteness surfaced, to borrow a word from one of Belgium's most prominent commentators, as a 'cryptogram' (Huyse 1996: 25).

However, while whiteness was not spoken, and in order for this whiteness to remain unspoken, its alleged opposite, darkness, did appear massively in the media between August 1996 and February 1998 (i.e. the moment when the second volume of the *Report* was published). It surfaced in myriad reports that sounded familiar to a Belgian audience or readership, as many of those reports rehearsed themes that had been building up for years in rumour and conspiracy theories. With each of the particulars of the Dutroux case becoming publicly known, connections were made in the press, time and again, with alleged 'incompetence', 'corruption' and 'conspiracies' (or 'networks' of 'protection'). Very quickly a picture emerged in the popular imagination as well as in the flood of news reports in the popular press, whereby 'the law' (the police and the judiciary), indistinguishable from 'politics', got associated with notions such as 'false', 'unworldly', 'bad', 'corrupt', 'lies, deceit, and cover-ups', 'crime', 'closed', 'chaotic', 'cold and impersonal', 'hiding behind a screen of silence' and therefore 'arrogant', and 'untruthfully hiding behind legal abstractions', such as 'professionalism' or 'impartiality' (on this see also, for example, Tanghe 1997). A televised scene showing the then Procurator-General (she was a key figure in the preparation of the so-called Spaghetti-decree) fleeing from reporters' cameras who relentlessly pursued her in stairwells and through lift doors provided television audiences with a powerful image that seemed to sum up years of rumour: her fleeing and ducking was labelled not as a sign of a desire for real judicial 'impartiality', but rather as a sign of 'cold', 'impersonal', 'arrogance' (Gies 2002). This imagery was not without its contradictions. On the one hand both 'the law' (and to a certain extent also 'politics') often were urged to adopt a more humane professionalism, to act with sensitivity towards victims, to act contextually and flexibly according to particular needs, and so on (and this one would of course expect in an emerging consumer culture). On the other hand they were also asked to be more predictable, less 'chaotic', less arbitrary, more systematic, more publicly accountable, more transparent (and this in turn would be expected in a de-welfarising and de-pillarising society where formerly trusted points of reference are crumbling), all of which presupposes, to a certain degree, much reviled 'neutrality' and 'impartiality'.

This 'cryptogrammic' gift of whiteness, helplessly unspoken but powerfully silent at the same time, imbued with (in the words of one of the future Inquiry Commission's appointed experts) 'a gigantic pattern of expectations' (De Ruyver, in Fijnaut *et al.* 1998: 86), prompted a countergift. It was cross-party 'politics' (and not 'the law') that took up the role of the giver. This giver, during the inquiry commission's proceedings, and in both this commission's *Report* volumes, gave the receiving party (a de-welfarising, de-pillarising, and consumerising population) a gift, i.e. a transformed criminal justice system – an emotionally charged consumer item *of*, as well as a newly rationalised piece of managerial technology *towards*, a victim democracy. Words like 'giver', 'receiver' and 'gift', used in the context of this chapter, do not mean to imply that the genesis and development of the *Report* were not marked by often bitter struggles and sharp conflicts. Surely there was struggle and conflict between all relevant parties, forces and movements, and often these were hopelessly divided internally as well. Some commentators have been at pains to unravel the (Euclidean) micro-politics of a few of these struggles and divisions, a real 'labyrinth of positions and trench wars' (Ponsaers and De Kimpe 2001: 107) that, although mostly and purposively hidden from public scrutiny, were part of an enormously complex network of coincidences and strategies, desires and rationales, whence the *Report* emerged, and into which, as a fragile immutable mobile, it would again scatter. But we are here interested in the gift, or the *Report*, itself, and in how this gift relates to social and political developments in Belgium that transcend the particulars of the Dutroux case or the problematic of an allegedly flawed criminal justice system.

The countergift

The first volume of the *Report* was published in April 1997, after some six months of televised and closely watched proceedings at the parliamentary, cross-party inquiry commission. It is interesting to note that the inquiry was framed as an inquiry 'into the handling by the police and the judiciary of the Dutroux and Consorts case'. Social problems and issues relating to the prevalence of or conditions for paedophilia, or its links to particular forms of informal economy (Marc Dutroux has also been found to be a highly skilled thief and fraudster, as were a few others named in this case), for example, were not the issue. Neither was government or governance. Without any significant criticism, this cross-party inquiry commission (or 'politics' in the popular imagery) managed to focus critical attention on the police and the judiciary (that is, on to those who were to form the future gift) and to redefine their own position as caring guardians of victims' needs. Indeed, the Inquiry Commission's task was to 'draft an inventory of all grievances', and aimed 'towards an improvement of legislation', wanted 'to gather facts in order to reconstruct the most important steps in the decision process' made by the police and the judiciary in the Dutroux case, and set out to 'describe how relatives of the victims were informed about the modalities of the investigation, on the progress of the investigation, and on the manner in which they were involved in the proceedings' (*Report*, Vol. I: 10). Victims' grievances and victims' needs were the focal point of this inquiry. In minute detail the *Report* then went on to list all the flaws of the police investigation into the Dutroux case, as well as the flaws in the way the judiciary handled the case. The Report concluded with a list of recommendations, some of which implied an almost complete overhaul of parts of the criminal justice system, while others would have (and later *did* have) constitutional consequences. We will concentrate on these recommendations in the next three sections of this chapter.

At first the commission members could not reach a unanimous consensus with regards to the contents of *Report I*. Party-political reflexes surfaced during the drafting of a list of names of individuals who were deemed to have been individually responsible for a number of errors. Political as well as corporatist divisions originally also prevented unanimity with regard to the recommendations for a complete reorganisation of all Belgian police forces into one 'integrated police service structured on two levels'. However, fear for a renewed public outburst of revolt that threatened, once more, to react violently against 'politics' as such, ultimately forced Parliament to accept and unanimously endorse the final *Report*. This forced consensus quickly proved too fragile to form the basis for a thorough reform of the criminal justice system and the momentum quickly withered away, only to gather again after yet another extremely tense event (Dutroux's escape during a transport in April 1998, but see on this Lippens and Van Calster 2002) that finally caused the major reforms that were recommended in the report to materialise into legislation.

Meanwhile, the inquiry commission set out to investigate whether 'networks of protection' had been at work in the Dutroux and Consorts case. A 'green telephone line' that was opened at the end of 1996 had prompted a number of (anonymous) women to report that, as a child, they were sexually abused in paedophile networks. Some of the women (their reports became known as the 'X-files') also hinted at involvement of well known politicians or people named in the Dutroux case who allegedly either took part in the abuse and/or 'protected' paedophiles from prosecution. Although much, if not most, in these testimonies was later found to be flawed or simply incorrect (and later dismissed as evidence), they did add considerably to the well publicised flow of rumour and conspiracy theories that burst out into the open in August 1996 and that never seemed to subside. Indeed, as researchers on urban legends and conspiracy theories have shown (Donovan 2002), the latter tend to have a built-in immunity against refutation (anyone who comes up with 'evidence' or arguments against is deemed to be part of the alleged conspiracy or cover-up) and this is particularly the case when societies (like Belgium) are in transition, with crumbling frames of reference and emerging new ones blending into an uneasy, hybrid mix. Confronted with this swelling flow of rumour, all members of the inquiry commission agreed to investigate whether the seemingly endless list of flaws and errors made during the Dutroux investigations were due to mere incompetence or negligence or whether indeed there were cover-ups and 'networks of protection'. It took the commission eight months to finally admit that they did not find any evidence for such networks or protection. However, fear of outright public rejection caused the commission to acknowledge that they *did* find some evidence, among some policemen and magistrates, of some degree of 'blurring of moral standards', 'ventures in risky milieus', 'developing and maintaining personal relationships with dubious characters', 'applying deontologically unacceptable methods' and 'corruptive behaviour' (*Report II*: 19), particularly in relation to the cases of 'car swindle' (one of Dutroux's criminal activities). This second volume of the *Report* (published in February 1998, two months before Dutroux's escape) was not accepted unanimously in Parliament. Rumour and conspiracy theories lived on, and thus the inquiry never managed to achieve 'discourse closure' (Burton and Carlen 1979: 138), at least not in this respect. When, in May 2002, a British journalist went to visit Belgium, she heard these very stories and, uncritically, reported them (Frenkiel 2002). Let us now have a closer look at the gift *of*, and the gift *towards*, a victim democracy.

The consumption of victim democracy

Zygmunt Bauman (e.g. 1999) claims that one of the defining features of our age is the fact that so many certainties and beacons of reference have fallen away, thereby opening up an uncertain and undecidable space of opportunities as well as danger and risk. Citizenship these days seems to boil down to walking an uneasy tightrope between the particularity of specific contexts and the universality of something like a public sphere. This holds true particularly in a country that, since about the mid-1980s, has seen the gradual erosion of welfare state provisions and the consumerisation of political and everyday life which brought the decline of the steady comforts that once used to be provided by the patronising though stabilising system of pillarisation. With the loosening of institutional and organisational ties, and therefore with ever-increasing gaps between them and the state, individuals, especially in a country like Belgium, during the late 1980s and throughout the 1990s, gradually found themselves adrift. Victim subjectivity often emerges in this gap between individual, de-institutionalising and (in the case of Belgium) de-pillarising consumers and a state apparatus that has not yet managed to develop new modes of governance that are more adapted to post-pillarisation conditions. Victim subjectivity provides usable 'scripts' (Messner, forthcoming) that allow particular, often highly diffuse concerns, to be flexibly managed within a 'public sphere' that somehow also expresses and simultaneously aspires to evoke something of the fast-fading solidarities of yore. Indeed, empirical research was later (a few months after the publication of the *Report*) to show how a majority of the participants in the so-called White Movement could be considered to be coming from more or less progressive segments of the population that had de-pillarised most (Walgrave and Rihoux 1997: 125) and whose motivation to take part in the White Movement, first and foremost, seemed to have been 'expressing solidarity', well before 'worries about paedophilia', 'reform of the judiciary' and 'political reform' (1997: 144ff.).

Victim subjectivity is of primary importance in the first volume of the *Report*. The recommendations section in the *Report* begins with ample recognition of the distress caused to 'victims' (the authority of 'politics', or the state, thus emerges as a benign and caring force). The *Report* then goes on to propose a reformed judiciary (a gift of a consumer item) that will lend a more humane ear to victims' experiences, and that constitutes them as consumers ('they and only they decide what's in their interest' – *Report* I: 161) of new legal opportunities that will allow them to take up a more active role during criminal investigations. Indeed, victim subjectivity in the *Report* appears not just as merely passive, merely consumptive, merely dependent consumer subjectivity. In a newly emerging active victim democracy that is sliding beyond the mere dependencies of a pillarised welfare society, this victim subjectivity also presupposes and indeed reinforces an *active* victim consumerism that offers voice (no more speechlessness, no more whiteness) to victims. The gift of a reformed judiciary here emerges not just as a consumer item, but also as a piece of technology that allows both the state and individual victims to share in the ongoing production and reproduction of a victim democracy. Indeed, 'today it's citizens who are on the move for the justice system. It's this movement that will bring about change' (*Report* I: 158). The energy that is being freed in the ongoing process of de-pillarisation and consumerisation is therefore destined to be put to use in a piece of technology that in turn should allow consumers to actively take part in their further constitution (by using an improved judiciary as what Foucault once termed a 'technology of the self'; see, for example, Martin *et al.* 1988) as citizens of and therefore contributors to a victim democracy.

Victim democracy's technology

Active victim consumerism and victim citizenship, in the gift of the *Report*, is acknowledged and indeed reinforced in the form of an offering of a piece of technology, i.e. a humane, victim-oriented criminal justice system. One may take all this very literally: the criminal justice system, in the *Report*, often appears as a machine where there is a need to 'do away with the rust in the cogs' (*Report I*: 172). Much of the *Report* evokes the judiciary as a cold and impersonal machinery where there is 'too much bureaucracy' and 'formalism', where officials live an impersonal and inhumane life 'too far from reality'. It is this machine that has to be readjusted to a changing world, and that, as the object of a gift, should be controlled by and accountable to both the state and its citizen consumers or 'customers' (on the resistance against this new terminology within the judiciary, see Kloeck 2002: 59ff.). Indeed, in an interview that took place a few years after the publication of the *Report* (quoted in Ponsaers and De Kimpe 2001: 78), the chairman of the Inquiry Commission – it should be added here that this chairman is of neo-liberal signature – reiterated that 'the police should not act *sui generis*' (as machines are not supposed to) but, on the contrary, 'should get their impetus from the public. This once used to be easier when the texture of social life was more appropriate to achieve this, but now, all this *should be activated*' (my italics). Once again a reformed criminal justice system (the police in particular) is imagined as a technology that should 'be dependent on authority ... and external control' (p. 78), an inert piece of machinery that, however, should obtain its energy and fuel from 'the public' who, alas, because of a 'social texture' that has crumbled away, will have to be 'reactivated' themselves in and through the use they will have to make, as victims/consumers/citizens, of this very machinery. There should therefore be a stop, according to the *Report*, to the 'infantilisation' of victims, who now, pushed as they are into 'passivity', are 'robbed of all responsibility' (p. 114). A reformed criminal justice system should be able to make use of new energies as soon as it sheds 'tradition' and 'juridicism' (*Report I*: 122ff.).

The machine itself, as an instrument that should function towards a post-pillarised and therefore post-fragmentation 'social texture', cannot any more remain fragmented itself. Indeed, the days of fragmentation, when 'all work on their square metre' (*Report I*: 173), the days of '*saucissonisation*' (a neologism that refers to the slicing of a sausage into separate slices, coined in the *Report* on p. 120), and the days of '*baronnies*' (p.107) competing against each other, are now over. The most crucial term in the *Report*, we think (see also Lippens and Van Calster 2002), seems to be 'integration', that not only seems to stand for co-operation or even unity, but also (particularly in view of *Report II* on 'networks of protection') for integrity. Much of the *Report*'s recommendations go towards the formation of a 'vertically and horizontally integrated' criminal justice system that should be able to hold 'chaos' at bay (*Report I*: 93) due to efficient and effective 'hierarchical' control and planned 'strategy' (p. 103). The flexible and active, spontaneous consumption of this newly integrated and trustworthy machine, as well as the strategically planned and hierarchically controlled use of it in a newly emerging victim democracy, are in turn expected to enhance ('activate') the production of yet more integration and integrity – the expected results of both the (self-)shaping of victim subjectivities and the gradually expanding reconstructions of communal solidarity and democratic citizenship which these victim subjectivities should manage to achieve on and out of the fragments of a crumbling, de-pillarising welfare society.

Devolution of emotional management

Societies in motion tend to be societies of *e-motion*. Emotions, during the inquiry commission's widely watched broadcasts, ran wild. One of the experts assigned to the commission later admitted that 'emotions (quite understandable in view of the victims' parents' experiences) constantly threatened to disturb the commission's activities' (De Ruyver, in Fijnaut *et al.* 1998: 81). It is hard not to read traces of the effects of Belgium's social and political transition in the extreme emotional eruption that surrounded the Dutroux '*fait divers*'. Indeed, one prominent commentator wrote how the country was in need of 'volcanologists' (Huyse, in Walgrave and Rihoux 1997: 11). Such emotionality may of course not be specific to Belgium (see on this Loader and de Haan 2002). However, the ongoing process of de-welfarisation and, more importantly, of de-pillarisation in that country did free emotional energy that was otherwise kept in check by the safety and predictability (however patronising) of pillarised service networks. In a transitional society like Belgium, this emotional energy can come from anywhere, and there is nowhere in particular where it can be dealt with. When the pillars start to show deficiencies and are therefore less apt to mould social issues (and the collective emotions which they imply) into pre-packaged forms and processes, while they lose their capacity as 'early warning systems' (Huyse 1996: 22), emotional energy tends to be left unattended, and will accumulate until, eventually, it may 'erupt' into the open. Subjectivities, in such an ambivalent zone of transition, are likely to yearn for some form of communal solidarity, while their newly won freedom, which has brought them anxiety, but also new opportunities, is not likely to be given up either. The Inquiry Commission's gift could therefore also be read as a management practice, i.e. as a practice of managing the enormous outburst of emotion at the time of the Dutroux affair (the inquiry commission, which was 'dragged into a maelstrom', really was 'in search of a new balance', wrote the commission's expert; De Ruyver, in Fijnaut *et al.* 1998: 79), but also as a gift of again a piece-of-technology-cum-consumer-item that, in future, should allow for a more effective and efficient handling of free floating emotionality. We will now develop this point.

Already during the (televised) sessions organised by the inquiry commission, it became clear that one of the major themes was the alleged lack of 'humane' sensitivity which so many professionals had shown during the Dutroux investigations. One investigating magistrate in particular was tackled severely and branded a 'rock-hard ice queen' (Winckelmans 1997: 292). The *Report* eventually redefined professionalism. This should henceforth not only include a measure of impartiality and neutrality, but also humane engagement and compassion towards victims/citizens. The piece of technology that was the object of the *Report*'s gift, in a way, should be a sentient, humane machine, a source of integration and integrity. As Lieve Gies (2002) has noticed, one of the consequences of the Dutroux inquiry could be described as a shift towards the 'personalisation' of both 'politics' and the 'judiciary', with information on the private life of politicians and magistrates, their *partiality* in a way, becoming an important issue that needs to be publicly available and that, in a few cases, has caused many to sympathise with public figures.

One of the *Report*'s most important recommendations (later to be implemented through a constitutional amendment) was the institution of a High Council for the Judiciary. This High Council mainly appoints magistrates in a 'de-politicised' manner (the previous system of party-political patronage has now ceased to function) and develops curricula for training and promotion of members of the judiciary. However, the High Council also acts as an 'ombuds-service' and introduces, within the judiciary, a consumer logic that should be able, in the words of its current president, 'with intellectual force and integrity', with 'sympathy', 'honesty', 'impartiality', 'reason and common sense', 'pragmatism and goal-orientedness' (Kloeck 2002: 60), to manage complaints and emotions in the somewhat ambivalent and uneasy zone between neutrality/ universality and partiality/contextuality, or between abstract justice (which is not wanted in an emotional age) and mere particularist sensitivity (which is not wanted in a de-pillarising society either). Here again, victim subjectivity appears to be dressed in the cloak of consumerism, with desires, reasons, anxieties and complaints that need to be dealt with in and by a devolved technology of emotional management.

Conclusion

This chapter has resulted from a close reading of the *Report* by the *Parliamentary Inquiry Commission into the Handling by the Police and the Judiciary of the Dutroux and Consorts Case*. Rather than assuming that this *Report* was a mere strategic ploy resulting from more or less coherent 'centres of calculation' striving towards hegemony, we have, inspired by Marcel Mauss's anthropological writings, read them as the hybrid result of a gift (and a countergift). Rather than an analysis of the 'labyrinth' of political and ideological struggles that one might be able to detect in the (Euclidean) space that produced this inquiry, this chapter has attempted a reconstruction of a newly emerging political imaginary which the inquiry and its subsequent *Report* have helped to bring about. This imaginary space, in our view, both expresses and simultaneously forms a space within which myriad political and ideological struggles take shape or dissolve. This imaginary space, i.e. the space of an emerging victim democracy, spans on the one hand the crumbling certainties of an eroding Belgian pillarised welfare society and, on the other hand, the undecidable and ambivalent blend of opportunity and risk that characterises a consumer culture and a consumer 'logic' that is gradually pervading political as well as everyday life in that country. The anxieties as well as the emotional energy that accompany this transition within Belgium's everyday life and political culture, in our reading, have forced themselves into the *Report*, but are also acknowledged there, and are both expressed in and channelled towards the *gift* of a reformed criminal justice system, the main dimensions of which could be described as the consumption of victim democracy, the production of victim citizenship and the devolved management of emotions. What seems to be particularly Belgian in this story of social transition is the speed and the intensity with which the events and the emotions involved have emerged and developed. Whereas other European countries also have undergone processes of de-pillarisation (e.g. the neighbouring Netherlands during the 1960s and 1970s are a case in point) and de-welfarisation, in Belgium these processes emerged and developed more acutely (a tremendous state budgetary deficit, the highest in the European Union during the 1990s, may have formed the backdrop to this), and their impact was felt much more deeply in everyday life contexts that, in the decade before the Dutroux affair, were simultaneously growing into a consumer culture.

References

Bauman, Z. (1999) *In Search of Politics*. Cambridge: Polity.

Belgian House of Representatives (1997–8) *Parliamentary Inquiry Report into the Handling by the Police and the Judiciary of the Dutroux-Nihoul Affair*, 2 vols. Brussels, April 1997 and February 1998.

Burton, F. and Carlen, P. (1979) *Official Discourse*. London: Routledge & Kegan Paul.

Donovan, P. (2002) Crime legends in a new medium: fact, fiction, and loss of authority. *Theoretical Criminology*, 6(2): 189–215.

Dupont, L. (1990) Terugblik op het Fenomeen 'Parlementair Onderzoek'. *Panopticon*, 11(6): 461–83.

Fijnaut, C., Huyse, L. and Verstraeten, R. (eds) (1998) *Parlementaire Onderzoekscommissies: Mogelijkheden, Grenzen en Risico's*. Leuven: Van Halewyck.

Frenkiel, O. (2002) Belgium's silent heart of darkness. *The Observer Review*, 5 May, pp. 4–5.

Gies, L. (2002) Up, Close and Personal: The Discursive Transformation of Judicial Politics in Post-Dutroux Belgium. Unpublished manuscript.

Gilligan, G. (2002) Royal commissions of inquiry. *Australian and New Zealand Journal of Criminology*, 35(3): 289–307.

Huyse, L. (1996) *De Lange Weg naar Neufchateau*. Leuven: Van Halewyck.

Huyse, L. and Verdoodt, A. (1999) Dertig Jaar Justitiebeleid: kroniek van een aangekondigde crisis. *Panopticon*, 20(1): 3–19.

Kloeck, K. (2002) De Hoge Raad voor de Justitie: een jaar ver. *Panopticon*, 23(1): 44–68.

Latour, B. (1990) Drawing things together. In M. Lynch and S. Woolgar (eds) *Representation in Scientific Practice*. Cambridge, MA: MIT Press, pp. 19–68.

Law, J. (1994) *Organizing Modernity*. Oxford: Blackwell.

Law, J. (2001) *Aircraft Stories: Decentering the Object in Technoscience*. Durham, NC: Duke University Press.

Licata, L. (2000) Identités Représentées et Représentations Identitaires. Unpublished PhD thesis, Université de Bruxelles.

Lippens, R. (1998) The White March as a Belgian body without organs. *Crime, Law and Social Change*, 29(1): 49–65.

Lippens, R. and Van Calster, P. (2002) Policing as forestry? Re-imagining policing in Belgium. *Social and Legal Studies*, 10(2): 283–305.

Loader, I. and de Haan, W. (2002) 'On the emotions of crime, punishment and social control. *Theoretical Criminology*, 6(3): 243–53.

Maffesoli, M. (1996) *The Time of the Tribes*. London: Sage.

Martin, L., Gutman, P. and Hutton, P. (eds) (1988) *Technologies of the Self: A Seminar with Michel Foucault*. Amherst, MA: University of Massachusetts Press.

Mauss, M. (1980) *The Gift*. London: Routledge & Kegan Paul.

Messner, C. (2004) Observing victims: global insecurities and the systemic imagination of justice in world society. In R. Lippens (ed.) *Imaginary Boundaries of Justice*. Oxford: Hart.

Mulder, M. de and Morren, M. (1998) *De Zaak Dutroux van A tot Z*. Antwerp: Icarus.

Ponsaers, P. and De Kimpe, S. (2001) *Consensusmania. Over de Achtergronden van de Politiehervorming*. Leuven: Acco.

Tanghe, F. (1997) *Het Spaghetti-arrest*. Antwerp: Hadewijch.

Walgrave, S. and Rihoux, B. (1997) *Van Emotie tot Politieke Commotie. De Witte Mars, Een Jaar Later*. Leuven: Van Halewyck.

Winckelmans, W. (1997) *De Commissie Dutroux. Het Rapport (met Commentaar)*. Leuven: Van Halewyck.

Chapter 11

Repairing the future: the South African Truth and Reconciliation Commission at work[1]

Stéphane Leman-Langlois and Clifford D. Shearing

Introduction

Political transitions require a coming to terms with the past by the new present. One varied set of institutions for accomplishing this has been labelled 'truth commissions'. While hard to define clearly because of their diversity they are usually understood as institutions intended to address some aspect of a political régime that is regarded as illegitimate and after a transfer of political power (Hayner 1994; 2001 Bronkhorst 1995). As the sign 'truth' suggests, Truth Commissions seek to do this by discovering and then making public to some extent the 'truth' about the past. This truth typically has to do with discovering the truth about what are now regarded as the old political authorities' illegitimate activities – these include such matters as investigating the whereabouts of persons who have disappeared, providing a basis for compensating victims, identifying the perpetrators of wrongful acts and correcting parts of the nation's history. This last feature of the discovery of truth is nicely illustrated in the name given to the Guatemalan Commission, namely the 'Commission for Historical Clarification'. Truth in these various guises is often seen as having consequences that will help promote a transition of political power and authority and enhance the new authority. These truth effects include such things as 'reconciling the nation' and 'restoring the moral order'. The management of these multiple objectives associated with truth commissions can and does present those responsible for forming, running and responding to them with a daunting task.

In this chapter we explore the finding of truth about a national past and the way in which this objective intersected with other objectives such as the truth of specific events. It also explores the complex relationship between the pursuit of an understanding of a national past and the social and political consequences this has (both intended and unintended and unanticipated). The socially constituted nature of truth-seeking within the context of truth commissions is immediately evident in the fact that truth commissioners are rarely chosen for their technical expertise as truth finders but for their 'representativeness'. Their selection is typically guided by a concern that the truth constitutes a 'balanced', 'equitable' version of the past. Representativeness expresses a desire to ensure that the reconstitution of an authoritarian past will reflect and strengthen a democratic present. The implicit assumption is that it is only because the nation is now free from the lies and the secrets of the past that it is able to look back and uncover the truth. A central goal of most truth commissions is to construct the new era as a break with and as free from the old, the new political authority as more legitimate, the new justice as more just, etc.

While the literature on truth commissions has grown and is growing exponentially it has been limited by and large to three broad types: normative or jurisprudential analysis (Ensalaco 1994; most of Rotberg and Thompson, 2000), 'therapeutic' evaluations (Minow 1998) and descriptive accounts (Hayner 1994, 2001; Krog 1998; Meredith 1999). The exploration of the social and political roots and consequences of these institutions that we have been hinting at has been relatively rare (see Wilson 2001 for an exception). Within the context of this literature our primary question is unconventional. We ask, with respect to the history-writing aspect of commissions that will be our focus, 'what is the *function of truth?*' To answer this question we examine the work of the South African Truth and Reconciliation Commission (TRC).

As our analysis proceeds, two levels of response will emerge. The first examines a particular assemblage of 'knowledge' authorised as truth. The second concerns what qualifies things as 'true'. We will not, of course given this perspective, offer a definition of 'truth' or an evaluation of whether the truth 'discovered' by the South African Commission is true in the positive sense that it conforms to reality. For our purposes, 'the truth' is simply what is authorised as truth. Our focus is on this process of authorisation and its purposes and consequences. We will argue that what truth commissions do is to enact possibilities deemed desirable within the new dispensation: enact transparency, enact justice, enact victim's dignity and enact right and wrong. Following Geertz (1973) we present the TRC as creating/enacting democracy and justice.

In order to explore these issues we will examine how the TRC established the truth about three main aspects of the past: victims, perpetrators and apartheid. The chapter has six sections. The first two offer a brief description of the TRC process and how the question of truth was constructed as a problem and a solution. The next three sections explore the TRC's handling of victims, perpetrators and 'history'. Finally we summarise our analysis of how the truth repaired the South African past and in so doing created the possibility of a present that could become the ground on which the possibility of a new and different future could be both envisaged and realised.

The TRC's main 'truth' committees: the Committee on Human Rights Violations and the Committee on Amnesty

The TRC is the only truth commission to date to have been instituted through a legislative act (the principal method has been for a government to issue a decree describing the institution and naming the commissioners). This legislative foundation equipped the TRC with powers of subpoena and seizure that other commissions have lacked. Its origins, however, meant that it was born out of an intense and drawn-out process of legislative and public debate. The possibility of a truth commission was mooted before the April 1994 'liberation' elections, and it was the first democratically elected South African government that introduced the Bill and guided it through a committee process before it was enacted into law on 26 July 1995.

The next step was the process of selecting the commissioners. Some 300 names were suggested to an *ad hoc* committee that presented 25 candidates to the President, who then appointed the 17 commissioners and named Archbishop Desmond Tutu as its chairperson. The commissioners met for the first time on 16 December 1995. Their first act was to assign themselves to one of the three committees specified in its founding Act. In addition one commissioner was made head of an investigation unit.

The Committee on Reparation and Rehabilitation is not important for our purposes, but it is necessary to briefly outline the other two. The Committee on Human Rights Violations (the 'HRC') had two principal tasks: (1) taking statements from victims of 'gross human rights violations' between 1960 and 1994; (2) holding 'institutional' and 'theme' hearings where members from the main South African social and political groups could present their understanding of the historical context of apartheid and the sources of human rights violations, either in general or around specific themes, incidents or groups (see Table 11.1). The hearings were intended to fulfil the TRC's mission to produce:

> ... as complete a picture as possible of the causes, nature and extent of the gross violations of human rights which were committed during the period from 1 March 1960 to the cut-off date, including the antecedents, circumstances, factors and context of such violations, as well as the perspectives of the victims and the motives and perspectives of the persons responsible ... (Promotion of National Unity and Reconciliation Act, 3, 1(a))

As the TRC's main committee the HRC findings were the principal resource relied upon by the Research Department in drafting the final report.

Table 11.1 Main hearings of the Human Rights Committee

'Theme' hearings	'Institutional' hearings
• Women as subjects of gross human rights violations • Youth and children • Caprivi trainees in KwaZulu-Natal • Moutse/KwaNdebele incorporation conflict • Soweto, 1976 • The killing of the 'Guguletu Seven' • The 'Bisho massacre' • The 'Seven Day War' in KwaShange/Imbali in 1990 • The 'Trojan horse' incident (Athlone, Cape Town) • The issue of compulsory military service • The special hearing on the disappearance of Siphiwe Mthimkulu in the Eastern Cape	• The prison system • The media • The legal system • The role of business during apartheid • The health care sector • The faith communities • The state security system • The role of the armed forces • The involvement of the former state in chemical and biological warfare

Source: TRC (1998: 1, 10, 14–15)[2]

The HRC took almost 21,000 statements from individuals claiming to have been subjected to gross human rights violations. It later subtracted some 2,000 that did not fit its frame of reference (outside the targeted historical period, absence of political objective, etc.). After some false starts a procedure for recording the huge numbers of victims' stories was established: 'Statement takers' recorded each victim's information on short standardised forms, which were entered into a computer database (for a detailed discussion of the problems of the database approach, see Wilson 2001: 38–61).

In April 1996 the HRC began a series of widely mediatised public hearings. In these hearings 2,000 of apartheid's victims were given the opportunity of telling their story in front of HRC commissioners, members of the public and television cameras. Hearings were held at different locations so as to ensure that the principal regions of the country would be adequately represented in the record. Before and following their appearance victims were met by psychologically trained support professionals and by 'briefers' who would explain to them the basics of the TRC's work and what was expected of them. Each witness was allowed as much time as they wanted to speak, and then were asked a few questions by the commissioners if clarification or expansion was needed. The questions were asked in a spirit of respect and dignity and never approached the style of even the mildest examination. According to the TRC

> [a]n important concern of the Human Rights Violations Committee was to ensure that the human and civil dignity of victims was restored by granting them an opportunity to relate their own accounts of violations (as emphasised in section 3(1)(c) of the Act). It was, therefore, incumbent on the Human Rights Violations Committee to make sure that the environment at the hearing was conducive to achieving these objectives. (TRC, 1998: 1, 10, 20)

Victims' submissions were aimed at producing *acknowledgment* and public, official recognition of the victims' suffering. In a separate process each story was briefly investigated to see if it could be corroborated.

Given this public process in which victims told their story, those who were identified as 'perpetrators' very often were concerned that their name might be brought up in the course of the testimony. Fearing judicial prejudice – as well as bad publicity – some sued in an attempt to muzzle witnesses. Most failed in these bids but gained the right to be heard at a later date if they were identified in an official Commission's 'finding'. While perpetrators could be present at the victims' hearings (they rarely were) they were not permitted to make submissions and if present were considered to be ordinary members of the audience. The hearings were to represent the victims' truth.

The other committee of interest was the Committee on Amnesty (AC). This committee was assigned the task of evaluating the 7,127 amnesty applications filed before the 30 September 1997 deadline. While it quickly rejected over 4,000 applications for not meeting the basic criteria, this still left a very sizable number of applications for a committee that was significantly smaller than the other two.[3] Given the magnitude of the task the AC could not finish its work with the rest of the Commission and continued to hear cases more than two years after the publication of the 'final' TRC Report. Its findings are to be released sometime in 2003 in a new version of the Report.

The AC granted individual amnesties to persons who would describe their actions in detail, including naming their accomplices. In addition, for amnesty to be granted the acts in question had to be recognised by the AC as 'politically motivated' and *proportional* to the amnesty seekers' motives. Once amnesty was granted the applicant was shielded from both civil litigation and criminal proceedings with regard to the acts specifically mentioned in his or her amnesty application. Amnesty was granted for actions rather than to perpetrators. This was intended to encourage full disclosure by the applicants and to 'break the ranks' by playing 'name names' thereby compelling others to apply for amnesty.

The typical amnesty hearing resembled conventional criminal court proceedings. After making a statement the applicant would be questioned by the AC 'leader of evidence' and by his own lawyer. Then lawyers for the victims would be allowed to question the applicants, which they often did at length, sometimes for days. In the vast majority of cases victims opposed amnesty applications, and were allowed to do so on the stand if they had evidence to present. They were then also questioned by their lawyer, by the leader of evidence and by the applicant's lawyer. In short, the perpetrators' truth was challenged so that 'the truth' would be revealed. In this forum it mattered that the 'truth' be 'true' and conventional judicial methods were deployed to establish the truth.

In each case the truth served a different constitutive purpose in making up a 'new South Africa'. In the case of 'victims' truth' the hearings were intended to provide an opportunity for the voice and suffering of victims of apartheid to be heard and acknowledged as real and legitimate. The hope was that this hearing and acknowledgment would enable perpetrators and onlookers to appreciate the terrible reality of apartheid and to move forward as South Africans to build a very different South Africa. It was also hoped that the catharsis of telling their story and having it heard and recognised would enable victims to move forward as well. The central theme of the Commission here, and one that the chairperson emphasised, was the possibility of shame and forgiveness that telling the truth of victims' pain enabled. In the case of the AC hearings the intention was also to enable those who acted to support and realise the culture and practices of the old South Africa to acknowledge the truth and shame of their participation. This would enable others to respond with forgiveness and empower them to remake themselves as citizens of the new South Africa. These truths, as different as they were, were both intended to be intersubjectively convincing, so that they would be accepted by all South Africans. The truths were to integrate a personal and individual face with a collective and social face. In the case of victims this required that their truth be experienced and viewed by others as authentic – as from the heart. For the AC hearings it was to be experienced as real and factual. In this case what was required were methods that would reveal an 'objective' truth that would command recognition across what had been, and were still, contesting South African constituencies. The truth elicited by each set of hearings was a truth shaped by a purpose.

History and the TRC's operational definitions of truth

Early on in the process that led to the construction of the TRC, the bill's drafters were well aware of the multiple truths with multiple purposes. Albie Sachs, now a Constitutional Court judge and an influential voice in the debate that shaped the TRC, spoke at a July 1994 conference on the truth commission of two kinds of truth: First, 'microscope truth' that is 'factual, verifiable and can be documented'; second, deliberative truth, that is 'dialogue truth', or 'social truth, the truth of experience that is established through interaction, discussion and debate' (in Boraine and Levy 1995: 105). Both of the committees we have discussed sought to elicit and then present one of these truths.

The TRC Report itself identified four truths (TRC 1998: 1, 5, 29–45). The first was 'factual or forensic truth', which according to the Commission included all information that could be corroborated by the Investigative Unit and used to produce 'findings' in the Report. This is Sachs' microscopic or positive truth. The other three are essentially subdivisions of 'dialogue truth'. The first of these is 'personal and narrative truth', that may or may not be corroborated or factually exact but is representative of *victims'* perceptions of their personal context. This truth is, within the construction of the TRC, only a victim's truth. The Report makes no mention of perpetrators' testimony in discussing this form of truth. To do so would have been to legitimate what was to be recognised as a dreadful past that was to be transcended. The second form of deliberative truth was identified as 'social truth'. Here the Commission's concern was with recognising as a matter of fact that in the past there had been different public views. This was recognised through the Commission's willingness to hear explanations and justifications offered by all recognised political parties. Once again what was intended was a truth that would help build the new South Africa – in this case a tolerant, understanding South Africa in which people who had had different views could now move ahead together. The Report states that the TRC's goal

> was to try to transcend the divisions of the past by listening carefully to the complex motives and perspectives of all those involved. It made a conscious effort to provide an environment in which all possible views could be considered and weighed, one against the other. (TRC 1998: 1, 5, 41)

The last category of truth was termed 'healing and restorative truth'. It is this truth that was central to the Commission's final report, and refers to the way truth was handled by the Commission. In order to achieve its goals of restoring the victims' dignity and then of moving forward to promote reconciliation through forgiveness the Commission sought to *acknowledge* the truth. Acknowledgment 'is an affirmation that a person's pain is real and worthy of attention' (TRC 1998: 1, 5, 45).

All four truths were *instrumental* truths with a constitutive purpose. Their differences were managed through a committee system that established boundaries between them – their domains were different. These boundaries were maintained within the final report. Where they were juxtaposed their differences were managed by locating them within the context of their purposes. Thus in the report 'forensic truth' is presented as necessary for amnesty decisions or to corroborate victims' statements. Where truths had to be juxtaposed, for example when statements establishing 'social truth' were contradicted by tangible facts, the latter were given priority as truth was here being used to justify an exercise of power. Another way of managing contradictory truths was to exclude them from the record. In managing truth and the relations between truths the Commission relied in part on its mandate. For instance, if a victim's 'healing truth' concerned a crime with no political motive, the Commission did not integrate it into its official record – this meant that no compensation would be offered.

A similar approach was taken with dialogue truth that was not material to the forensic findings of the Report and was not integrated into a general argument but rather appeared as illustration of facts established in other ways. They were only deployed to accomplish a political, constitutive mission to illustrate and support 'national reconciliation' and to enact and manifest new boundaries between *right* and *wrong*. Each truth had its place and its uses.

The TRC was not writing history in a conventional sense. It was establishing *facts* from a judicial perspective and with judicial standards when and where this was needed to enact amnesty. Elsewhere it explored the 'background' of human rights violations to uncover elements useful to determine individual responsibility and not to create a historical narrative. As it was 'incident-driven', this background was only deployed as it related to human rights violations. When the 'role of the media' was investigated the main question and justification for the hearing was, 'what did the media do to encourage the continuation of human rights violations?' and not, for instance, 'what part did the media play in maintaining apartheid?' Keeping the focus on gross human rights violations, the Report states in its introduction to the chapter on the media that:

> The South African media played a crucial role in helping reflect and mould public opinion during the years under review. However, could the media also be said to have been directly responsible for gross human rights violations? And to what extent were they responsible for the climate in which gross human rights violations occurred? (TRC 1998: 4, 6, 1)

Truth commissions, as the TRC nicely illustrates, do not combine facts and interpretations to establish a richer historical account, as is commonly suggested (Maier 2000). Even if this were to have been an aspiration for the TRC it would have been very difficult to put into practice. For example, it would have been difficult to integrate the different domains the Commission had established to hear truth, to integrate and relate victims' accounts and perpetrators' admissions: more than half the victims' statements regarded the 1990–94 period, while extremely few of the amnesty applications did.

The fundamental reason was of course that the Commission had other objectives besides 'historical truth'. While the record established by the Commission might be useful to historians, it is not itself a history even though it was presented and is read as a record of what happened. It offers a past meant to enable a different future. This future meant that some of the things that a thorough examination of the past might require were not done. For example, the requirement for appeasement – the most basic manifestation of 'national reconciliation' – meant that the TRC failed to subpoena some political leaders who were obviously responsible for political violence (Mangosuthu Buthelezi, leader of the IFP, for instance; see the TRC's explanation, 1998: 5, 6, 55; also Wilson 2001: 70). What the TRC provides is multiple stories, particularly of human rights violations, meant to create a new collective world that has attempted to shift the way apartheid is intersubjectively understood. For instance, it has made denials that abuses occurred nearly impossible. Yet this does not constitute a historical truth as a historian would understand it. Rather it is intended to provide a disjointed set of judicially selected examples of right, wrong, magnanimity and vindication. A history that is at once not a history – it repairs rather than establishes a past.

The TRC's goals, methods and results were different from those of historians, anthropologists or sociologists – its truths are not 'scientific truth'. The TRC Report was not science, and it was not meant to be. Commissions, and the TRC, provides excellent examples, establish truths but they are not truth-finding in a scientific sense. They are rather modern morality plays that mobilise facts to articulate and promote normative agendas.

The truth about victims

The TRC is sometimes presented as 'victim-centred' (as in du Toit 2000), and sometimes as (usually *unduly*) 'perpetrator-centred' (for instance, Asmal *et al.* 1996). The first point of view is supported by an explanation of how HRC hearings gave victims an unconstrained opportunity to be heard and to accuse their aggressors, that victims were the object of two of the three TRC committees, that the TRC Law suggests that compensation should and will be offered and that through the TRC the new state officially acknowledged their suffering. As we have just suggested, this is not an uncontested view. It has been pointed out, by those sympathetic to victims and their 'rights', that acknowledgment has been a mixed affair where some have found solace while others appear to have suffered more, that the Reparation Committee was only empowered to make *recommendations* and that these will not be followed (the government announced in the beginning of 2003 that victims would get about one-sixth of the amount recommended by the Commission). This has all been contrasted with the situation of perpetrators, where recommendations for amnesty were given immediate effect.

These and similar contests merely point to the fact that what has taken place was a process of constitution, a play, with a script with somewhat unruly actors and varied, equally unruly audiences, all of whom at times contested and sought to rewrite the script. In this section we explore the place of victims in this play.

Supporters of the TRC frequently portrayed it as a replacement justice institution that would essentially take the place of trials and civil action. To accomplish this it was important to position the institution within this context. One of the most often used devices for doing this was to constitute the commission as an instance of 'restorative justice' (see Hayner 2001; on restorative characteristics of the TRC, see Boraine 2000; Kiss, 2000; Leman-Langlois 2002b; Villa-Vicencio 2000). This, as we have already noted, was done by the Commission itself, for example in arguing that the truth it revealed was restorative because one of its effects was to promote healing. An example of the Commission's thinking and the way this was presented is the following:

> The tendency to equate justice with retribution must be challenged and the concept of restorative justice considered as an alternative. This means that amnesty in return for public and full disclosure (as understood within the broader context of the Commission) suggests a restorative understanding of justice, focussing on the healing of victims and perpetrators and on communal restoration. (TRC 1998: 1, 5, 54)

Restorative justice within the TRC had five specific principal meanings: (1) restoring the victims' dignity by giving them an opportunity to speak; (2) recognising, and thereby legitimating, victims' perpectives; (3) providing victims with the information they want about what had happened (often through the voices of perpetrators); (4) providing victims with social assistance (education, health, etc.) and symbolic recognition; (5) financial compensation for victims (TRC 1998: 1, 5, 89–95).

These restorative possibilities assume and require victims who will find these possibilities restorative. The packages that the Commission offered thus were at once packages for delivering restoration through the truths associated with each victim, as well as packages for making up victims as people and communities who could be restored through these processes. Accordingly, creating processes to facilitate restoration and reconciliation was also intended to select and create process-compatible victims. A corollary of this was the view that victim participation in the Commission's processes was seen as legitimating the Commission and its truth-establishing processes of restoration. In this reciprocal process 'truth' about victims was produced and reinforced.

The required victim participation was elicited in three main ways. First, victims were 'recruited' into the TRC process with a promise of eventual reparations. A 1995 government pamphlet states that '[a]ny person who is of the opinion that he or she has suffered harm as a result of a gross violation of human rights may apply to the Committee for reparation' (South Africa 1995: 17). (The pamphlet did not state, however, that the Committee had no funds for reparation.) Second, victims were assured that making a statement to the Commission would alleviate their psychological suffering. An example of how this was done is to be found in the first issue of the TRC newsletter *Truth Talk* which cites the words of a victim whose daughter was murdered: 'It allowed me to release the acrimonious feeling I harboured and the burden of responsibility as the incident took place in my home' (*Truth Talk*, 1 (1): 3). Finally, victims were enticed by the possibility that making a statement would trigger an investigation into the matter which might result in new information being uncovered. In each of these ways the TRC used seduction to recruit victims to its processes. They were invited to participate in and thereby conform with an already determined model that promised to deliver various benefits including personal empowerment (on the power of conforming, see Crozier and Friedberg 1977, esp. ch. 1). In other words, participating in the process would be better than staying at home.

Once victims had agreed to participate in the TRC process they were assigned to the roles of *truth-holder* and/or *truth-seeker* (for a more detailed analysis of the victims' situation see Leman-Langlois 2000a). Truth-holders were made up as the dignified bearers of a piece of South African history which they would entrust to the TRC, not merely for what personal benefits this might bring, but for the greater good of the nation as a whole. They were thus constructed as persons and members of communities that would and did incorporate and integrate both egoism and altruism. The deputy Chairperson of the Commission put it this way on the first day of HRC hearings in Johannesburg:

> ... because the Commission is mandated by the Act to receive all who are victims of violence or human rights violations I want you to know that you are welcome and that we are very grateful to you that you have come to tell your story, because all these stories are part of the whole fabric of South Africa which we are trying to unravel. (Case GO/O135, TRC 1996)

'Truth-seekers' were those whose loved ones disappeared in unclear circumstances and who wanted to know what happened and who was responsible. This was the role assigned to victims in the typical amnesty hearing. This was facilitated in particular by the constitutive rules of the AC that permitted victims to oppose amnesty decisions on the basis that applicants had failed to make 'full disclosure' of their past actions. In one incident – the Heidelberg Tavern massacre amnesty hearing – the presiding Commissioner apologised after being accused of making light of certain aspects of the case in a letter written by the victims present at the hearing. The letter said, among other things, that

> [w]e are under the impression from the proceedings thus far that the legal representatives [of the applicants] are constrained to present the minimum facts required to satisfy those requirements for amnesty. We are all of the view that a proper and full disclosure of the facts has not been made'. ('Heidelberg Tavern Attack: Amnesty Applications', letter to the AC made publicly available at the hearing by the 12 signatories)

The sheer fact of a victim's participation, including his or her associated adoption of the TRC/AC functional structure and discourse – even when criticising the process – made virtually all victims TRC compatible.

These elements were brought together to form the greater institutional narrative of the TRC – a narrative that was about a 'shameful past' that legitimated and celebrated the efforts of the new administration to redress and compensate as a way of building a peaceful and just nation. That the truth that made this narrative possible was seldom corroborated or verifiable was secondary – what was important was the *truth-telling* itself and the story of pain and reconciliation it made possible.

The truth about perpetrators

Much can be said about the ways the TRC dealt with perpetrators of gross human rights violations, and this section will not attempt a summary. Rather, we will examine one narrow example of Commission-produced instrumental truth – in this case, the creation of politically appropriate and TRC-compatible perpetrators. Unlike the creation of TRC victims, however, unfolding events worked to 'impose' a transformation of the Commission itself.

'Restoring victims' dignity' within the Commission's processes meant, in part, assigning (or perhaps better *reassigning*) blame. In this case it is not the victims' self-perception that was at stake but the remaining members of the public who might still think that victims were communists and subversives and either deserved what happened to them or are now simply making up a fictional account for political or financial gain. Restoring victims' dignity also meant restoring 'the moral order' through a recognition of those who fought for victims' rights during the apartheid years: 'the leaders and fighters for freedom in South Africa will forever be heroes. Those who fell are martyrs of the struggle' (the Minister of Justice, second reading debate on the TRC Bill, Senate Hansard, 27 June 1995: 2210). The moral order to be constructed (restored) had important consequences for South Africa and its various political constituencies. Accordingly, the status of victims and the associated status of perpetrators was a politically charged matter.

From its beginnings in public and then parliamentary debates the TRC's national reconcilliation mission implied that perpetrators of crimes (during their amnesty hearing) and all others who offered support or tolerated their activities (during the 'institutional' and 'theme' hearings) would make themselves up through the processes of the Commission as contrite and apologetic – even if there was a fundamental, though buried, disagreement in Parliament as to who exactly needed to apologise, and for what (on this aspect see Leman-Langlois, 2002a). During these debates, it seemed implicitly obvious that wrongs would immediately appear as such, at their mere description. At the basis of this asssumption/ objective was the desire to ensure that 'history' would not be, and could not be, 'sanitised' and that crimes of the past would no longer be denied.

Kader Asmal, minister in the new government and collaborator on the early drafts of the TRC law, explained in his book (Asmal *et al.* 1996: 17) how the TRC was given enough leeway to demand contrition from perpetrators:

> its Amnesty Committee ... has ample statutory discretion to impose a contrition requirement in its amnesty procedures. A contrary interpretation [of the law] would undermine an overriding aim of the Act, which is to restore the human and civil dignity of victims. (Asmal *et al.* 1996: 17)

The view that victims' dignity is linked to contrition was carried over to the proceedings of the TRC. Even though the AC did not in fact require it in any form, and neither did the HRC during its 'theme' and 'institutional' hearings, it is clear that, at the outset at least, most commissioners looked for and wanted to hear apologies. At the South African Defence Force (SADF) institutional hearing, Deputy Chairperson Alex Boraine commented on a general's presentation:

... my overall impression is that this submission is breathtaking in its one-sidedness. I find it almost unbelievable that in 80 pages there can be no acknowledgement or acceptance that the SADF in implementing a policy of apartheid could bear no responsibility for a single death. (SADF hearing transcript, not paginated see TRC, 1997)

Chairperson Tutu, in his introduction to the Report, comments on this failure of perpetrators to be made up as (that is to be) contrite and apologetic persons as follows:

It is to give substance to our cry from the heart that politicians should really stop playing ducks and drakes with our future – for the greatest sadness that we have encountered in the Commission has been the reluctance of white leaders to urge their followers to respond to the remarkable generosity of spirit shown by the victims. This reluctance, indeed this hostility, to the Commission has been like spitting in the face of the victims. (TRC 1998: 1, 1, 67)

What is clear from these and many other similar statements is that Commissioners became frustrated in their expectations of what perpetrators should be if the Commission was to realise its hopes. Contrition and apologies, quite simply, were not forthcoming in many, many of the hearings. While 'uncovering the facts' often effectively destroyed the validity of the usual denials it did not always (or usually), as was hoped, demonstrate past wrong doing and criminality – except of course for those who already considered their acts as crimes and came to the Commission not to escape prosecution but to unburden their souls. Very often the amnesty requirement that applicants state proportionally strong political motivations for their acts (a requirement designed to limit amnesty applications) in practice was taken up as an opportunity for public justification rather than contrition.

The truth to be presented and legitimated by perpetrators, which was expected to help the Commission fulfil one of its main objectives as a 'victim-oriented' institution, was not often delivered. Perpetrators were not as TRC-compliant as victims. A truth that was to 'restore the moral order' very often gave way to a litany of justifications which threatened to actually undermine this order. And yet in his closing remarks before the vote on the TRC Bill, the Justice Minister had explained that:

It is very important that the new South Africa be different from the old. If we want it to be different from the old, there has to be a radical break with the past in terms of the morality of society, in terms of the rule of law, and in terms of our respect for human rights. (Parl. Hansard, 17 May 1995: 1438)

This was a key objective, a crucial hope, but it was not one that most perpetrators shared. In response the commissioners adjusted their language and started condemning perpetrators openly and suggesting that appearing before the AC was a form of punishment. As Chairperson Tutu explained to a journalist at the closing of the Commission:

[h]e had to say in public, in the full glare of television lights, I killed, I tortured. And maybe his wife and children are hearing about it for the very first time. His community are hearing about it for the first time. It is a very high price they are paying. (Beresford 1997: 5)

In short, as it became evident that most perpetrators and their supporters would not play their assigned role, would not be hailed as contrite, the commissioners adjusted the script in ways that would enable them to produce, if not ideal, then at least satisfactory results.

The truth about the past

Forensic truth, as a series of corroborated incidents, was the least controversial or disputable and hence seen as the most objective of the Commission's truths. But this did not mean that it spoke for itself and did not require interpretation as a feature of the Commission's story of the emergence and the necessity of a new South Africa. A past described as a succession of violent incidents can just as easily be understood as a *contentious* past as it can one of oppression, dispossession, etc. A simply contentious past might require recognition but it does not require the vast restructuring of a nation that the Commission was designed to contribute to. In short, resolving *conflict* does not necessarily require a moral reconstruction in the same way that resolving oppression and dispossession does. As the Commission notes:

If political circumstances – literally power arrangements in a social order – constitute the primary explanation [for human rights abuses], such circumstances must be changed. In South Africa this has already been effected. (TRC 1998: 5, 7, 147)

If this has already happened there is nothing more to be done. That is in part what Wilson (2001: 225) meant when he argued that viewing reality through human rights was overly reductive. The task of the TRC was not simply to add to an instrumental reconstruction that had been done or was to take place through other means. This was not the new South Africa that it was called on to create. Its task was the forging of a new moral reality, a new South Africa understood in a symbolic, figurative sense.

The TRC's Report does not suggest that all is well in South Africa or that the Commission had alone done what needed to be done. On the contrary, in chapter 5 it clearly states that most of the work of moral reconstruction remains to be done. The Commission's work is presented as preliminary brush clearing so that the work that lies ahead in building a new country with a solid moral foundation can continue. Yet by insisting that the 'new' or 'post-apartheid' South Africa had already transcended the political conflicts of the past, and by referring to its work as 'post-conflict' and 'restorative' justice, the TRC projects suggests that South Africans have already accomplished much and that a new reality has already been born. It seeks its cake and eats it, to project a path that still needs to be walked while at the same time arguing that the absence of signs of significant conflict in the present signifies national reconciliation:

> when that white Army officer asked for forgiveness they did not rush to strangle or assault him. Unbelievably they applauded. Yes, this is a crazy country. I said at that point, let us keep silent because we were in the presence of something special, of something holy. (Chairperson Tutu's Press Club speech, October 1997, no longer available)

South Africa, it is suggested, is a work in progress: not what it was but not yet what it will be once personal conflicts are resolved.

We have already noted that the 'conflicts of the past' were presented in the Report both as more background, context and as an explanation of gross human rights violations. Being 'incident-driven' the Commission showed little interest in this background beyond this. For instance, Chairperson Tutu concluded the 'media' hearings with a question:

> Is silence from that quarter [the media] to be construed as consent, conceding that it was a sycophantic handmaiden of the apartheid government?' (TRC 1998: 4, 6, 57)

The question is not answered. In this silence lies a strategy of reconciliation that the Commission fostered. While institutions like the media were at fault for *following* the policies of apartheid, they were not to blame for its existence – and therefore neither were their constituents (the Afrikaner readers of the Afrikaans language press). In the story on which reconciliation was to be founded political motives could be mistaken, but not blameable. Reconciliation was to be possible, was possible, because the South African constituencies were not evil, rather they had been led astray by currents of history, by a 'background'. These South Africans were prodigal sons who could become part of a new family in a 'rainbow Nation'.

There is irony here. This essentially unexamined background is the very collection of the things that have changed *the least* since the de jure, official rejection of apartheid. Hence the need to leave it unexamined. What *had* disappeared with the demise of apartheid were precisely the 'gross human rights violations', especially the state-sponsored violations, which were the TRC's main focus. The TRC's focus was on things that offered the greatest contrast with the past to be left behind. This strategy was not the Commission's. It was built into its mission – a built-in feature of a project originated by the new elites and shaped and tailored by politicians. They were the authors of the moral strategies that then shaped their world. The commissioners and all those who became engaged with them were important players who improvised considerably. Yet they were constrained and their thoughts, meanings and actions were shaped by the script that had been written for them.

Conclusion

It is a truism that the present shapes the ways we choose to remember the past. What is less obvious, however, is how these memories then serve to define the present and what will be left of it tomorrow. We have argued that the TRC is perhaps best understood as a morality play in which a new moral order was enacted, reinforced and justified (Shearing and Ericson, 1991), where ways of being a 'new' South African were exemplified and made stronger by deeply moving stories (Geertz 1973).

We have not tried to show how the TRC built a state-sanctioned or ANC-approved version of history. It did *not* do that. The primary defining element of TRC truth isn't 'party political' – though pressure from various formations was always felt. Rather, it was shaped and constructed through an integration of the lens of 'gross human rights violations' and the confines of national reconciliation. While its Report consistently eschews the distinction, the TRC focused far more intensely on right and wrong than it did on true and false.

A solution is always a simplification, a reinvention of the problems it is meant to address. The TRC project is no exception. What is interesting, and what we have tried to elucidate, is the specific ways in which reality was simplified. This process of simplification was not determined although it was shaped and constrained – it was contingent and contextual. In the TRC's story we have seen how victims and perpetrators engaged with commissioners within the constraints of a set of institutional scripts aimed at the creation of a moral order. Not one that was entirely intended but not one that was entirely foreign either.

The TRC's account of the past would from the perspective of scientific accuracy be judged woefully incomplete (see Pigou 1998). But it is precisely this incompleteness that provides the space and flexibility to reconstruct a past, to construct a present and to imagine a future. Its factual incompleteness is not a flaw but a feature of its work. It allowed for the creation of a past and a vision of a future that would provide a foundation for a fledgling democracy and legitimise a new order. Truth was deployed to restore justice, reconcile a nation, educate people and rehabilitate the victims. A nation moved from open conflict to simmering tensions with a dream of a better tomorrow. Enemies were reconstructed as competitors, forward-looking and capable of ruling together. Its truths enabled the TRC to present a history compatible with these possibilities.

Notes

1. Research for this chapter was financed in part by a grant from the Quebec Government's *Fonds pour la formation de chercheurs et l'aide à la recherche* (FCAR).
2. Because of multiple existing versions of the Report, references here refer to volume(s), chapter(s), paragraph(s).
3. On 16 December 1995 the numbers were as follows: AC three commissioners, HRC eight and RRC five. Shortly thereafter some additional 'committee members' with equivalent powers were appointed to each committee, bringing the numbers to five for the AC, 21 for the HRC and ten for the RRC. A June 1997 amendment to the Act allowed the AC to have 11 members. Finally, after the official October 1998 closure of the TRC the AC was brought up to 19 members (though some resigned) to speed up the process – which would take another 30 months to complete.

References

Asmal, K., Asmal, L. and Suresh Roberts, R. (1996) *Reconciliation Through Truth: A Reckoning of Apartheid's Criminal Governance.* Cape Town: David Philip/Mayibuye.

Beresford, D. (1997) Fisher of men, seeker of truth. *Mail and Guardian,* 19 to 23 December, p. 5.

Black, D. (1989) *Sociological Justice.* New York: Oxford University Press.

Boraine, A. (2000) *A Country Unmasked: Inside South Africa's Truth and Reconciliation Commission.* Oxford: Oxford University Press.

Boraine, A. and Levy, J. (eds) (1995) *The Healing of a Nation?* Cape Town: Justice in Transition.

Boraine, A., Levy, J. and Scheffer, R. (eds) (1997) *Dealing with the Past: Truth and Reconciliation in South Africa,* 2nd updated edn. Cape Town: Justice in Transition.

Bronkhorst, D. (1995) *Truth and Reconciliation: Obstacles and Opportunities for Human Rights.* Amsterdam: Amnesty International Dutch Section.

Crozier, M. and Freidberg, E. (1977) *L'acteur et le système,* Paris, Seuil.

du Toit, A. (2000) The moral foundations of the South African TRC: truth as acknowledgement and justice as recognition. In R. Rotberg and D. Thompson (eds) *Truth v. Justice: The Morality of Truth Commissions.* Princeton, NJ: Princeton University Press, pp. 122–40.

Ensalaco, M. (1994) Truth commissions for Chile and El Salvador: a report and assessment. *Human Rights Quarterly,* 16: 656–75.

Geertz, C. (1973) *The Interpretation of Cultures.* New York: Basic Books.

Hayner, P. (1994) Fifteen truth commissions: a comparative study. *Human Rights Quarterly,* 16: 597–655.

Hayner, P. (2001) *Unspeakable Truths: Confronting State Terror and Atrocity.* New York: Routledge.

Kiss, E. (2000) Moral ambition within and beyond political constraints: reflections on restorative justice. In R. Rotberg and D. Thompson (eds), *Truth v. Justice: The Morality of Truth Commissions.* Princeton, NJ: Princeton University Press, pp. 68–98.

Krog, A. (1998) *Country of My Skull: Guilt, Sorrow and the Limits of Forgiveness in the New South Africa.* New York: Times Books.

Leman-Langlois, S. (2000a) Mobilizing victimization: the construction of victims as determinants in the South African Truth and Reconciliation Commission. *Criminologie,* 33(1): 145–66.

Leman-Langlois, S. (2000b) *Constructing Post-Conflict Justice: The South African Truth and Reconciliation Commission as an Ongoing Invention of Reconciliation and Truth.* PhD thesis, Centre of Criminology, University of Toronto.

Leman-Langlois, S. (2002a) Constructing a common language: the myth of Nuremberg in the problematization of post-Apartheid justice. *Law and Social Inquiry,* 27(1): 79–100.

Leman-Langlois, S. (2003) La mémoire et la paix, la notion de 'justice post-conflictuelle' dans la Commission vérité et réconciliation en Afrique du Sud. *Déviance et société,* 27(1): 43–57.

Maier, C. (2000) Doing history doing justice: the narrative of the historian and of the truth commission. In R. Rotberg and D. Thompson (eds) *Truth v. Justice: The Morality of Truth Commissions.* Princeton, NJ: Princeton University Press, pp. 261–78.

Meredith, M. (1999) *Coming to Terms with the Past: South Africa's Search for Truth*. New York: Public Affairs.

Minow, M. (1998) *Between Vengeance and Forgiveness: Facing History After Genocide and Mass Violence*. Boston: Beacon Press.

Pigou, P. (1998) Truth Commission's work is unfinished. *Sunday Independent*, 7 June.

Rotberg, R. and Thompson, D. (eds) (2000) *Truth v. Justice: The Morality of Truth Commissions*. Princeton, NJ: Princeton University Press.

Shearing, C. and Ericson, R. (1991) Culture as figurative action. *British Journal of Sociology*, 42(4): 481–506.

South Africa (1995) *Truth and Reconciliation Commission*, Cape Town: Justice in Transition on behalf of the Ministry of Justice, 28pp.

South Africa (1994–96) Hansard. *Debates of the National Assembly Interpellations, Questions and Replies of the National Assembly; Debates of the Senate Interpellations, Questions and Replies of the Senate*. References according to date and column in official paper version.

South African Truth and Reconciliation Commission (TRC) (1997) *Complete Transcripts of TRC Hearings*. Availabel at: http://www.doj.gov.za/trc/index.html.

South African Truth and Reconciliation Commission (TRC) (1998) *Report of the South African Truth and Reconciliation Commission* (paper edition). Cape Town: Juta Books; on line at: http://www.doj.gov.za/trc/index.html.

Villa-Vicencio, C. (2000) Restorative justice: dealing with the past differently. In C. Villa-Vicencio and W. Vervoerd (eds) *Looking Back Reaching Forward: Reflections on the Truth and Reconciliation Commission of South Africa*. Cape Town: University of Cape Town Press, pp. 68–76.

Wilson, R. (2001) *The Politics of Truth and Reconciliation in South Africa: Legitimizing the Post-Apartheid State*. Cambridge: Cambridge University Press.

Chapter 12

Peace or punishment?

Nils Christie[1]

Punishments

The gallows

Not far from Krakow is Auschwitz and, next to Auschwitz, the major death-camp Birkenau. Where the railway tracks end in Lager Birkenau, a gallows was raised after the Second World War. Here they hanged the Commander.

I have never been able to understand it. One life against one and a half million! One broken neck against all these suffocated, starved to death or plainly killed in that camp. To me, the execution became a sort of denigration of the 1.5 million victims. Their worth became, for each of them, 1.5 millionth of the worth of the Commander.

But what else could be done? So asked my Polish colleagues when I revealed my doubts a long time ago. And I had no answer, except this: maybe a hearing had to be carried out. Day after day, survivors would have to reveal what happened. All sorts of victims would be able to express their despair, rage and wish for vengeance. The Commander would also express his position, his reasons for acting as he did, in front of the survivors and a panel of administrators of the hearing.

But then, for the panel, if it was a free one and not simply executioners hired by the rulers, what should they in the end decide?

One possibility, and this would be my preference, would be that the chairperson in the panel should express the following to the Camp Commander: 'You have clearly done it. You have administered the death of more than a million human beings. Your acts are morally repulsive to an extent beyond what can be imagined. We have heard it. Everyone in the civilised world will get to know about your horrible acts carried out at this horrible place. No more can be said and done. Go away in shame.'

Of course, I know that could not happen. I had, in the beginning of the 1960s, long talks with Professor Batawia in Warsaw. He was a professor in forensic psychiatry, and had carried out long conversations with Rudolf Höss, the commander of Auschwitz. We compared notes. I had worked in the same field, interviewing guards who tortured and killed in *Nacht und Nebel* (Night and Fog) camps in the North of Norway. We found that we had two common experiences. First, neither of us had met any monsters from the camps. Bad news for those hoping to find beasts behind the atrocities – by and large they are not there. Secondly, neither the Polish, nor the Norwegian society was particularly interested in getting acquainted with our results. Batawia was flatly forbidden to publish, and my small articles were ignored. It was not until a new generation had grown up that I could publish the whole report as a book (Christie 1974). Before then, with closeness to the atrocities, it was revenge that was asked for, not analysis.

The execution of an idea

But nonetheless, they might have been right, those who hanged the commander. They did not only hang the commander, but a whole system. His broken neck symbolised a broken idea. By hanging the commander, values were re-established. It was the Nazi ideology which hung in those gallows. Societies need clear and fast answers when their most fundamental values have been under attack such as happened in the Nazi era.

A block against understanding

I agree, of course I agree, how could I not? But nonetheless, in a little corner of my sociological conscience lurk some doubts. We killed the commander, yes. We even killed the major initiators after Nuremberg. We exterminate the evil ideas and their major carriers, swiftly, unanimously. We make it crystal clear that certain acts such as genocide and extermination of unwanted minorities are crimes so far out of the human imagination that no mercy is possible. My doubt is only this: do we thereby hit the whole target? By hanging the commander and also those bosses in Nuremberg, a good feeling of accomplishment is created; vengeance, often called justice, is carried out, but at the same time the discussion of the causes behind the atrocities and also of related phenomena is effectively cut off.

The commander was probably guilty and from a legal perspective he might have deserved his destiny. But nonetheless, at the very same time he also functioned as a scapegoat, as did his chiefs who were hanged in Nuremberg. Behind those hanged were some undetected forces, long chains of evil influences, determining factors. These forces were left untouched, left in peace, by hanging the last link in the chain. Justice, as it is understood when we enforce this through the criminal law, had taken place, and it was not necessary to dig deeper. Atrocities, when met with punishments on those individuals who have committed them, might prevent the development of a more full understanding of the underlying phenomena and the general forces behind them. It was not until 1989 that we got into the deep layers of understanding of the concentration camps with Zygmunt Bauman's book *Modernity and the Holocaust* (Bauman 1989).

By hanging commanders, and while the judges in Nuremberg focused on finding personal guilt for atrocities, other phenomena were also left in peace, left to grow. Three themes were not discussed in Nuremberg, naturally enough in a court with judges from Great Britain, the USA and USSR:

- Dresden;
- Hiroshima and Nagasaki;
- The Gulags.

Dresden was made into a no-town in less than 24 hours, and with at least 135,000 victims. It has since been difficult to find rational military reasons for their extinction. Hiroshima and Nagasaki were made into church-yards with one atom bomb to each town. The reasons behind these mass-killings of civilians seem unclear. But no one – even if they tried – could have raised the question in Nuremberg or before any other international court: precisely because these formal inquiries were conducted in the manner of a court, rather than some broader commission which wanted to examine 'the truth', for good or bad. It has been difficult to find rational military reasons for what happened. A better-founded hypoth-esis seems to be that the dropping of the bombs was intended as a sign of warning to the USSR, a glorious introduction to the Cold War.

And then there are the Gulags. Of course they could not be discussed in Nuremberg with a prominent Russian among the judges. But while they decided on death in Nuremberg, the Gulags bulged.

General prevention

But by hanging the individuals most closely related to the atrocities, we also teach everybody a lesson. Mass-killers will end in the gallows! Maybe we are preventing other people from going into the service of evil forces. So goes the theory of general prevention.

These are the conventional arguments for all severe punishments. And I am afraid they have even less validity here than in more ordinary cases. Perpetrators of this type of evil act see themselves as servants of states, most often of national states surrounded by aggressors. Or they are just functionaries, as Adolph Eichman in his office. Or they see themselves as soldiers in an inevitable and also just war, as when today secret forces from Israel kill or kidnap persons far outside the borders of the Middle East. So it is not reasonable to think that this will influence the next potential traitor. The situation will be another, the cause will be another. And the next person in will see him/herself as an obvious winner. It is the bandits on the other side who will be brought to court.

If impunity reigns

But of course, I do also know what would have happened if the commander of Birkenau and some of the Nazi bosses had not been killed. The anger around them was over-whelming and uncontrollable. In many concentration camps, the guards were torn into pieces on the very day of liberation.

The urge for vengeance has to be respected in such circumstances. But it then has to be tamed, channelled into the penal law apparatus and calmed by being placed in the hands of the state. If impunity reigns, peace cannot be re-established.

This is a major argument for formal penal action. It is a good one. But it points to a solution with severe costs attached, costs that often appear much later in the life of a nation. Let me illustrate with experiences from my own country, Norway.

Quisling

During the Second World War, the word 'quisling' was widely used as a synonym for 'traitor'. In Norway, this is still so. That is not strange. Vidkun Quisling was a Norwegian military officer. He was the founder of our National Socialist party in 1933. He visited Hitler in 1939. On 9 April 1940, the Germans invaded Norway. Vidkun Quisling declared himself Prime Minister that same day. He remained the leading collaborator until the German surrender in May 1945. He was arrested the day after, brought to court, defended by a highly regarded lawyer but sentenced to death. An appeal to the Supreme Court was dismissed and he was executed on 24 October 1945.

Quisling became a synonym. But he was not alone in collaborating with the occupiers. Of a population of 3.5 million at that time, 80,000 became members of the Nazi party. And many more assisted the occupiers – some as workers, others as informers or directly as torturers in the service of the Gestapo. A special term was used: collaborators were called *landssvikere*. This meant something worse than just being traitors. It meant letting down the whole nation, which during war especially is a particularly important base for identity and sovereignty.

The purge

I still remember the big headlines on the very first newspaper that appeared in Norway the day after German capitulation: RO – ORDEN – VERDIGHET. TRANQUILLITY, ORDER, DIGNITY, do not take private action, let the state authorities administer the punishment which certainly and justly will follow. And indeed, it followed. The prisons bulged. All members of the Nazi party, even completely passive ones, were brought before the judicial authorities. Particularly during the first years after the occupation the sentences were severe in the extreme. More than 40,000 persons received some sort of punishment, 17,000 in the form of imprisonment. Thirty-one Norwegians were executed.

Preventing private vengeance

Quisling did not get away with it, nor did his followers. The thought of meeting Quisling in the streets of Oslo some time after the end of German occupation was close to inconceivable as well as completely intolerable. Some sort of peace was re-established through what happened to Quisling and his collaborators.

This calmed the situation just after the German occupation. Private vengeance was relatively rare, except for degradation ceremonies carried out against women who had had relations with German soldiers, and also grim actions taken against their children (Olsen 1998). In such ways, a country of peace had regained some of its peace.

But that was a peace with costs attached. Let me illustrate with a visit to the city of Narvik.

Narvik, October 2002

In October 2002, quite an extraordinary meeting took place in Narvik, a city high up in the North of Norway. Narvik became famous in 1940 for the most fierce fighting taking place there between German forces on the one side, and British, French, Polish and Norwegian forces on the other. A great number of soldiers died. They are buried at the graveyard in the centre of Narvik. Two years later, new catastrophes developed close to the town. A ship of misery arrived. It had Yugoslavian prisoners on board, prisoners deported to the far North as part of Hitler's programme of *Nacht und Nebel*. A camp was raised. Next summer, only 30% of the prisoners were still alive.

And then to the meeting in 2002, 60 years after these occurrences. It was a meeting for peace and reconciliation. Here we were, representatives for all the involved nations. Some war veterans and also young soldiers from the various nations, ambassadors, the President of the Norwegian Parliament, the mayor of Narvik and also some academics. We met at the graveyard; German graves to the left, Allied graves lined up in front and to the right. We met in church with bits of prayers in all languages represented. And we met at seminars on the theory and practice of reconciliation.

We were all there.

Or were we?

German war veterans had been invited and had accepted. But veterans are old now, and sick. The German ones did not appear. What a relief. Norwegian war veterans had grudgingly agreed to meet them. Now they were spared, and only the German ambassador arrived.

But another category was not invited at all. That was the Norwegian collaborators. Not a single former collaborator was observed. 'I could not have been here if they had been invited,' said the leading Norwegian veteran, who was also a survivor of the concentration camps in Germany. I know him as a kind and decent man. 'Well,' he added, 'if they clearly had admitted their old wrongdoings, that would have been a different situation.' In a heated debate, the chairman exclaimed, directed at me: 'Would you accept a former torturer here, for reconciliation?'

I would.

The monument

We were also visiting the site of the old concentration camp just outside of Narvik. A monument was raised here. According to the text on the stone, this was 'a gift of gratitude from the Norwegian and Yugoslavian people to the memory of the more than 500 Yugoslavs, victims of nazism, who died in the German ... camp 1942–43'.

Died? They were killed.

German camp? Yes, organised by German SS. But the guards were Norwegians, several hundred. After the war, 47 of them were brought before penal courts and given very severe prison sentences. I knew them well. As mentioned above, I had talked with most of them some time after the end of occupation, and also with those guards who in the same camp had not behaved particularly badly. The court cases were thoroughly reported in the Norwegian media.

The delayed costs of punishment

What happened in Narvik that October is no evidence, but an illustration. The collaborators and war criminals were all severely punished after the occupation had come to an end. But the grand-scale punishments had not evicted the resident hatred. The collaborators are still despised in Norway, their children feel like outcasts, and their grandchildren keep quiet about their family history. A considerable segment of the population is thereby up to this day outside respectable society. And most Norwegians continue to think that killing in concentration camps was an activity reserved for Germans.

Reconciliation as an alternative

When strength becomes weakness

Penal law has great advantages *if pain is to be delivered.*

Penal law is oriented towards deciding on responsibility and guilt. This has consequences for the pattern of thinking within the institution. Penal law is built up on dichotomies, guilty or not guilty. A decision of 'half guilty' does not count. It is the decision of either–or that counts.

In addition to decisions on guilt, the essence of the penal process is delivery of pain. This makes it an even more serious matter. Most states develop mechanisms for control of this activity. The emphasis on proportionality between harm done and amount of punishment given is one such mechanism. The emphasis on equality is another. Equal pain to equal crimes. But crimes are seldom equal, and offenders are rarely identical twins. Central to penal law is therefore the striving towards ways of handling the differences between harms done and punishments that can be inflicted, particularly by reducing the number of factors to be taken into consideration. This is primarily done through elaborate systems of training or socialisation into what sort of information is accepted as 'legally relevant information'. Legal training is, to a large extent, training in relevance, or to be more precise, in irrelevance when it comes to issues of truth and justice. Many among us have been in situations where we have been told by our lawyers that what we think of as our best arguments in a legal conflict should not be mentioned at all in court. The judge would think that we were out of our minds and that the lawyer was a bad one by bringing in what to us was the essence of the case – what was true, and what would lead to justice. This is, though, probably necessary in a legal system. Here, it is essential since, before it all starts, the lawyers and court officials are likely to have established some sort of agreement on relevance. But this arrangement is not necessarily good for the exposure of the total story of what happened. The strength of the classical penal courts might at the same time be their weakness for two important tasks if reconciliation is attempted:

- Penal law prevents people presenting their whole story, as they see that story themselves.
- Penal law might hinder conflicting parties in creating a mutual understanding – and a lasting peace.

But there are alternatives.

Conciliation as a solution

Due to developments in modern industrialised societies, we find nearly everywhere a growth in the penal apparatus, including a growth in the prison population. But at the same time, as an attempt to curb this development, we also find a renewed interest in alternative forms of conflict solutions. We find attempts to civilise conflicts and re-establish mediation and/or reconciliation as a solution.

As described above, penal law creates strict limits on what is seen as admissible information. But conciliatory bodies do not have that restriction. In such settings, what is relevant is what the parties find relevant. They can and shall listen to the story, as the parties see that story.

This links to another contrast. Penal courts might have their bursts of strong emotions. But basically, it is a 'dry' and 'dull' process, encouraging affective neutrality. Conciliatory meetings, on the other hand, encourage emotional displays. The Truth Commissions in South Africa were arenas for emotional explosions, for display of sorrow and grief, for hatred, but also for forgiveness.

And also in contrast: conciliatory bodies are not forced to think in clear cut dichotomies. They are open for continuous variables, and thereby for the whole story. They can leave the dichotomies and accept a presentation of a totality as the parties see that totality.

Doing this, presenting the whole emotionally coloured story in its totality, they help the participants to preserve their personal histories, and also to recall what they might have forgotten.

Within penal law it has also to be a personalised guilt. Not a 'system-guilt', not a historical development, but the behaviour of one specific person. Truth Commissions have more to work with, greater possibilities for raising questions closer to a sociologically oriented understanding of the phenomenon.

But are penal courts good for reconciliation?

Alternatives to penal courts were not attempted after the Second World War. Commissions for peace and reconciliation were not in our minds at that time. But now they are, and central questions are raised as a result. Penal courts are clever organisations when pain is to be delivered. But can they help us to create peace in any other meaning than keeping the wishes for vengeance under control? And more important, can they help us towards reconciliation between parties in conflict? *Or is the opposite the case, that they may simply drive them further apart, by believing one but not the other? Is it so, that the strength of the penal courts in preventing vengeance is their weakness when it comes to reconciliation?*

I think this is the case.

What reconciliatory bodies are good at

Comparing the penal process and conciliatory activities, some contrasts are clearly visible.

Within penal law it has to be a personalised guilt. Not a 'system-guilt', not a historical development, but the behaviour of one specific person. Truth Commissions have more to work with, greater possibilities for raising questions closer to a sociologically oriented understanding of the phenomenon.

For the purpose of *preventing errors* in the delivery of pain, the penal law arrangements – when they are functioning properly – and sometimes they are not – are probably the best that can be invented. But when it comes to a more thorough exposure of what happened, and when it comes to giving the participants an opportunity to tell their own stories and expose their own emotions, conciliatory arrangements have obvious advantages.

Creating peace

In conventional penal cases, penal courts might, to some, help towards reconciliation and peace. A person might have broken a generally accepted norm. He has stolen from a poor widow or raped an innocent girl. He shares the values, is filled with shame, sees the punishment as just, endures the sentence and comes home where the father slaughters the calf and receives him with that famous meal that makes his brother so angry. Fine.

But political struggles are often conflicts about priority of values. The Nazi members of Norway had ideas. Wrong ideas, in my opinion, but not in theirs. A sentence would in a great number of cases be experienced as a political sentence, as a diktat. And diktat is a long way from reconciliation.

An essential element in any process of reconciliation is the listening to the other party, the whole story of that other party. For that activity, the question of a specified guilt according to a specified law is not of necessity a good procedure. Keeping 'irrelevant' information out of the proceedings and hunting for dichotomised answers are not the best conditions for creating peace. On the contrary, it seems more reasonable to state that where values are in great contrast, the strengths of the penal courts are their weakness when it comes to creating a peace to live with, a solution somewhat more acceptable to all parties involved.

International tribunals and penal courts

With the background of these general views, how do the most recent penal answers to atrocities look?

The international tribunals

The Nuremberg court was clearly a court established by the winners. It was a military court, and international only in the sense that the four judges came from the four major countries that defeated Germany. And it was a court deciding over an enemy that had suffered total defeat.

In more recent attempts to establish international standards, this has to some extent changed. Some courts have gone international. The International Criminal Tribunal for former Yugoslavia in The Hague and the similar one for Rwanda situated in Arusha in Tanzania are the most recent examples. I am far from convinced that they are successful.

While I was first preparing some writing on this theme in spring 2001, Yugoslavian authorities were under enormous pressure to send Milošović to the Tribunal in The Hague. If the government sent him to The Hague, they would receive money from the West to rebuild the country. If they only brought him to court at home, they would receive nothing. They sent him to The Hague. The next day they received a promise of money – $11.9 billion against one piece: Milošović.[2] The prosecution raised the claim to get Milošović to The Hague before the NATO war against Yugoslavia had come to an end. It seems probable that these claims prolonged the war.

The International Tribunal for Rwanda creates other types of trouble. The Tribunal is situated in Arusha in Tanzania. It costs annually millions of dollars to run. It is created for the 'elite' suspects – some 100 people awaiting trial in a decent prison nearby. The idea behind it was that the major culprits ought to be sentenced first. But this means that the smaller fishes have to wait. They do that waiting in prisons across the border, in Rwanda. Some 120,000 prisoners have here been stored away under conditions bound to kill many more among them than the total number to be sentenced by the International Tribunal in Arusha. In 1999, 3,000 died in prisons in Rwanda.[3] Happily, Rwanda, in the year 2002, started a system with Gacaca-tribunals, a system based on lay-people and with a purpose closer to mediation and restoration.

The International Penal Court

Then to the new International Penal Court. This will be a civil court with judges and prosecutors from several different countries. It is a long step forward compared to Nuremberg.

And certainly, in contrast to what has happened in Afghanistan, proceedings before an international penal court would have been highly preferable. An international criminal court might have helped towards more civil ways of handling this conflict. With an international penal court in action, the arguments for sending suspects to The Hague rather than to ceremonies of degradation in Cuba would have been obviously strengthened.

Such a court might also have calmed the wild demands for vengeance that appeared after September 11th. We might have evaded plans for military courts, and maybe also the way in which, post-September 11th, actions against terror step-by-step were converted to a war against those resisting the West. The Axis of Evil, as we have been told. But the old problems follow the new arrangements.

First: will it again become the winners' court?

Western legal order emphasises the value of being sentenced by equals and according to laws given by elected representatives. Even within the most peaceful among national states, these values are not always adhered to. Or maybe I should rather say, they are never fully realised. Jury members as well as judges are nearly always older, better educated and of more privileged class background than those they are to decide over. Laws are mostly better suited to controlling the poor than the rich, and to controlling those without power more than those with power, and they are given by and *for* the more successful citizens of the population.

With international courts or tribunals, it is even more difficult to play according to the basic rules of the *game*. It will *not* be a drama according to national laws, it will *not* be a trial carried out by national judges, and it will *not* be trial by an ordinary jury. In my little country, some 80,000 collaborators were convicted after the Second World War. Of course no Nazi members served as prosecutors, jury members or judges. Such people were by definition not worth listening to.

And international courts have extraordinary problems in preserving their independence, and making that independence visible. Large and powerful states, and small ones with *good* connections to the large ones, are better protected against being brought before international courts than small states without power and/or with miserable connections to the great powers. It was the total losers that were hanged in Nuremberg. When the International Criminal Court comes into being, new problems will arise. Turks might be expected before the Court due to their treatment of Kurds. Some might expect to see Sharon before the Court for both old and new acts, facing indictments from further afield than just the Belgian courts. Some Russian generals might also be asked to come to answer for their methods in Chechyna.

What has happened during recent months was bound to happen: the strongest among states are not willing to be brought before such a court. The US had signed up, but recalled its signature and exerts these days an enormous pressure on other nations to give the country guarantees that no American is to be brought before the International Criminal Court. Russia has signed, but not ratified. China has not signed, nor has it ratified. Israel is in that same category. A pathetic illustration on how the International Penal Court also becomes the court of the winners.

The problem of independence is reflected in the budgets for the International Penal Court. The Court has been officially functioning from 1 July 2002. Money is needed. The budget up to the end of 2003 is 30 million Euro. Germany has guaranteed to stand 22% of the costs. According to Christian Schmidt-Hauer (2002) this means that Germany therefore can claim a fifth of all positions in the court.

Will reconciliation be harmed by the International Penal Court?

One question is inevitable: if we find conciliation a value, will that activity be helped or harmed by the introduction of the International Criminal Court?

I fear the new court will harm reconciliatory activities.

First, the whole idea is growing out of the traditional penal thinking, and will further bolster the idea of pain as the obvious answer to evil acts.

Secondly, in my reading of the rules for the International Criminal Court, I fear that this court will block the use of alternative ways of handling conflicts. At least it will not encourage alternatives.

The rules for the International Criminal Court say that cases can be prosecuted even if the national penal courts are against this course of action. In my reading of the rules, I find it highly doubtful that reconciliation will be seen as an acceptable alternative to a penal process.

I have no definite answers to the problems here raised. What I cannot hide, and will not hide, is an ambivalence, bordering on scepticism, regarding the International Penal Court as an answer to atrocities. Penal law always creates restrictions on the flow of information, and is therefore not the best instrument to clarify what happened. International penal law is inevitably the law of the winners, and therefore of dubious utility in attempts to create social peace. It is an instrument to describe certain parts of what happened in the past. But we need systems that look forward. We need instruments that both clarify the past and help the future. Systems for truth and reconciliation seem to be solutions in need of encouragement rather than being harmed by an extension of the traditional ways of meeting harms done.

There are no good answers

Maybe there are no good answers to atrocities. Such a conclusion is not a heroic one; it is not one that will initiate strong actions, or immediately create new defences against evil forces. But maybe by admitting to the non-existence of good answers we create a foundation on which to build peace. If the hunt for good answers is in vain, we are forced back to ordinary ways of handling conflicts. In particular we have to tap experience from peace research and civil ways of handling conflicts.

We have to live with sorrow and misery in the shadow of atrocities. But – if you will forgive me for expressing my own morality – we must at the same time also try out some old-fashioned ways of solving conflict, restore – and forgive – maybe even before the culprits have moved so far as to ask for it. We do not want amnesia. But, after all the information has been brought to the surface, imprinted into all our minds and all human history, we might in the end have no better final solution than forgiveness.

Notes

1. Parts of this chapter have been presented in seminars and lectures in various countries in Europe and will also be published in my forthcoming book: *A Suitable Amount of Crime?* (Routledge 2003).
2. Milošović may be a bad man and also be found guilty. I have no opinion on that.
3. Penal Reform International, *Annual Report 2000*, p. 7.

References

Bauman, Z. (1989) *Modernity and the Holocaust.* Cambridge: Polity Press.
Christie, Nils (1974) *Fangevoktere i konsentrasjonsleire (Guards in Concentration Camps).* Oslo: Pax.
Olsen, Kåre (1998) *Krigens barn. De norske krigsbarna og deres mødre (Children of the War).* Oslo: Forum/Aschehoug.
Scmidt-Hauer, (2002) In Namen der Völker/På folkenes vegne. *Die Zeit/Morgenbladet,* 5–11 July.

Part 4
Official discourse reconsidered

Chapter 13

Official discourse, comic relief and the play of governance

Pat Carlen

'The play's the thing.'[1]

When Frank Burton and I wrote *Official Discourse* twenty-five years ago we had been heavily influenced by the anti-epistemological stances of poststructuralist and postmodernist writers. As we interrogated the reports of the official inquiries, however, we were not at all comfortable with the infinite regress of epistemological agnosticism and political nihilism which constantly hovered around the edges of our analyses by way of assumption, intention or implication. Our constant questioning of *Official Discourse*'s project, however, was not for personal reasons. None the less, even though neither of us was looking for truth or epistemological certainty, we did have difficulty in keeping in mind, and believing in, the purpose of our critique. For if there is no authorised knowledge, nothing beyond analytic deconstruction, how is it possible to break out of the hermeneutic circle into effective political action, into just action, into knowledge? If there are no guarantees of truth and justice, how can the pursuits of knowledge and law ever be moral or political projects? Why, indeed, bother?

One of the reasons for our concern was inherent in the nature of our subject matter – reports of inquiries into possible miscarriages of justice. For though there may be good enough reasons for embracing agnosticism and nihilism as personal creeds, issues of criminal justice are more difficult of examination through the lens of existential ethics. When it comes to assessing official inquiries into possible miscarriages of justice there are certainly more important concerns than reducing one's own ontological and epistemological insecurities and inconsistencies: concerns, for instance, about legitimate governance and the righting of wrongs.

Contemplation of the horror of wrongful imprisonment soon sharpens epistemological questions (about the possibility (or not) of buttressing knowledge claims with evidential appeals to either common sense or legitimated scientific protocols) into more urgent political questions about the role poststructuralist knowledge and critique can claim to play in the politico-legal arena. For if no knowledge has any referential truth outside the discourses in which it is known, why ever bother to construct, deconstruct and reconstruct official discourse? And by the same token, if knowledge, law and justice know no truth, what are the struggles in the academy, the courts and politics all about? Do knowledge, justice and law ever have any force beyond their own recognition and denial?

In this essay, I once again examine the concept of 'miscarriage of justice' – and for the same reason that we deconstructed some miscarriage of justice inquiries in *Official Discourse*; because official inquiries raise in juridico-political form a vital question also posed by anti-epistemological stances in relation to the construction of knowledge/science/theory: about the relationships between procedural rule/method/convention and law(justice)/theory/knowledge. For greater stylistic ease, I will in this chapter keep mainly to the language most relevant to miscarriages of justice, though I will occasionally make analogies with science/knowledge in parenthesis. Throughout, and again for stylistic purposes, I will vary the vocabulary used, employing the terms law, justice, knowledge, science and theory as being, for the purposes of this project only, coterminous with each other.

The overall argument of the chapter is that the very desire for both justice and/or knowledge emanates from similar assumptions about the impossibility of their procedural and substantive attainment – and that it is therefore in the impossibility of their desire that the utopian imperatives of criminal justice must be cherished. Rejection of totalising conceptions of knowledge, law and justice need not result in the abandonment of utopianism in criminal justice and politics. For the local, official and routine deconstruction of justice and knowledge claims, together with the global denial of social justice in general, repeatedly demonstrates that criminal justice projects are always and already like knowledge projects; they are both desirable and undesirable; both possible and impossible; and they make sense only within a concomitant recognition and denial of both their probity and their Others. At that moment of incongruity there is a comic relief that cuts through irony to a glimpse of the new, and through critique to a birth of the possible.

Modernisms and law's rationality

The terminology in which modernism, postructuralism and postmodernism has been discussed has been so varied and confusing that an explanation of the author's intended meanings for them in this chapter (and for the time being) may be helpful.

In the following discussion the term *systemic modernism* refers to the Enlightenment project of rationalising social organisation in the service of capitalist industrial production; *critical modernism*[2] refers to the writings of thinkers such as Saussure and Freud whose works called into question the more positivistic and empiricist tenets of systemic modernism – though without rejecting assumptions that the construction of a rational science is possible. *Poststructuralisms* refers to the mix of postmodernist anti-epistemologies which, in contrast to systemic modernism's project of the progressive rationalisation of both knowledge and society, reject the notion that any master-narrative can guarantee truth and, instead, stress that all discourses require a constant deconstruction in search of their conditions of existence and, concomitantly, the secrets of their power (Burton and Carlen 1979).

How do these stances relate to each other? And what are the implications for the possibilities and desirability of developing a critical theory of the administration of criminal justice (or the construction of knowledge) without invoking the positivistic yardstick of an always and already known procedural rationality against which the degree of criminal justice (or knowledge) achieved might be measured?

It has nowadays become routine for writers on poststructuralisms to stress that many elements of poststructuralist critiques of epistemology and knowledge were always and already the other of Enlightenment projects in pursuit of rationality and truth (e.g. Harvey 1989; Smart 1992). Around the same time that Max Weber was outlining the 'ideal type' of rational–bureaucratic justice based on the impersonal unbiased, logical application of legal rules to particular 'cases' (Weber 1969, originally published early 1920s), Ferdinand Saussure was emphasising that there is no necessary (but always an arbitrary) relationship between linguistic signs and their referents (Saussure 1974, first published in 1916). Scepticism was endemic in jurisprudence too. In 1930, Jerome Frank was already reminding lawyers that though laws may be born in recognition of the paradoxical liberal fiction that constraint is a condition of freedom, jurisprudence itself was born of rule-scepticism (Frank 1970, first published 1930). Likewise in literature: readings of Shakespeare, for example, perennially and differently demonstrate that 'premodern' magic (*The Tempest*), 'modernist' rationality and scepticism (*Merchant of*

Venice) and 'postmodern' recognition and denial of both constraint and creativity (*Hamlet*) can be archeologically reconstructed as at least possible discourses (even if not dominant or prevailing ones) in ages other than their own.[3] None the less, debates about their legal, political and ethical implications tend to set up 'ideally typical' versions of both modernisms and postmodernisms. In this essay the distinction provided by Douzinas and Warrington (1991: ix) will be used.

> The orthodox jurisprudence of modernity constructs theories that portray the law as a coherent body of rules and principles, or of intentions and expressions of a sovereign will... Postmodern theory... distrusts all attempts to create large-scale, totalizing theories in order to explain social phenomena. It refuses to accept that there is a 'real' world or legal system 'out there', perfectly formed, complete and coherent, waiting to be discovered by theory. (Douzinas and Warrington 1991: ix)

The 'strong' version of postmodernism which denies that rules become embedded (for the time being at least) in structures having an effectivity independently of the 'truth' of any particular rule has provoked the censure of theorists adamant that in law, theory and politics a 'postmodernist' closure is as undesirable as any other would be. Furthermore, both Hunt (1990) and Thompson (1993) have argued that denial of the 'truth' and legitimacy of the master narratives does not in itself empower those who have always and already been written out of the scripts. Deconstruction of legal or theoretical discourses neither explains why the master narratives in law and theory have the powers they do, nor protects against the illegal coercions of the powers that be.

Denial of master status to poststructuralisms themselves is obviously very relevant to discussion of poststructuralist critiques of the rationalising rhetorics of modern criminal justice administrations or scientific methods, and, as I have already said, it was one of the major questions teasing Frank Burton and myself as we read the reports of the public inquiries at the end of the 1970s. Of equal concern, however, was the more conventional liberal demurrer – that a poststructuralist (deconstructionist) approach to criminal justice is incompatible with the criminal law court's project of seeking/constructing the truth about contested situations, and the utopian hope that the courts may be the only space wherein the weak and poor can ever be protected from the strong and wealthy. However, before critiques of both systemic modernism and poststructuralisms are discussed further (together with the implications for knowledge, justice, law), the uses and abuses of the rational – bureaucratic model of criminal justice require further elaboration.

As is well known, Weber himself was in two minds about bureaucracy. He seemed to admire what he described as the rationality of the ideal typical bureaucratic system, administration that proceeded according to impersonal rules rather than whim or charisma. But, at the same time, he expressed anxiety about the potential of bureaucracies to foster elitism and secrecy. Ideally, the bureaucratic model should promote the just (fair) administration of criminal process by preventing bias and arbitrariness, and making sure that the law-enforcers themselves have been constrained by, and are answerable to, the criminal law's procedural rules. These latter, of course, are only partly (in theory) and partially (in practice) constitutive of the 'rule of law'. In practice, a host of courtroom studies (e.g. Carlen 1976 and Ericson and Baranak 1982) have demonstrated that the competent performances (Chomsky 1971) of courtroom professionals are directed at furthering a variety of interests other than those of an 'ideal' criminal justice – though it might safely be assumed that Weber always and already knew that without need of empirical illustration.

More radical critiques of bureaucratic law have emphasised the hypocrisy of judicial systems dependent upon a formal (and fictional) assumption of equality before the criminal law in societies where those subject to laws are substantively unequal – both in their capacity to get a fair trial (Pashukanis 1978) and in their capacity to bear punishment (Carlen 1989; Hudson 1994). Yet, ultimately, and despite their very different critical perspectives, both Pashukanis and Weber thought that bureaucratic administration should be favoured because of the space it creates wherein class antagonisms might be revealed (Pashukanis 1978:) and administrators and officials called to account for their actions. 'What is decisive', wrote Weber (1969: 355) 'is only that, in principle, behind every act of purely bureaucratic administration there stands a system of rationally discussable "grounds."' For the time being, at least, this principle is still both necessary and desirable to a progressive politics of knowledge and criminal justice, even though it is also necessary and desirable concomitantly and continuously to engage in deconstructionist erasure of presently discussable grounds in order to achieve the comic relief of simultaneously glimpsing the new and not new – that moment of recognition when the conditions for change are known to have changed, and when also, to borrow a phrase from Shearing and Leman-Langlois (Chapter 11, this volume) 'repair of the past' becomes possible.

Poststructuralisms and criminal law denied

Poststructuralisms are many, though they all recognise and deny structuralism. The poststructuralist insights which raise most questions about the possibilities for pursuing justice via the formalities and egalitarian myths of bureaucratic criminal law courts are: first, that there are no master narratives which guarantee the truth (or not) of statements or discourses; and second, that, because there are no essential and fundamental truths against which the 'consistency' and 'bias' of other narratives can be assessed, rationalist critique should be replaced by hermeneutic deconstruction. For:

> Unlike critique, deconstruction cannot call on some other, supposedly superior form of truth to take the place of what has been dissolved, for this would be to remain in the mode of critical overcoming and thus in the mode of modernity itself. (Snyder 1988: xlix)

If, however, no 'superior form of truth' can be called upon, what hope is there of either assessing criminal justice, or of attaining it (in terms of redressing wrongs without increasing social inequalities still further) in criminal courts where evidence is constituted as such by pre-given rules and where the final judgment and sentence are end-products of a series of negotiations and decisions taken outwith the formal legal process (Hudson 1987; de Haan 1990; Carlen 2000)?

As was suggested above, the major concerns of critics hostile to poststructuralist projects in law, knowledge and politics are twofold. First, there is a fear that once all master narratives have been called into question it will be impossible to set up criteria against which the degree and quality of justice attained in any specific case can be assessed. Secondly, it is asserted that hermeneutic deconstruction cannot in itself destroy the force and effectivity of the power of law or the rationalist and primarily empiricist protocols on which it is based. In reply to those critics, a poststructuralism is herein advocated which in both recognising and denying structuralism can also recognise law's power without celebrating it as truth. Additionally, it will be mooted that a poststructuralist approach to criminal law requires an uncoupling of the notions of law and justice/knowledge via conceptions of law as 'project' and justice/knowledge as 'desirable possibility'.

The poststructuralism advocated here both recognises and denies structuralism.[4] In relation to criminal justice, the effectivity (power) of the structures of social and legal process, and social and legal identity, common-sensically grouped (and often conflated) under the signs of 'crime', 'criminal' and 'criminal justice', are recognised. But they are then denied any necessary unitary being in theories, subjectivities or practices. Such a poststructuralism is structuralist in so far as it attributes an effective, recognisable, nominalist reality (see Fuss 1989) to the concepts of 'crime', 'criminal' and 'criminal justice'. It is poststructuralist (for the time being) when it adopts the methodological protocol of Bachelard (1940) that systems of thought must deny their own conventions and conditions of existence. It is structuralist in so far as it is mindful of Saussurian linguistics which demonstrate that individual words have no essential meaning but only acquire meaning via syntagma which through differentiation assign the value of a specific sign (Saussure 1974). It then becomes poststructuralist (for the time being) by raising the spectre of otherness (Lacan 1975) or the desire for (and knowledge of) meanings which lie beyond the text (or context). These latter also make possible (via 'differance' – Derrida 1976) the construction and simultaneous deconstruction of the text (context, theoretical object) itself. In other words, the poststructuralist perspective on law's justice which is argued for here is one that allows recognition of the value (i.e. effectivity, power) of already-known structures of criminal justice (or knowledge) production at the same time as denying that they have ever necessarily achieved justice, either in any specific 'case' or for any or all of the parties involved in any particular trial.

Then how can advocates of a poststructuralism that denies law's truth argue either for a form of legal-bureaucratic criminal process or public inquiry that cannot deliver the goods, or for a justice/knowledge that can never be recognised as such? It is because formal legal process (or conventional scientific methodology) is, for the time being, the best set of tools (project) known for fashioning a glimpse of a desirable yet undesirable, possible yet impossible, desire (justice), and moreover, because the power of the tools inheres not in the conventions themselves but in the comic relief they produce as they self-destruct in the never-ending play of governance. This claim will now be supported: first by discussion of how conservative and liberal fears that the term 'miscarriage of justice' must be an oxymoron can be rendered irrelevant by the force of law's alterity; and second by a brief description of how deconstruction of recent official discourse on women's crimes and women's imprisonment in England showed not only that such revisionist discourse had always and already been made both possible and impossible by reformist rhetoric and deconstructionist (unofficial) discourses, but also the conditions under which a specific play of governance results in both official and unofficial discourses becoming so visibly divorced from their extra-discursive objects that their flawed credibilities implode/explode in comic relief.

Miscarriages of Justice and The Force of Law

A 'miscarriage' means literally a failure to reach an intended destination or goal. A miscarriage of justice is therefore, *mutatis mutandi* a failure to attain the desired end result of justice. (Walker and Starmer 1993: 2)

But what is the 'desired end result of justice'? Walker and Starmer offer the following definition of 'miscarriage of justice' in the context of criminal justice:

A miscarriage occurs as follows: whenever individuals are treated by the State in breach of their rights; whenever individuals are treated adversely by the State to a disproportionate extent in comparison with the need to protect the rights of others; or whenever the rights of others are not properly protected or indicated by State action against wrongdoers. (Walker and Starmer 1993: 4)

They then go on to give several examples of each type of miscarriage. In this essay a much narrower definition will be used. 'Miscarriage of justice' will apply to all those cases (known and unknown, officially recognised, or officially denied) wherein persons have been convicted of crimes of which they are innocent (either in so far as they did not commit the actions constituent of a behavioural violation of the law, or did not commit them with the guilty intent necessary for conviction). Thus 'miscarriage of justice' will here refer neither to the systematic failure of the criminal justice system to punish the crimes of the very powerful (Levi 1987) nor to its systematic discrimination against the powerless (Mauer 1998; Morgan and Carlen 1999). Instead, 'miscarriage of justice' will mean what it most frequently means in popular discourse: the conviction of an innocent person.

In 1991 in England, the Royal Commission on Criminal Justice was set up to assess, among other things, 'the arrangements for considering and investigating miscarriages of justice' (Walker and Starmer 1993: 1). In 1993 a series of research studies investigating various aspects of the criminal justice process attempted to pinpoint the areas of the investigative and trial processes most liable to contribute to wrongful convictions (see especially

McConville and Hodgson 1993). Other instructive studies have been produced by campaigners on behalf of miscarriage of justice victims and by academics (e.g. McConville, Sanders and Leng 1991, and Walker and Starmer 1993). Two types of causes of wrongful conviction are identified here: immediate causes and essential causes.

The immediate causes of wrongful conviction can most usually be located in either the criminal (or negligent) malpractices of the police or other players in a case (for example, fabrication of evidence by police or witnesses) or in what I will call 'no-fault judicial misadventures' when, despite the complete propriety (under the law) of the pre-trial, trial and post-trial procedures, the court interprets evidence in such a way that an innocent person is convicted. Both types of immediate cause are made possible by the essential causes of miscarriages of justice which inhere in: (1) the *alterity* of law's truth; (2) the *judicial erasure* of law's force; and (3) the *impossiblity of constructing judicial guarantees* of justice.

Suggested remedies for the immediate causes of miscarriages of justice have espoused two apparently opposed strategies: either procedural reforms and an extension and strengthening of the criminal justice bureaucracies; or, and alternatively, a weakening and displacement of the formal rules of *judicial procedure* in favour of a courtroom informalism in search of a *justice* more relevant to the extra-courtroom conditions which give rise to 'cases' in the first place.

Procedural reform of criminal justice is based on an implicit assumption that a constantly reformed law is the best instrument for creating a space wherein the truth of contested events can be constructed outwith the inequalities of power wherein they originally occurred – an assumption that is always and already rendered both desirable and absurd by the courts' routine production of convictions flawed by forced confessions and fabricated evidence. Conversely, proponents of a greater informalism in the administration of criminal justice argue that inequalities of power outside the courtroom are reproduced and magnified in court by a bureaucratic logic and formalism far removed from everyday, common-sensical modes of communication in use outside the law courts (Carlen 1976). Greater degrees of courtroom informalism, they imply, would promote the more democratic modes of communication essential for fair trials. Concomitantly, the number of flawed convictions would be reduced. But again, experience of informalism in legal process has always and already triumphed over optimism (see Matthews 1988). Evidence from a range of studies indicates that outwith the limits to punishment and the proprieties of courtroom interaction imposed by formal legal process, defendants may receive even more excessive punishments than they would normally be awarded in the formal courts (de Haan 1991). Likewise, their cases are often more adversely affected by the unregulated bullying or other unfair tactics of accusers in informal settings than they are in formal courts where they receive at least some protection (and space for appeal) from a bureaucratic procedure set up to declare in advance the legal prerequisites for the construction of criminal justice.

Again, why bother? If to date the known alternatives to formal legal process have been proven to be no more successful in reducing miscarriages of justice than the ever-reforming law bureaucracies they have sought to replace, why bother with poststructuralist critiques of systemic modernism's attempts to deliver justice via bureaucratic legal systems and rationalist modes of inquiry? Why not just go on chipping away at conventional judicial reform and take comfort from the notion that, given the known alternatives, we are doing our best?

Why not, indeed? In democracies law must always and already seek an empiricist erasure in any case. But that is no reason why we should not also take seriously the poststructuralist insights which simultaneously point towards both the *essential* causes of miscarriages of justice, and the roots of the desire forever to do better in attempting to prevent them. In the rest of this section I will discuss three of those essential causes. Together they help constitute the impossible desire for law's justice (and knowledge's truth) – which, in other words, is actually why we bother with – and are forever bothered by – the play of governance.

The alterity of law's truth

The first essential cause of justice's impossibility via law inheres in the alterity of law's truth, that is in all the social inequities which, even though they are known and recognised for what they are outwith the criminal justice process, nonetheless remain beyond the jurisdiction of the criminal court trying a specific case. Yet a knowledge of such inequities is essential to an understanding of why any particular case takes the form it does. Innumerable examples could be given to illustrate the point, but a pertinent and recent one is to be found in Hillyard's (1993) account of how an institutionalised racism directed towards the Irish community in England helped create the racist climate wherein so many innocent Irish people have been arrested and detained under the Prevention of Terrorism legislation since 1974. This Other of law's force was recognised by a law lord himself. 'Hence Lord Denning's comment in response to the Guildford Four case that even if the wrong people were convicted, "the whole community would be satisfied'" (Walker and Starmer 1993: 12, quoting from *The Times*, 17 August, 1990, p. 12). And there it is! The gasp of shock and comic relief when the law's *alter ego* pokes its way into the action.

The erasure of law's force

In his essay *Force of Law: 'The Mystical Foundation of Authority'*, Jacques Derrida (1992) claims that just as law has always had its origin in force so, too, does justice always presuppose force. For Derrida, law is a *coup de force*. And it is this *coup de force* which is the excluded knowledge (Other) of judicial proceedings. Indeed, it could even be claimed (though Derrida does not say so) that the essential skill in constructing the case for the prosecution inheres in the art of translating the *coup de force* into the *coup de théâtre* whereby the force of law is endowed with a fictive legitimacy. Obligingly, the same English law lord has also provided strong evidence in support of this point ... and, again, with reference to the wrongful conviction of Irish defendants.

After the Birmingham Six 'had begun civil proceedings for assault against the police, Lord Denning struck out their action' with the comment:

> If the six men win, it will mean that the police were guilty of perjury, that they were guilty of violence and threats, and the confessions were involuntary and were improperly admitted in evidence and that the convictions were erroneous. That would mean that the Home Secretary would either have to recommend that they be pardoned or he would have to remit the case to the Court of Appeal. This is such an appalling vista that every sensible person in the land would say: It cannot be right that these actions should go further. (Jackson, 1993: 161)

More incongruity, more comic relief. This time at the absurdity of a judge being lured by the alterity of law's force to both recognise and suppress the force of what, from that incongruous moment of its recognition, becomes much less suppressible.

The impossibility of constructing guarantees of law's justice

The most fundamental cause of miscarriages of justice resides in the impossibility of ever encapsulating the alterity and force of law's power within judicial proceedings (or of capturing the alterity and force of theory in methodology). The Other which lies beyond all discourse, (thereby rendering it both possible and impossible) is in law courts, the force of a law which in its closure is always and already the death of justice, as well as being the force of its desire.

> In short, for a decision to be just and responsible, it must, in its proper moment if there is one, be both regulated and without regulation: it must conserve the law and also destroy it or suspend it enough to have to reinvent it in each case, rejustify it, at least reinvent it in the reaffirmation and the new and free confirmation of its principle. Each case is other, each decision is different and requires an absolutely unique interpretation, which no existing, coded rule can or ought to guarantee absolutely. (Derrida, 1992: 23)

Therefore, Derrida (1992: 15) argues, 'Deconstruction is justice.' For, like all poststructuralist approaches to truth and justice, deconstructionism denies the law's *coup de théâtre* its closure and, in seeking the extra-legal social, political and ideological conditions which make possible the prosecution's case, also seeks justice via law's destruction. At the same time, of course, the death of law is impossible. Law and convention are fundamental both to the human condition of 'being in the world' and to making sense of it (see, for instance, Vattimo, 1988). What deconstruction does is to point to all the alternative modes of case (or knowledge) construction which had to be suppressed in order that the case (knowledge) in question could take the form it did. It is in that sense that Cornell, Rosenfeld and Carlson (1992: 1x) are quite right to claim that 'deconstruction is ... aligned with the marginalised'.

So ... deconstruction stands in permanent opposition to the already-known – whether that already-known be knowledge, law or justice. But even though I recognised in 1978 that academic critique should be engaged in this kind of permanent revolution, the questions of social responsibility continued to nag at me for years – increasingly as, throughout the 1980s, empiricist paradigms of knowledge gained more and more ground in political and policy circles – and despite the position I had embraced at the end of *Official Discourse* where I had written:

Foucault is [not] patient with theorists who ... under the sign of ... 'progressive politics' ... attempt to regain control over the effects of a discourse: 'they do not want to lose *what they say*, this little fragment of discourse' (Foucault, 1978: 76). But they *will* lose what they say, and neither the intelligibility (or not) of the discourse nor its accessibility (or not) remain within authorial control. This is not to say that this work has not been done without regard to the constraints of theoretical protocols... It is to say that the discourse within which we write allows us neither *privilege to be within nor licence to stand without* the discursive effects of the text... At the limits of theory there is no sovereign language which will guarantee meanings independently of the discursive and non-discursive effectivities within which the order of language is constantly renewed. (Burton and Carlen 1979: 136)

In 1979 the full absurdity of that lesson had yet to be experienced by its author.

Comic relief and the play of governance

Since 1983 I have been involved with a group campaigning both for the reduction of the female prison population and for better conditions for women prisoners based on an official recognition that the needs of female prisoners are different to those of their male counterparts. The aims of the group have always been supported by many feminist groups as well as by criminal justice personnel. Yet, at the end of the 1990s neither of the main political parties in England was prepared to contest populist conceptions of the necessity and efficacy of imprisonment as the symbolic centrepiece of a punitive (if ineffective, in terms of crime reduction) criminal justice system. The only opposition to the increased use of imprisonment for both men and women came from anti-prison theorists, the long-term campaigning organisations such as Women in Prison, the Howard League, the Prison Reform Trust and NACRO, together with the Prison Inspectorate and some of the more enlightened among the judiciary and Prison Service personnel.

By the mid-1990s, the strongest case for prison reductionism was being presented in relation to women's imprisonment. Women criminals were not seen as posing the same risks to the general public as men and, moreover, their claims to special treatment as mothers were receiving sympathetic publicity. To meet the threat of this ideologically obstructive Other, the Prison Service for England and Wales set up a Women's Policy Group to ensure that women prisoners' interests and different needs were in future taken seriously (in effect, authoritatively defined and circumscribed) by the Service itself. In other words, the Prison Service wanted to reassert ownership of a part of the prison population that it was constantly being accused of neglecting.

At the same time, many in the campaigning organisations were questioning the utility of their oppositional, 'outsider' and often abstract critiques of women's imprisonment. Therefore, in order to make their prison-reductionist arguments more politically effective they began to modify them to appeal to the common-sense of a still punitive public which might be prepared to sympathise at least with women prisoners who had suffered abuse, or with children of prisoners damaged by their mothers' imprisonment. They were met halfway by the Prison Service's new Women's Policy Group which, in an attempt to diffuse the mounting criticism of all aspects of women's imprisonment, went out of its way not only to consult with a range of campaigning, statutory and voluntary organisations but also to employ them as programme providers within the women's prisons.

The anti-prison campaigners were caught offguard. Dispirited by their previous lack of success in reducing the female prison population (during the 1990s it had doubled in size), and seeing an opportunity to help shape a more liberal policy on women's imprisonment, many abandoned the theoretical critique of the legitimacy (and social costs) of imprisoning non-violent women for minor crimes, and (unmindful of the advice of Julia Kristeva (1972) to 'those committed to a practice of challenge' *not* to 'abandon their discourse as a way of communicating the logic of that practice') packaged their criticisms in the language of common sense with a populist (and official) appeal. From then on, instead of arguing against the promiscuous use of imprisonment for women on the basis of some quite complex theoretical grounds, many campaigners (myself included) were on occasions content merely to argue, for instance, that it was important to treat women prisoners well because they were mothers and guardians of the next generation; that women in prison would be less likely to commit crime if they received some kind of therapy in prison; that women prisoners had been treated as victims by too many writers on women and crime when in fact there were many strong women in prison who would be even stronger if their custodial sentence could be made into a much more positive experience ... and so on. The dominant message, therefore, seemingly coming from both official and oppositional discourses, was that women in prison should resist the 'deterministic' victimhood conferred upon them by critics of penal welfare; they should take responsibility for their lives by recognising their own needs; they should engage in activities that might enable them to be crime-free in the future; and they should have the opportunity to convert their period of imprisonment into a positive period wherein they might recuperate from the problems they had suffered outside prison. In its hunger for recognition the campaigning message had lost its theoretical power. Thereafter, the embryonic threads of a new official discourse justifying women's increased penal

incarceration were nakedly waiting to be metonymised from oppositional discourses which had originally been born of a desire both to
reduce the frequency and change the nature of women's imprisonment.
It did not take long for officialese to stitch them together in a new form –
though still according to the old strategy of erasing from the new official
discourse all reference to the material conditions of existence (characterised by poverty, racism and sexism) of a majority of female
prisoners. They replaced it with an 'imaginary' realignment of signifiers
(in this case the literal words and slogans of the prison critics) and
signifieds – that is, differently contextualised meanings of those very
same words.

Displaced from their original theoretical contexts, words such as
'responsibility', 'victim', 'need', 'citizenship', 'risk', 'accountability',
'rehabilitation' and 'choice' now took on very different meanings and
referents. Within the new official discourse on women's crime and
women's imprisonment, they were destined to have entirely different
effects from those envisaged by their radical authors, and soon provided
new justifications for sending more and more female lawbreakers to
prison.[5] At last it came home to me that, in the play of governance, the
force of an oppositional discourse's alterity (like that of an official
discourse) is never entirely neutralised, though recognition of an
oppositional discourse's absurd metonymynisation[6] in an official
discourse can, indeed, provide comic relief as the Other of officialese is
thereby, in its turn, simultaneously recognised and denied[7].

And so, to return to the fundamental project of this essay: to question
whether it is still worth bothering to struggle for a law and a knowledge
'that would respect both the desire for justice and the desire for the
unknown' (Lyotard, 1986: 67).

In this chapter, it has been argued that both modernist and
poststructuralist approaches to law and knowledge should be taken
seriously, and that by working on the contradiction that the claims of
law and knowledge to legitimacy must always and already be both
recognised and denied, we can cherish a humanity that, in its impossible
desire for a just law and a true knowledge, is constituted also in the
comic relief of knowing that all knowledge, both official and unofficial, is
also always and already otherwise. Only 'the play's the thing'...

Notes

1. William Shakespeare: *Hamlet*, Act II, scene ii.
2. Both terms were taken from Hassard and Parker (1993) who were quoting

Cooper and Burrell (1988).

3. See French (1972) for intimations of how pre-modern magic prefigures modern science; see also Pratt (2000) on the late twentieth-century renaissance of pre-modern shaming punishments.

4. This formulation was developed by the present author in Carlen (1998).

5. A more detailed analysis of the way in which oppositional discourse on women's imprisonment in England and Wales was incorporated into a new official discourse on women's imprisonment for the new millennium is given in Carlen (2002).

6. See, for example, Lord Denning above and note 5 above. For a similar discussion about the uses of irony, see Young (2002: 271). For penetrating analyses of the relationships between modernist and postmodernist ethics in general see Bauman (1993) and Bauman and Tester (2001).

7. An example of one of the most comical incorporations of unofficial into official discourse occurs in a remarkably clever document entitled *The Government's Strategy for Female Offenders* (Home Office 2000). In it, the arguments which had been put forward by some qualitative researchers that women committed crime because it appeared to them that they had few legitimate options (see Rosenbaum 1983; Carlen 1988) were turned on their head. Implicitly allowing the symbolic-interactionist claim (and, incidentally, justification for qualitative, as opposed to the quantitative, 'evidence-based' research upon which the government usually insists) that their ways of seeing the world shape people's actions, the solution of the *Government's Strategy* is simple: change women prisoners' beliefs about the world; the problem is in their heads, not their social circumstances:

The characteristics of women prisoners suggest that experiences such as poverty, abuse and drug addiction lead some women to believe that their options are limited. Many offending behaviour programmes are designed to help offenders see there are always positive choices open to them that do not involve crime. At the same time, across Government, we are tackling the aspects of social exclusion that make some women believe their options are limited. (Home Office 2000)

References

Bachelard, G. (1940) *The Philosophy of No*, trans. G.C. Waterson. London: Orion Press.

Bauman, Z. (1993) *Postmodern Ethics*. Oxford: Blackwell.

Bauman, Z. and Tester, K. (2001) *Conversations With Zygmunt Bauman*. Cambridge: Polity Press.

Burton, F. and Carlen, P. (1979) *Official Discourse*. London: Routledge & Kegan Paul.

Carlen, P. (1976) *Magistrates' Justice*. Oxford: Martin Robertson.

Carlen, P. (1988) *Women, Crime and Poverty*. Buckingham: Open University Press.

Carlen, P. (1989) Crime, inequality and sentencing. In P. Carlen and D. Cook (eds) *Paying for Crime*. Buckingham: Open University Press.

Carlen, P. (1998) Criminology Ltd: the search for a paradigm. In P. Walton and J. Young (eds) *The New Criminology Revisited*. Basingstoke: Macmillan.

Carlen, P. (2000) Against the politics of sex discrimination. In D. Nicolson and L.Bibbings (eds) *Feminist Perspectives on Criminal Law*. Oxford: Cavendish.

Carlen, P. (2002) New discourses of justification and reform for women's imprisonment in England. In P.Carlen (ed.) *Women and Punishment*. Cullompton: Willan.

Chomsky, N. (1971) Topics in the theory of generative grammar. In J. Searle (ed.) *The Philosophy of Language*. Oxford: Oxford University Press.

Cooper, R. and Burrell, G. (1988) Modernism, postmodernism and organizational analysis: an introduction. *Organization Studies*, 9(1): 1–23.

Cornell, D., Rosenfeld, M. and Carlson, D. (eds) (1992) *Deconstruction and the Possibility of Justice*. London: Routledge.

de Haan, W. (1990) *The Politics of Redress*. London: Unwin Hyman.

Derrida, J. (1976) *Of Grammatology*. London: John Hopkins Press.

Derrida, J. (1992) Force of law: 'The Mystical Foundation of Authority'. In D. Cornell, M. Rosenfeld and D. Carlson (eds) *Deconstruction and the Possibility of Justice*. London: Routledge, pp 1–67.

Douzinas, C. and Warrington, R. with McVeigh, S. (1991) *Postmodern Jurisprudence*. London: Routledge.

Ericson, R. and Baranak, P. (1982) *The Ordering of Justice*. Toronto: University of Toronto Press.

Foucault. M. (1978) Politics and the study of discourse. *Ideology and Consciousness*, 4(2).

Frank, J. (1970) *Law and the Modern Mind*. Gloucester, MA: Peter Smith.

French, P. (1972) *John Dee: The World of an Elizabethan Magus*. London: Routledge.

Fuss, D. (1989) *Essentially Speaking: Feminism, Nature, Difference*. London: Routledge.

Harvey, D. (1989) *The Condition of Postmodernity*. Oxford: Blackwell.

Hassard, J. and Parker, M. (eds) (1993) *Postmodernism and Organizations*. London: Sage.

Hillyard, P. (1993) *Suspect Community: People's Experience of the Prevention of Terrorism Acts in Britain*. London, Pluto Press.

Home Office (2000) *The Government's Strategy for Women Offenders*. London: Home Office.

Hudson, B. (1987) *Justice Through Punishment*. London: Macmillan.

Hudson, B. (1994) *Penal Policy and Social Justice*. London: Macmillan.

Hunt, A. (1990) Postmodernism and critical criminology. *Critical Criminologist*, 2(1): 79–85.

Jackson, J. (1993) Trial procedures. In C. Walker and K. Starmer (eds) *Justice in Error*. London: Blackstone Press.

Kristeva, J. (1975) The system and the speaking subject. In T.A. Sebeok (ed.) *The Tell-Tale Sign*. Peter de Ridder Press: Lisse, Netherlands.

Lacan, F. (1975) *The Language of the Self*. New York: Delta.

Levi, M. (1989) *Regulating Fraud*. London: Macmillan.

Lyotard, J.-F. (1986) *The Postmodern Condition: A Report on Knowledge*. Manchester: Manchester Univeristy Press.

McConville, M. and Hodgson, J. (1993) *Custodial Legal Advice and the Right to Silence*. London: HMSO.

McConville, M., Sanders, A. and Leng, R. (1991) *The Case for the Prosecution*. London: Macmillan.

Matthews, R. (ed.) (1988) *Informal Justice*. London: Sage.

Mauer, M. (1998) *Race to Incarcerate*. New York: New Press.

Morgan, R. and Carlen, P. (1999) Regulating crime control. In P.Carlen and R. Morgan (eds) *Crime Unlimited? Questions for the Twenty-First Century*. Basingstoke: Macmillan.

Pashukanis, E. (1978) *Law and Marxism*. London: Ink Links

Pratt, J. (2000) The return of the wheelbarrow men: or, the arrival of postmodern penality? *British Journal of Criminology*, 40(1): 127–45.

Rosenbaum, M. (1983) *Women on Heroin*. New Brunswick, NJ: Rutgers University Press.

Saussure, F. (1974) *Course in General Linguistics*. London: Fontana.

Smart, B. (1992) *Modern Conditions, Postmodern Controversies*. London: Routledge.

Snyder, J. (1988) Translator's introduction. In G. Vattimo, *The End of Modernity*. Cambridge: Polity.

Thompson, P. (1993) Postmodernism: fatal distraction. In J. Hassard and M. Parker (eds) *Postmodernism and Organizations*. London: Sage.

Vattimo, G. (1988) *The End of Modernity*. Cambridge: Polity.

Walker, C. and Starmer, K. (eds) (1993) *Justice in Error*. London: Blackstone Press.

Weber, M. (1969) *Max Weber on Law in Economy and Society*, ed. Max Rheinstein, trans. E. Shils. Cambridge, MA: Harvard University Press.

Young, J. (2002) Critical criminology in the twenty-first century: critique, irony and the always unfinished. In K. Carrington and R. Hogg (eds) *Critical Criminology*. Cullompton: Willan.

Index